FAMILY ART PSYCHOTHERAPY

A Clinical Guide and Casebook

FAMILY

ART

PSYCHOTHERAPY

A Clinical Guide and Casebook

Helen B. Landgarten, M.A., A.T.R.

Professor, Director/Chairperson,
Graduate Department, Clinical Art Therapy,
Loyola Marymount University;
Coordinator, Art Psychotherapy, Cedars-Sinai Medical Center,
Thalians Community Mental Health Center,
Family and Child Department of Psychiatry,
Los Angeles

BRUNNER/MAZEL, *Publishers* • New York

Library of Congress Cataloging-in-Publication Data

Landgarten, Helen B.
  Family art psychotherapy.

  Bibliography: p. 283
  Includes index.
  1. Family psychotherapy. 2. Art therapy.
I. Title. [DNLM: 1. Art Therapy. 2. Family
Therapy—Methods.   WM 430.5.F2 L256f]
RC488.5.L349   1987   616.89′156   86-28380
ISBN 0-87630-456-0

Published by
BRUNNER/MAZEL, INC.
19 Union Square
New York, New York 10003

MANUFACTURED IN THE UNITED STATES OF AMERICA

10 9 8 7 6 5 4

With love and respect
to
my husband, Nate, and children, Aleda and Marc,
my siblings, Manuel, Vera, and Max,
and
my professional family of origin, Saul, Frank, Ellen, Marjorie, Helen,
Zan, Daisy, Tom, and Mary

Foreword

I believe this volume makes an important contribution to the modality of family therapy. Helen Landgarten has given us lucid examples of her clinical work, condensed from her very broad experience. Moreover, it has stimulated me to think about why art therapy allies so naturally with the modality of family therapy.

Family therapy is manifestly an interpersonal and a here-and-now experience. It offers a way of retrieving what may have become lost in the interpersonal life of a particular family, and it provides a unique opportunity for reorganizing relationships in the family with the individual growth that can occur as a result. What so often becomes lost in family life is the intimate emotional connection between the marital partners that may have had at least a brief flowering in the years of courtship. The early intensity of emotional relationship in that time in life is difficult to sustain, and a continuing closeness requires constant nurturance and attention. Unfortunately, complex life circumstances, the stresses of parenting children, death of parents, economic struggles, failed ambitions, the inevitable "knocks of life" challenge and may severely erode the earlier passions and tend to undermine the mutuality of deep relationship as the years go by. These affect not just the marital couple but, of course, all the members of the family.

Carry-overs from childhood and the early experiences of each of the marital partners may limit their capability for sustained close relating as adults, and may affect their ability to parent their children effectively. Emotional deficits or unresolved conflicts within each lead to an acting-out within the family life of self-defeating patterns of relationship. Examples vary from the obvious to the subtle: the once-upon-a-time abused child, now a parent, who provokes interactions in the family that reevoke the childhood feeling of victimization; the once-upon-a-time prematurely mature child who now in adulthood covertly longs for dependency, but cannot allow it and instead becomes overcontrolling of spouse and/ or children; the conscience-ridden child who now in adult years places oppressively perfectionistic demands on self and others—spouse, children, employees, etc. These and innumerable other situations, many so well presented in Helen Landgarten's book, have been extensively written about in the family therapy literature. As these distortions in personal relationship reveal themselves in the family sessions, opportunity is present for significant change—but not easily and not always without some pain, the more so because of the inevitable circularity of patterns of behavior, each drawing upon and evoking reciprocal reactions in the others.

Many psychoanalytically trained therapists in the years prior to the emergence of family therapy had begun to emphasize the importance of here-and-now phenomena in therapeutic sessions. They believed that emotions induced and worked with in that way were essential for change to occur. The avenues for here-and-now therapeutic work were, in the beginning, developed through the Sullivanian focus upon interpersonal relations, through the Gestalt schools' use of action techniques within therapy sessions, through the notion of "corrective emotional experience" developed by Franz Alexander, through the intense experiences of psychodrama so impressively demonstrated by John Moreno and others, through the modality of group therapy, and through the application of psychological field theory and of general systems communication theory applied to interpersonal process. Permeating all of this for many therapists have been the teachings of skilled child therapists, such as Frederick Allen and Donald Winnicott, who knew how to translate a child's emotional life into simple interactions and visual symbols. Child therapy of necessity addresses immediate events occurring within sessions, and the use of art media (drawing, puppetry, clay) has been a traditional vehicle for this.

Into this matrix of theory and practice of the 1960s came a new clinical modality defined as "Art Therapy." Helen Landgarten, drawing upon her background as an artist, and working with children as well as adults, was able to integrate those experiences and move into the newly evolving field with unusual clarity of purpose and an outstanding ability to teach. She brought to her work, so clearly illustrated in this volume, certain minimal requirements for effective clinical function with families, and I will say just a little about this.

To do art therapy with families one must begin with a deep conviction about the value of the modality. In my observation, there is not much room for therapist vacillation or ambivalence. It is an authoritative (*not* authoritarian), strongly educative method. The art therapist must feel free to take hold of a family in each session, firmly provide an assignment, and just as firmly guide the family through. Statements about what is happening between the family members, what is being communicated, how connections are being forged or avoided, who is allying with whom and against whom, all can be offered tactfully, cautiously, and even tentatively. But the first step in each session, the providing of materials and the initiation of the activity, is a firmly organizing one and this provides a subliminal message to the family. In effect it states, "We are here together for a serious purpose and we have a common task to perform," and it calls upon the will to change.

Furthermore the message is: "Here is an opportunity to be together, to work together, to relate honestly to each other, and to learn about what blocks us from doing so." The experience shows to the family that various difficult feeling states—shame, hurt, anger, and also love—can be expressed and tolerated instead of avoided or denied. In doing together, there can be pleasure even while there is discomfort, and out of this comes hope.

So in the crucible of the here-and-now of family interacting, new ways of relating become possible. Expressed emotion must accompany this. Art media used with certain families, if skillfully managed, makes this possible. The method is visual and nonverbal, and it derives from the deepest layers of human experience—the infant gazing into the mother's eyes, the toddler checking mother's and father's facial expressions, adults searching each other's faces for signs of love or hate or danger.

In spite of all that our technological age has done to change our social structure, the need for humans to live in families has not ended. The essential pathways for gratifying life in families are only beginning to become known to us. Much discovery lies ahead. Art therapy, as it is presented in this volume, offers us an optimistic vehicle for moving forward, both to treat and to prevent pain in family relationships.

Saul L. Brown, M.D.
Director, Dept. of Psychiatry
Cedars Sinai Medical Center;
Clinical Professor of Psychiatry
University of California
Los Angeles

Acknowledgments

My ardent appreciation goes to *my husband Nathan*, whose continued support helped me to maintain the drive to complete this book; to *my daughter Aleda Siccardi*, both for coordinating the families' artwork and for photographing my portrait which appears on the book jacket; also to *Laura Gates Kazazian* for the expressive and evocative drawing which is on the cover of the book jacket.

I extend my gratitude to *Lori Gloyd*, my secretary at Loyola Marymount University, for typing the major portions of this text and for struggling along with me throughout the stages of the book's development; to the editor, *Ann Alhadeff*, for her valuable help and interest; and to the Cedars-Sinai Medical Center librarian, *Louise Lelah*, for her willing assistance in obtaining reference material.

I also wish to thank: *John Howells*, editor of the *International Journal of Family Psychiatry*, for granting permission to utilize my article "Family Art Psychotherapy" (which was published by the International Universities Press New York) in volume 2, number 3/4, 1981; *Darcy Lubbers*, for proofreading the galleys; *Adrienne J. Guss*, for photographing the three-dimensional artwork; and the various typing services which were filled by *Carol Cordier*, *Janet Munoz*, *Irene MacLean*, *Heide Prout*, and *Pat Newkirk*.

Contents

Illustrations

Preface

I began my career as a family art psychotherapist at the Thalians Family Child Department of Psychiatry in Sinai Hospital (currently Cedar-Sinai Medical Center), Los Angeles, in 1967. In spite of my 20 years of practice I am still amazed at the accuracy of art psychotherapy for diagnostic purposes, the expeditious effect during treatment, and the valuable use of the art products as a review during termination.

In my first book, *Clinical Art Therapy: A Comprehensive Guide*, I related the theory and application of this approach for clients of all ages, showing a variety of individual, conjoint, family and group work, and portraying art psychotherapy practices within the various types of institutional settings. In this book, *Family Art Psychotherapy*, I address family diagnosis and treatment through case history presentations.

My motivation for writing this book was initiated by the frustration with the meager literature on this topic for teaching purposes. Aside from providing a text for art therapists, I also believe it is timely to broaden the helping professionals' vision of this field as a possibility for enhancing their family work. I came to this conclusion while addressing mental health audiences, who questioned me about the relationship of family art psychotherapy to the approaches of Ackerman, Bowen, Whitaker, Minuchin, Satir, Haley, as well as others. It is therefore important that art psychotherapy be understood as a psychotherapeutic technique, syntonic with all existing family therapy theories.

The case histories cited herein will demonstrate *why* and *how* clinical art therapy is an asset to the family's work process. Even though the goals and treatment plans of the art psychotherapist are similar to those of other clinicians, it is the *means* that are different. The unique aspect of this approach is the *family art task*, a *directive designed for family participation and as a therapeutic instrument.*

Readers will not find explanations of the theories of family therapy in this book, since it is written primarily for persons who are already acquainted with the field. For the novice, a preliminary literature review is strongly recommended.

The family work in this text contains a variety of presenting problems, with different ages among the family members. The cases include brief, short-term, and long-term treatment. The latter is described in detail, in the two lengthy chapters 5 and 7. In several histories, aside from the family meetings there are concomitant individual sessions. All the case illustrations presented in this volume have been sufficiently disguised in order to protect the identity of those individuals concerned.

It is my hope the readers will realize there is a loss of details in each chapter. For this reason, my work may come across as easier, less complex, and less involved than it actually is. Although this is not my intent, please be aware of this defect.

Chapter 1, the *Introduction*, portrays family art psychotherapy as a modality which is based upon, and synergistic with, the various theories of family therapy. The role of the art medium is included.

A step-by-step account of my *standardized evaluation techniques* is presented in Chapter 2. It includes two vignettes. The first displays a mother and child engaged in an art task, which quickly exposes the parent's maladjustment and sadistic tendencies. The second case is a *diagnostic* example of a five-member intact family. The parents sought help for the two latency-age boys due to the latter's acting-out behavior. Within a single session, the art tasks revealed the family members' inappropriate role assignments. This chapter lists specific dynamics which are to be observed and interpreted during the diagnostic phase of treatment.

Crisis intervention is an important part of the therapist's practice. It is frequently a poignant, yet brief and essential form of treatment. Chapter 3 describes my work with a seven-year-old boy who was molested by a stranger. The author met with the parents, the child, and the family to work on the trauma of the sexually abusive event and the preparation for a court appearance.

With an increase in the rate of divorce, the issue of *parental separation and loss* is frequently dealt with in therapy. Chapter 4 gives an account of two latency-age children whose parents were in the process of separation. The treatment revolved around the offsprings' reactions to the forthcoming divorce and their preparation for a new, binuclear lifestyle. A joint custody plan is included.

Family therapy is essential for work on *encropresis*. Chapter 5 refers to a case on this subject. The patient was a nine-year-old boy. The major focus of family treatment was communication, insight, and management. Individual treatment for the designated patient included: awareness, self-management, and the expression of his underlying anger and fear. This case history offers a *detailed account of long-term family therapy.*

Abandonment by a parent affects everyone in the family. Chapter 6 reports art psychotherapy with a group of individuals who manifested different types of symptoms in reaction to their rage and anxiety. Mother, depleted and depressed, became immobilized and unable to maintain control over her children. The designated patient was the eldest child, an adolescent who acted out through his oppositional behavior and poor school performance. The middle child blatantly exhibited the family's anxiety through nervous behavior, which included nightmares, nail biting, and running around the house in a frenzied, out-of-control fashion. The youngest child acted-in by becoming a selective mute, withdrawing verbally, and communicating important messages through notes.

Although the author's primary goal was to deal with the loss of father and the feelings that accompanied this event, a powerfully *family-bonded resistance* circumvented the therapist's plan. The treatment was focused on communication and the problems each individual displayed. Because symptom removal was successful, treatment was terminated by the participants. The author sees this case as a failure, since the family utilized their *"flight to health"* as a defense, denying themselves the working-through process of abandonment.

Therapy with an intact family containing two adolescent girls is demonstrated in Chapter 7. The older child, who was ordered into treatment for violating traffic laws, also exhibited additional acting-out behavior. The father's separation anxiety, due to the daughter's struggle for individuation, caused conflict in the relationship and turmoil for the family. A report of all the treatment sessions reflects intrapsychic and interpersonal work, as well as a shift in roles.

Art psychotherapy for a three-generation family is portrayed in Chapter 8. The focus was on helping the family to face the eldest woman's near demise and to bid farewells. Home site visits were a part of the therapy.

This book is coordinated in a developmental sequence. The age of the family members ranges from early latency through geriatrics. It is hoped that through these case illustrations the reader will gain insight into the use of family art psychotherapy as a highly effective form of treatment.

CHAPTER 1

Introduction to Family Art Psychotherapy

FAMILY THERAPY CONCEPTS

Family art psychotherapy as practiced by this author is built upon *dynamically oriented art therapy theory* (Naumberg, 1966) in conjunction with *family systems theory* (Ackerman, 1958; Bell, 1953; Bowen, 1960; Haley, 1971). The major vehicle for diagnosis and treatment is the art task, which functions as an applied psychotherapeutic technique.

All family art therapy is based on a single or a combination of family work theories. These may include: psychoanalytic, experiential, Bowenian, structural, strategic, communications, and behavioral. For this reason art psychotherapy is synergistic with all of the concepts listed above. Whether the practitioner is a psychiatrist, psychologist, social worker, or marriage and family counselor, the methods inherent in this modality may serve to complement the clinician's current mode of treatment.

GOALS

In spite of the specific goals that are set forth by the various family therapy schools, in recent years there has been a consensus on two points: 1) the resolution of presenting problems; and 2) the facilitation of family tasks which parallel the developmental phases in the family life cycle (Duvall, 1971; Howells, 1975). (See Tables A and B on pp. 11 and 12.) Commenting upon the therapists' role in symptom relief and effecting longer-term growth of the family, Green (1981) states:

3

. . . Any or all of the following goals may be set, depending on the specific nature of the family's difficulties: (1) more, or less, involvement with extended family and persons outside of the nuclear family; (2) clearer communications and greater acknowledgment of communication; (3) differentiation of self; (4) a collaborative approach to conflict resolution; (5) a strong parental alliance and spouse subsystem that provides appropriate leadership of the system and nurturance of the children; (6) direct person-to-person (dyadic) involvements without triangling in others in times of conflict and anxiety; (7) greater autonomy, initiative, and self direction of family members; (8) undoing transference and projective distortions and achieving more realistic perceptions among family members; (9) greater spontaneity and appropriate sharing of affect among family members; and (10) greater optimism, satisfaction, and joy in family life. (p. 16)

ADAPTABLE ART TASKS

The emphasis during family treatment depends upon the clinician's view of "conditions for behavior change" (Nichols, 1984). Regardless of the focus, art therapy tasks are adaptable to the many aspects of family therapy—for instance, unlayering the participants' early experiences, exploring the family of origin, examining past and current histories, surfacing preconscious material, defense reduction, gaining insight, emotional experiencing, understanding cause and effect, observing transactional configurations, pointing out dysfunctional behavioral patterns, differentiation of family members, uncovering conflict, improving parenting and problem-solving skills, as well as grief and mourning work.

The manner in which the art directives are utilized will depend upon the clinician's perceptions of their role. For example, the *psychoanalytic* practitioner (Ackerman, 1966) may choose to be in a neutral position, offering interpretations based on individual and family behavior as observed during the creative process or relative to the content of the art. The *experientialists* (Satir, 1971; Whitaker, 1976; Whitaker & Keith, 1981), who take an active part in treatment while helping the client's developmental growth, may provide the family with innovative art experiences that deal with feelings, spontaneity, genuineness, awareness, and understanding. The *Bowenians* (Bowen, 1978), with a direct style emphasizing triangulation, can point out this aspect as it is revealed in the unit's artwork; they will engage the clients in tasks that stress differentiated autonomous functioning. *Structuralists* (Minuchin, 1974), who are active directors, may calculate art project interventions that purposely interrupt the family's usual transactional behavior and require members to rearrange their roles. They may also designate directives that manipulate a trial realignment of subsystems and change boundaries.

On the other hand, the *communication* therapists (Jackson, 1961; Satir, 1967; Watzlawick, 1966), using the circular causality model of a chain reaction effect, will observe the family's communication patterns and methods of decision making, while engaged in a joint art venture. Treatment will include family constructs which contain rules for clear communication and problem solving. The *strategic* viewpoint (Haley, 1976; Madanes, 1981), with the systemic stance, may use the artwork as a vehicle for prescriptive and paradoxical intervention, giving attention to the resolution of problems. *Behavioral* clinicians (Friedman, 1972) can offer art directives for educational purposes, modifications, and positive reinforcement.

FAMILY SYSTEMS BLUEPRINT

Since this author places emphasis on family systems theory (Landgarten, 1981), individual members are examined within the context of group process with various actions triggering off responses. The system is examined through the way in which the family functions as a unit while creating an art form together. The value of the art task is threefold: the *process* as a diagnostic, interactional, and rehearsal tool; the *contents* as a means of portraying unconscious and conscious communication; and the *product* as lasting evidence of the group's dynamics. This art psychotherapist perceives the initial mutually created art as a *floor plan of the family's basic structure*. As early as the first session, the clinician can offer insightful feedback, much to the amazement of the family. Participants are surprised to discover how their creative renderings can offer information about their interactional patterns and rules. Since clients are taught to understand the correlations between their artwork and themselves, the *metaphoric blueprint concept* is put to use from the outset of treatment. This factor has a positive effect as it tends to hasten a positive transference which is especially necessary for family therapy.

The clinical art therapist injects an "agent of change" (Bell, 1964) by intruding upon the unit's system in an attempt to upset the old balance and to help organize a more satisfying one. The *invading device is the art directive, which contains the appropriate media and is clinically sound*. It is essential for the reader to realize that the author's instructions, which are reviewed in this book, are *dictated by the dynamics of each session with consideration to short- and long-term goals*.

Whenever the family is engaged in creating an object, a salient factor is the therapist's constant vigilance for the *overt and covert messages that are revealed through the artwork, as well as the subtle nuances displayed while the family members execute their art.* Familial dysfunction may be portrayed during the art production as well as in the artwork. For example:

Undifferentiated ego mass (Bowen, 1978) may be present. This concept refers to blurred boundaries and entanglement. This can be exemplified through "lumped together" artwork, where it is difficult or impossible to identify the contribution of each member due to overlapping, merging, and connecting forms.

Triangulation (Bowen, 1978) may be evident. It is displayed during the art process when two people focus their dissatisfaction onto a third person.

Parentification (Boszormenyi-Nagy & Spark, 1973) exists when there is inappropriate reversal of the parent–child roles while creating their product.

Marital schism and marital skew (Lidz, Cornelison, Fleck, & Terry, 1957) may be highlighted by the art task. In the "schism," incompatibility is exhibited with conflict and hostility. Harmony exists for the skewed pair and is displayed in their artwork since the roles are complementary; the dominant individual's independence dovetails with his/her spouse's dependency.

Pseudomutuality (Wynne, Ryckoff, Day, & Hirsch, 1958) presents a family façade of positive relationships. Their cooperative artwork has a tendency to be on the compensatory, pleasant side. In this situation the family's united front layers over any conscious divergencies or splits. At the same time the family's alignment serves to deprive them of affectional depth. While any threats to the family unity are denied, intimate relationships are also circumvented. In this way the unit manages to keep an equilibrium. There is a *family resistance to change* (Brown, 1966) while in treatment, since the members collude to maintain their *family homeostasis* (Jackson, 1957; Satir, 1967).

A double-bind (Bateson, Jackson, Haley, & Weakland, 1956; Sluzki & Ransom, 1976) might be revealed. It is a pathological, mixed communication which sets up entrapment through obscure and/or contradictory instructions. A double message is sent out while the family is engaged in the art. One message is on a face value level, and an opposing one is hidden beneath the surface. The person receiving the dual communication is in a "no-win" situation. If the superficial overt instruction is followed, the covert one must be denied even though it was perceived correctly.

Professionals who explore the use of clinical art therapy will see the family's roles, alliances, communication patterns, and group gestalt in short order. Therefore, readers who choose to integrate this modality into their practice are advised to be *selective* regarding the *use* of the *material* revealed by their clients. One must *assess the timing for sharing and/or using exposed information*. It is also imperative for the clinician to understand the twofold potency of the art experience. First, emotions that deal with specific issues are intensified by the directness of the art focus. Second, the product provides concrete evidence not only to the therapist, but also to the creator and the rest of the family. For these reasons, caution must be taken since the artwork frequently makes latent material symbolically manifest.

This author warns clinicians to pay heed to the techniques that evoke strong emotions, bring about confrontations, and/or expose family or individual secrets. Each therapist must consider the therapeutic value of eliciting these situations. Nevertheless, the art experience facilitates interactions, an attitude of openness, insight, and the adoption of new skills. It also furnishes the family with a stage for rehearsing new roles and communication styles since art therapy participants can afford to take a chance on dealing with each other in a new way through the nonthreatening art experience. *Families soon learn that their symbolic art therapy efforts serve as trials for taking grander risks at home.*

One of the art therapist's simpler motivations for having the family work together is that the collaborative effort can prove to be enjoyable. This dimension, which is prophylactic and indigenous to the art therapy modality, offers the family a means to discover some of its strengths and acts as a catalyst for positive change.

An element intrinsic to the task orientation is the use of the art materials. Aside from the creative function, the medium serves additional purposes (Landgarten, 1981). For example, it can heighten or lower the client's affective state, influence the freedom of self-expression, and circumvent defenses. Due to these factors, the size and properties of the media are given consideration. Materials can be viewed on a 10-point continuum from the least to the most controlled (see media chart below).

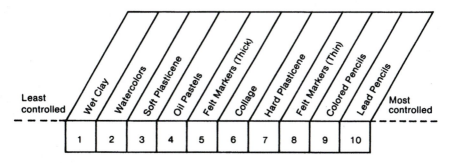

In the realm of family treatment, the central media (numbers 3–8) are most frequently used. The media and spatial considerations must relate to the objectives of the directives. For example, *disengaged* families (Minuchin, 1974) display this dynamic in their art. At some time in treatment, projects requiring a small, closed-in space are utilized to symbolically focus the work on bringing this unit physically and psychologically closer together. In contrast, the enmeshed family (Minuchin, 1974) requires a *variety* of media and *separate* products to evoke the family's awareness and work towards individuation.

For family units that need structure and boundaries, trays and boxes are employed since limitations are defined by the raised sides and tend to prevent acting out in the art. In other cases, where the directive is meant to increase family esteem through immediate gratification or problem solving, it is prudent to provide media that are simple to use and will help the participants to succeed as quickly as possible. On the other hand, where it is therapeutic to delay satisfaction, a project requiring careful planning and extended involvement may be considered. In this situation, a complicated project with multimedia would be most suitable.

Regardless of the clinician's directives, he/she watches the way in which materials are used, as well as the individuals' reactions to them. These observations reveal additional clues to the interpersonal transactions. For instance, during the evaluation phase a child may demonstrate low frustration tolerance to a medium that is difficult to manipulate. The family's responses to the child's actions will expose the way this type of situation is handled at home. If inappropriate roles or behavior are revealed, then the therapist may choose to use this same art material again in the future in order to reopen and deal with the issue.

To recapitulate, it is mandatory for the art therapist to have a cognitive perspective on the art materials, directives, and process. A cardinal factor during evaluation and treatment is the family art psychotherapist's responsibility to function on two tracks simultaneously. One is based on the knowledge of *clinical art therapy;* the other is framed upon a *family therapy foundation.* These two theories are creatively wed during the application process while families are helped to take action towards symptom removal and to increase the quality of their lives.

REFERENCES

Ackerman, N. W. *The Psychodynamics of Family Life.* New York: Basic Books, 1958.
Ackerman, N. W. *Treating the Troubled Family.* New York: Basic Books, 1966.
Bateson, G., Jackson, D. D., Haley, J., & Weakland, J. Towards a theory of schizophrenia. *Behavioral Science, 1,* 251–264, 1956.

Bell, J. E. Family group therapy: A new treatment method for children. *American Psychologist, 8*, 515 (7), 1953.

Bell, J. E. The family group therapist: An agent of change. *International Journal of Group Psychotherapy, 14*, 72–83, 1964.

Boszormenyi-Nagy, I., & Spark, G. L. *Invisible Loyalties: Reciprocity in Intergenerational Family Therapy.* New York: Harper & Row, 1973. (Second ed. published by Brunner/Mazel, New York, 1984.)

Bowen, M. A family concept of schizophrenia. In D. D. Jackson (Ed.), *The Etiology of Schizophrenia.* New York: Basic Books, 1960, pp. 346–372.

Bowen, M. *Family Therapy in Clinical Practice.* New York: Jason Aronson, 1978.

Brown, S. L. Family interviewing viewed in light of resistance to change. *Psychiatric Research Reports of the American Psychiatric Association*, No. 20, Feb. 1966, pp. 132–139.

Duvall, E. M. *Family Development.* New York: Lippincott, 1971.

Friedman, P. H. Personalistic family and marital therapy. In A. A. Lazarus (Ed.), *Clinical Behavior Therapy.* New York: Brunner/Mazel, 1972.

Green, R. J. An overview of major contributions to family therapy. In R. J. Green & J. L. Framo (Eds.), *Family Therapy: Major Contributions.* New York: International Universities Press, 1981.

Haley, J. Approaches to family therapy. In J. Haley (Ed.), *Changing Families: A Family Therapy Reader.* New York: Grune & Stratton, 1971.

Haley, J. *Problem Solving Therapy.* San Francisco: Jossey-Bass, 1976.

Howells, J. G. *Principles of Family Psychiatry.* New York: Brunner/Mazel, 1975.

Jackson, D. D. The question of family homeostasis. *Psychiatry Quarterly, 31* (Suppl.) Part I, 79–80, 1957.

Jackson, D. D. Interactional psychotherapy. In M. T. Stein (Ed.), *Contemporary Psychotherapies.* New York: Free Press of Glencoe, 1961.

Landgarten, H. B. *Clinical Art Therapy: A Comprehensive Guide.* New York: Brunner/Mazel, 1981.

Lidz, T. Cornelison, A., Fleck, S., & Terry, D. Intrafamilial environment of schizophrenic patients. II: Marital schism and marital skew. *American Journal of Psychiatry, 20*, 241–248, 1957.

Madanes, C. *Strategic Family Therapy.* San Francisco: Jossey-Bass, 1981.

Minuchin, S. *Families and Family Therapy.* Cambridge, MA: Harvard University Press, 1974.

Naumberg, M. *Dynamically Oriented Art Therapy: Its Principles and Practices.* New York: Grune & Stratton, 1966.

Nichols, M. *Family Therapy: Concepts and Methods.* New York: Gardner Press, 1984.

Satir, V. *Conjoint Family Therapy.* Palo Alto: Science and Behavior Books, 1967.

Satir, V. The family as a treatment unit. In J. Haley (Ed.), *Changing Families.* New York: Grune & Stratton, 1971.

Sluzki, C. E., & Ransom, D. C. (Eds.). *Double Bind: The Foundation of the Communicational Approach to the Family.* New York: Grune & Stratton, 1976.

Watzlawick, P. A. A structured family interview. *Family Process, 5*, 256–271, 1966.

Whitaker, C. A. A family is a four dimensional relationship. In P. J. Guerin (Ed.), *Family Therapy: Theory and Practice.* New York: Gardner Press, 1976.

Whitaker, C. A., & Keith, D. V. Symbolic experiential family therapy. In A. S. Gurman & D. P. Kniskern (Eds.), *Handbook of Family Therapy.* New York: Brunner/Mazel, 1981.

Wynne, L. C., Ryckoff, I., Day, J., & Hirsch, S. I. Pseudo-mutuality in the family relationships of schizophrenics. *Psychiatry, 21*, 205–220, 1958.

RECOMMENDED READING

Andolfi, M., et al. *Behind the Family Mask*. New York: Brunner/Mazel, 1983.

Beavers, W. R. *Psychotherapy and Growth: Family Systems Perspective*. New York: Brunner/Mazel, 1977.

Bell, J. E. *Family Therapy*. New York: Jason Aronson, 1975.

Berger, M. M. (Ed.). *Beyond the Double Bind*. New York: Brunner/Mazel, 1978.

Bloch, D., & Simon, R. (Eds.) *The Strength of Family Therapy: Selected Papers of Nathan W. Ackerman*. New York: Brunner/Mazel, 1982.

Boszormenyi-Nagy, I., & Framo, J. L. *Intensive Family Therapy: Theoretical and Practical Aspects*. New York: Harper and Row, 1965. (2nd ed. published by Brunner/Mazel, New York, 1985.)

Bross, A. (Ed.) *Family Therapy: Principles of Strategic Practice*. New York: Guilford Press, 1983.

Brown, S. L. Family therapy. In B. Wolman (Ed.), *Manual of Child Psychopathology*. New York: McGraw Hill, 1972.

Brown, S. L. The developmental cycle of families: Clinical implications. *Psychiatric Clinics of North America, 3*, (3), 369–381, Dec., 1980.

Carter, E. A., & McGoldrick, M. (Eds.), *The Family Life Cycle: A Framework for Family Therapy*. New York: Gardner Press, 1980.

Dreikurs, S. E. Art therapy: An Adlerian group approach. *Journal of Individual Psychology, 1*, 69–80, 1976.

Farber, A., Mendelsohn, M., & Napier, A. *The Book of Family Therapy*. Boston: Houghton-Mifflin, 1973.

Framo, J. L. *Explorations in Marital and Family Therapy*. New York: Springer, 1982.

Hoffman, L. *Foundations of Family Therapy*. New York: Basic Books, 1981.

Jackson, D. D. (Ed.). *Therapy Communication and Changes*. Palo Alto: Science & Behavior Books, 1968.

Kwiatkowska, H. Y. *Family Therapy and Evaluation Through Art*. Springfield: Charles C Thomas, 1978.

Kwiatkowska, H. Y., Day, J., & Wynne, L. C. *The Schizophrenic Patient, His Parents and Siblings: Observations Through Family Art Therapy*. U.S. Dept. of Health Education and Welfare: Public Health Service, 1962.

Lidz, T. *The Family and Human Adaptation*. New York: International Universities Press, 1963.

Riley, S. Draw me a paradox: Family art psychotherapy utilizing a systemic approach to change. *Art Therapy, 2*, (3), 116–125, Oct., 1985.

Selvini-Palazzoli, M., Boscolo, L., Cecchin, G., & Prata, G. *Paradox and Counterparadox*. New York: Jason Aronson, 1978.

Sluzki, C. F., & Ransom, D. C. (Eds.). *Double Bind: The Foundation of Communicational Approach to the Family*. New York: Grune & Stratton, 1976.

Watzlawick, P., Beavin, J. H., & Jackson, D. D. *Pragmatics of Human Communication*. New York: Norton, 1967.

Williams, F. S. Family therapy. In J. Marmor (Ed.), *Modern Psychoanalysis*. New York: Basic Books, 1968, pp. 387–406.

Williams, F. S. Family therapy: A critical assessment. *American Journal of Orthopsychiatry, 37* (5), 912–919, Oct., 1967a.

Zuk, G. *Family Therapy: A Triadic Based Approach*. New York: Behavioral Publications, 1971.

Table A
Developmental Phases in the Family's Life Cycle, with Typical Tasks to Be Mastered at Each Phase

Phase	Developmental Tasks
Courtship	Contending with partner-selection pressures from parents; giving over autonomy while retaining some independence, preparing for marriage, including mutually satisfying sex life; becoming free of parents.
Early marriage	Sexual compatibility; sporadic contact with a partner becomes permanent; dealing with relatives; preparation for children; increased living standard with both partners working; interdependence.
Expansion	Children—new roles as parents, reduced income if wife loses earning power; agreements between spouses re: birth control, pregnancy, child care; greater interdependence; dealing with rivalries between children; dealing with one or the other parent's overinvolvement with the children.
Consolidation	Family has no new additions but problems of school, adolescence. Sexuality in children must be dealt with; high earning power required of one or both parents; greater independence in children; generation clashes between parents and children.
Contraction	As children leave, the major activity of the couple—being parents—is gone; need for new interests; loss of involvement with children; increased economic prosperity.
Final partnership	Wife's return to work if she has not done so previously, new roles as spouses, alone with each other; height of husband's career; high economic status.
Disappearance of family	Retirement with lower economic status and reduced prestige; increased dependency on others; maximum contact time between partners; problems of death—loss of partner, bereavement, loneliness.

Adapted from *Principles of Family Psychiatry*, by J. G. Howells. Copyright 1975 by Brunner/Mazel, Inc. Reprinted by permission.

Table B
Stage-Critical Family Developmental Tasks Through the Family Life Cycle

Stage of the Family Life Cycle	Positions in the Family	Stage-critical Family Developmental Tasks
1. Married couple	Wife Husband	Establishing a mutually satisfying marriage Adjusting to pregnancy and the promise of parenthood Fitting into the kin network
2. Childbearing	Wife-mother Husband-father Infant daughter or son or both	Having, adjusting to, and encouraging the development of infants Establishing a satisfying home for both parents and infant(s)
3. Preschool-age	Wife-mother Husband-father Daughter-sister Son-brother	Adapting to the critical needs and interests of preschool children in stimulating, growth-promoting ways Coping with energy depletion and lack of privacy as parents
4. School-age	Wife-mother Husband-father Daughter-sister Son-brother	Fitting into the community of school-age families in constructive ways Encouraging children's educational achievement
5. Teenage	Wife-mother Husband-father Daughter-sister Son-brother	Balancing freedom with responsibility as teenagers mature and emancipate themselves Establishing postparental interests and careers as growing parents
6. Launching center	Wife-mother-grandmother Husband-father-grandfather Daughter-sister-aunt Son-brother-uncle	Releasing young adults into work, military service, college, marriage, etc., with appropriate rituals and assistance Maintaining a supportive home base
7. Middle-aged parents	Wife-mother-grandmother Husband-father-grandfather	Rebuilding the marriage relationship Maintaining kin ties with older and younger generations
8. Aging family members	Widow/widower Wife-mother-grandmother Husband-father-grandfather	Coping with bereavement and living alone Closing the family home or adapting it to aging Adjusting to retirement

From *Family Development*, Fourth Edition by E. M. Duvall (J. B. Lippincott). Copyright © 1957, 1962, 1967, 1971 by Harper & Row, Publishers, Inc. Reprinted by permission.

CHAPTER 2

Family Evaluation

INTRODUCTION

Family art psychotherapy is an effective modality for diagnosis. Although this author works within a dynamically oriented and systems theory framework, readers will find the methods described herein applicable to their own theoretical beliefs and styles.

The essential instrument, the *art task*, is a tool that provides the therapist and the participants with a vehicle for exploration. During the evaluation phase the art task offers the family a focus for an interactional experience. This technique, which delineates communication patterns, is viewed primarily through the process and secondarily through the content. Even within the limitation of a single session, the clinician witnesses a linked chain of events which formulate the family system as well as the group gestalt. From the moment the family is involved in creating a product, a record of each member's actions is documented onto the construct. Thus, cause and effect are observable, enabling the clinician to assess both the strengths and weaknesses of the total family and the members therein.

DIAGNOSTIC PROCEDURE

The art psychotherapy family systems diagnostic procedure is simple to administer. During the first meeting the entire family is told that they will partake in a quasi-art experience. It is presented as somewhat game-like and often enjoyable. It is not unusual for clients to indicate their resistance to the art-related exercise. This reluctance is lessened when the family is notified the art exercise is a *standardized method* for examining the way in which the family functions as a group. This statement gives credence to the use of art therapy as a clinical approach. If concerns about performance are mentioned, the therapist offers assurance by declaring, "The art, per se, is unimportant since there are no expectations either about the way in which the art is created or about the end product itself." Further encouragement is given as the participants are notified that each family is unique and finds its own style for self-expression. Some individuals work in a scribblelike fashion; the art of others contains organized designs; and then there are persons who prefer representational images. The main message is the *unqualified acceptability of their efforts*.

FIRST PROCEDURE: NONVERBAL TEAM ART TASK

The assessment phase is initiated through a nonverbal team task. It starts when the family is asked to divide up into two teams; the composition of each unit indicates family alliances. Control power can also be witnessed by the way in which the two teams are formed.

With the teams set, everyone is asked to *select a color marker that is different from the others and is to be used for the entire session.* This unique color rule facilitates the therapist's observation of each person's contribution.

Each team is notified that they will *work together on a single piece of paper.* (Where colored plasticene or construction paper is utilized, each person still maintains his/her own "special color.")

The clinician informs the members that they are *not permitted to speak, signal, or write notes to each other while working on the art, and when finished, they are merely to stop.*

After the tasks are completed, the *verbal ban is lifted,* and the teams are told to name their artwork and write the title onto the product.

SECOND PROCEDURE: NONVERBAL FAMILY ART TASK

The second diagnostic technique requires the entire family to work together on a single sheet of paper. Once again, they are to refrain from communicating with each other verbally or nonverbally. As previously, they may speak while titling their creations.

THIRD PROCEDURE: VERBAL FAMILY ART TASK

The family verbal task is the third technique. The participants are instructed to *make a single piece of artwork*. However, during this exercise *talking is permitted*.

POINTS FOR OBSERVATION

Throughout the three procedures listed above, the therapist must be an astute observer and recorder. Notes may be taken to retain each member's contribution. Every gesture and mark provides a clue to the family system. It is important to pay attention to the 17 points listed below:

1. Who initiated the picture and what was the process that led up to this person making the first mark on the page?
2. In what order did the rest of the members participate?
3. Which members' suggestions were utilized and which were ignored?
4. What was the level of involvement on the part of each person?
5. Which participants remained in their own space versus those who crossed over?
6. Did anyone "wipe out" another member by superimposing their image on top of someone else?
7. What type of symbolic contact was made and who made these overtures?
8. Did the members take turns, work in teams, or work simultaneously?
9. If there was a shift in approach, what precipitated the change?
10. Where are the geographical locations of each person's contribution (central, end, corner, all over)?
11. How much space did each person occupy?
12. What was the symbolic content of each person's contribution?
13. Which members functioned independently?
14. Who acted as initiators?
15. Who were followers or reactors?
16. Were emotional responses made?
17. Was the family's working style cooperative, individualistic, or discordant?

The above-mentioned observations, plus the verbal and nonverbal interchanges, provide the therapist with information regarding the family system. This includes ego strengths and weaknesses, assigned roles, behavioral patterns, modes of communication, and the gestalt of the family's style of interaction.

Although the knowledgeable therapist is aware of the meaning behind the evolution of the artwork, family members rarely recognize the subtleties they have revealed, since the art represents an undefended form of communication.

As the product is completed, it is essential to help the family maintain a focus on the here-and-now experience. This method does away with family history reporting, a defense that is often used by parents.

When the family art psychotherapist facilitates a discussion about the participants' perceptions of the roles that each person played, the family is engaged in an introspective exploration. Before the session ends, this author believes it is important for therapists to state their observations, in order to give support to the reality of the family process. The clinician's verbalized interactional assessment gains credibility through the visual proof of the product itself. The artwork is always referred to as the source for the psychotherapist's insight to lessen omnipotent fantasies about the therapist within the transference phenomenon.

The vignettes described below illustrate the methodology for the assessment procedures.

DIAGNOSTIC CASE ILLUSTRATION #1

Mrs. Hartzell, a young mother, requested treatment for her six-year-old child at the school's insistence. Johnny was withdrawn in the classroom and had a learning disability. Initially, the therapist met with Mrs. Hartzell to gather Johnny's developmental history. The child's progression appeared normal. Mother reported her boy was conceived out of wedlock. Although she had never lived with the child's biological father, he maintained contact with his son.

Nonverbal Team Art Task

During the first conjoint session, colored plasticene was offered to both mother and son, with instructions for the *nonverbal mutual art task*.

The parent initially held herself back as she nonverbally cued her child to begin the project. The boy selected colored plasticene which matched his own skin color. As he manipulated the medium, his mother sat still, watching her son's activity. Johnny formed a *little nude boy*, then looked around the room to discover a *toy bathtub*. Helping himself to the prop, he carefully placed his *figurative sculpture into it*.

Mother's face became alive as she responded with interest to her boy's gesture. She began to smile as she helped herself to a piece of plasticene, quickly rolling it out into a *snakelike* form. The woman looked at her son and laughed as she placed the *snake on three sides of the toy tub's rim*. Johnny, obviously upset, asked his mother, "Why did you put a snake around the boy?" Still smiling, Mother ignored the question, replying, "Oh, you realized it was a snake!" The child, unsettled and frustrated by his parent's response, turned his body away from his partner (Figure 1).

In this example, the underlying message of a dangerous or unprotected environment is both blatant and dramatic. One can quickly see the mother's inappropriate responses to her child. Her threatening metaphor displayed an unconscious hostility which alerted the therapist to the possibility of a passive-aggressive or physically aggressive child abuser.

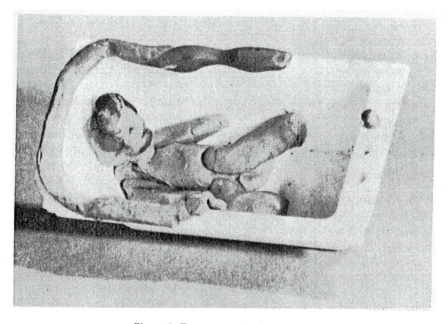

Figure 1. Dangerous environment

Dynamics

Mother's role was displayed by the following:

1. Initially she cued her child to begin, thus placing him in the role of "initiator."
2. Mrs. Hartzell was passive while "on watch," as she waited to see what her son would do. In this way Mother used the child to provide herself with the role of the "responder."
3. Mrs. Hartzell's laughter conveyed her sadistic enjoyment while symbolically placing the child in danger.
4. When Johnny questioned his mother about her response, she brought her defenses into play by refusing to answer him or to deal with the issue.

Johnny's role during the dyadic interchange was as follows:

1. The child waited for his parent to cue him before he acted.
2. When given permission to begin he created a little boy with whom he identified.
3. His immediate reaction to his mother's inappropriate response was fear and anxiety.
4. Although the rule of the exercise prohibits verbal exchange, the child, to relieve his anxiety, asked his mother for clarification of her action.
5. The mother's lack of explanation or comfort, after her threatening actions, caused Johnny to be fearful, then hurt, by her lack of attention. His feelings of helplessness finally resulted in withdrawal.

Verbal Art Task

The second technique is a verbally oriented art task. Mrs. Hartzell and her son were instructed to *make another piece of art together*. They were reminded to *select the same color plasticene again, but this time talking was permitted*.

Johnny, following the rules, again picked up the same colored plasticene, and again hesitated, waiting for his mother to give him permission.

Mrs. Hartzell, breaking the rules, chose to use a different color. Although Johnny reminded her it was necessary to retain the former colored plasticene, his mother merely laughed as she played with the media, ignoring his advice regarding conformity.

The child failed to make a move until his mother urged him to "go ahead already." He formed the *face* of a *little boy*. When mother responded by pushing in the nose on his little sculpture, Johnny began to cry, accusing his parent of being "mean." Mrs. Hartzell attempted to distract the child by saying she was going to form a tree for him. After shaping the *tree* Mrs. Hartzell took the plasticene sculpture of the *boy's face and placed it onto a limb of the tree*. Johnny, still teary-eyed, asked his mother what she was doing, but his questions were in vain since they went unanswered. At that point the child shifted from being frustrated to feeling rejected. As his psychic energies collapsed, he withdrew and became silent in an obvious depressed state.

Dynamics

The dynamics during the duo verbal art exercise revealed that in spite of the opportunity to talk, Mother *did not communicate*. Once again her gestures, which were symbolically destructive, led the author to wonder about the issue of child abuse, either as a physically active or as a negligent parent.

The psychological material that was gathered during the first conjoint session included: 1) Mother's insensitivity to her child's needs; 2) the unprotected environment in which Mrs. Hartzell placed her son; 3) the boy's anxious responses and his sense of helplessness and depression.

The author presented to Mrs. Hartzell a simplified version of the dyadic dynamics with a great deal of sensitivity and tact. This was particularly important to develop a therapeutic alliance. Since children remain in treatment only if their parents so choose, the clinician must be seen as an ally. Mrs. Hartzell was helped to examine the parallel between the artwork and the roles she and her son played out in their daily lives. The therapist told the mother she might be unaware of areas of danger for her child, citing possible examples such as crossing streets alone or access to kitchen utensils that are inappropriate for him to handle, or playing on top of chairs or beds.

A few additional assessment sessions led the therapist to confirm the suspicion of emotional child abuse and physical neglect. The case of Mrs. Hartzell and her son was reported to the Department of Protective Social Service. An investigation proved Johnny's mother to be an inadequate, neglectful parent and a destructive force in her son's psychic structure.

DIAGNOSTIC CASE ILLUSTRATION #2

The Grey family consisted of a father, 42 years old; a mother, age 40; a daughter, age 16; and two sons, one eight, the other six years old. Mrs. Grey made the phone call requesting counseling for the boys due to their "troublesome behavior."

Nonverbal Team Art Task

During the first family visit the group was asked to *divide up into two teams*. The Greys' alliances portrayed a division between the females and males in the family.

The following describes the teams' *nonverbal* art task process.

Female Team

Selecting a dark pink felt marker, Mother began to *scribble* loosely on the page. The teenage daughter picked a red color similar to her mother's, then proceeded to place a *frame* around her mother's scribble. Mother appeared unaware of the frame as she continued to draw *lines* all over the page. The adolescent held herself back as she paid a great deal of attention to Mother's drawing, assessing the activity very carefully before she decided to assert herself. The girl reshaped her mother's forms into *representational objects* (Figure 2). When the pair were finished, they agreed, "The exercise was fun." Both participants claimed they experienced themselves "as equals," believing they both enriched their partner's endeavors. The couple was pleased with the picture's title, called "Sharing," since they believed it was indicative of a favorable joint venture.

Male Team

The males, in contrast to their female counterparts, functioned differently. Father began the picture by drawing a house in the middle of the page. Both boys, verbally active, competed with each other as they vied for the greatest amount of space. They pushed and shoved one another, struggling to make symbolic contact with their Dad by adding features onto his initial structure.

When Father saw his sons taking over the entire picture, he withdrew from further participation. The eight-year-old, who sighted his father's retreat began to draw *over* his brother's contribution. The younger child retaliated by scribbling on his sibling's drawing. In a short time the boys

Figure 2. Daughter adds structure

destroyed the entire picture. Both children were agitated and angry. The three-member team agreed on the title, "Something Terrible."

Dynamics

The *female team* revealed the mother's impulsiveness. She did not respond to her daughter's attempts to engage her in a representational design. Mother's symbolic looseness or freedom threatened her daughter, who tried to ease her discomfort by setting boundaries through a "frame." When that gesture failed, the adolescent exerted power by transforming her partner's amorphous lines into definite shapes and objects. This appeared to be a symbolic attempt to tighten psychological reins on her mother. The gestures were most likely on a subconscious level as both women agreed upon the "equality" of their involvement, stating that neither person acted as a "leader or follower." Whether the mother was capable of providing structure for herself or whether she was merely being playful was unknown at that time. However, she did reveal an insensitivity to her daughter's nonverbal communication by being oblivious to the reality-oriented cues.

The *male team* showed Father's minimal involvement. Although he initiated the project, he made only one contribution. He failed to respond to his sons' chaotic activity when he discontinued his participation. The boys' sibling rivalry was blatant, and the eldest boy, resenting his father's withdrawal, displaced his rage onto his younger brother. When the father did not put an end to his sons' behavior, either physically or symbolically, both children acted out. The title, "Something Terrible," exhibited the team's dissatisfaction with themselves and with each other.

Nonverbal Family Mural

The entire family was instructed to *do a nonverbal mural together and to abide by the same rules as the nonverbal team project. Everyone must also be certain his or her color is unique.* Before the project began, numerous questions were asked of the art therapist: "Should the picture be on one piece of paper?" "Do you want us to work together or should we take turns?" The clinician did not respond with any specific answers, instead telling them they were free to approach the task in any way they desired.

Mr. and Mrs. Grey simultaneously began working on the picture. Father created an automobile, which was going off the page to the right. Mother, spotting her husband's picture, made an abstract image of a sailboat which was headed in the opposite direction.

The boys began to push each other in an attempt to get near their Dad and his picture. The eight-year-old drew an auto directly behind his father. When the six-year-old placed a person in his father's car, the older brother covered the page with raindrops. The youngest child responded to this symbolic gesture by putting a portion of a sun in the corner.

The last person to draw was the teenage daughter, who added waves under her mother's boat, a road under the automobiles, and a traffic sign in the middle of the page with the word STOP on it.

When a title was requested, the eight-year-old recommended, "It's raining and the cars bump into each other." Father, with little effort, quietly suggested, "Vehicles that Move." Mother said the title should deal with people, for example, "Everyone Going Their Way." When the daughter asked her younger brother what he wanted, he refused to answer, because he resented his brother's graphic negation. A few minutes went by without any conversation. The adolescent, sensing a lack of a resolution, produced the title, "Transportation, rain or shine." When comments were not forthcoming, the girl took the initiative to write down her title (Figure 3).

Figure 3. Family drawing

Dynamics

The roles in the family nonverbal art task were consistent with the teamwork nonverbal art, except for that of Mother. Once again *Father* played the too-brief role of leader by starting the picture with an automobile. *Mother*, responding to her husband's image, also drew a vehicle, although it was abstractly drawn, was not grounded, and was directed away from her spouse. This was in contrast to her loose design when she interacted with her daughter alone (in the female team project). Mrs. Grey also did not display the pleasure that she had while working as a dyad with her daughter. The *boys* still sought their father's attention. Their interaction was less destructive in spite of the eight-year-old's hostile gestures. The *daughter's* actions remained consistent in an authority role, shown by the way she decided upon the title, grounded the family structure by providing a baseline for both her parents, and through her "stop sign," which contained a message to the family to cease their negative actions.

At this time the author did not lead the family into any discussion nor were any observations shared. It is essential to complete the third technique of the verbal family art task before proceeding with the exploration of perceptions and insights. The contrasts in nonverbal and verbal communication must be observed to see if there is consistency or dissonance between the two modes.

Verbal Family Art Task

Following the nonverbal team approach, the next step was the *total family's participation in an art task where verbal interchange was permitted.* The Grey family was notified of the rules and was told to create a colored construction paper sculpture. Each person was given scissors and glue. However, only four sheets of different colored paper were placed in the center of the table instead of five. The therapist purposely shorted the family of one sheet to see how such a situation would be solved. This technique is used with caution. The therapist must assess if there is sufficient ego strength in the family to handle the added stress. If shortage of media is counterindicated, the correct amount of materials are supplied to the family.

The project began when both boys immediately grabbed their own pieces of paper. Father was the next person to make a selection. The female members were then faced with the dilemma of having only *one* remaining sheet of paper. Mother looked dejected but did not venture to say anything. Her daughter picked up the paper, folded it in half, tore it down the middle, and shared it with Mother.

Father, who did not pay attention to anyone else, was quick to create a *cone shape*, declaring it was a "teepee," as he placed it in the center of the table. His daughter decided to cut out a *small person*, which she glued onto her Dad's teepee. In the meantime, Mother, who had cut out a *spiral*, could not decide what to do with it. She finally dropped the design down on the table directly in front of herself.

While the parents were involved with their own project, the adolescent observed her brothers as they made two *Frankenstein* figures. Pushing Father's teepee aside the boys set down their cutouts in the middle of the table.

After some thought, the daughter decided to pick up Mother's spiral and entwined it around the brothers' Frankenstein figures. This gesture brought an argument from the boys. They complained to their parents but received neither support nor admonishment. Frustrated by a lack of response, the younger children began to shove one another. The pouting eight-year-old grabbed his Frankenstein figure and ragefully tore it up.

When the author requested a title for the construction, the boys refused to make any suggestions. Father said, "One Frankenstein Destroyed;" Mother suggested, "The Problem of the Spiral;" the daughter followed with the idea of "Frankenstein on an Indian Reservation." The last person to offer a name was the eight-year-old boy, who grumbled "Monsters Are Strong." The final decision was made by the daughter, who without consultation, wrote on a slip of paper, "The Frankenstein Was Destroyed Because of the Problem of the Spiral Since They Lived on the Indian Reservation which Let Monsters be Strong." All the family members agreed that was a good way to solve the title problem because she had included everyone's ideas (Figure 4).

The content of the artwork, as well as the suggested titles, added to the data on the family dynamics. However, during the initial evaluation session the clinician must make important decisions about *what* and *how much* information is to be shared. The therapist's observations that are made during these beginning art tasks are frequently referred to later in treatment as analogous examples of the family's daily actions.

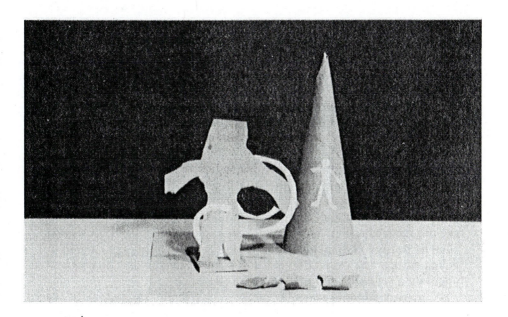

Figure 4. Construct defines roles

Dynamics

Father was unaware a problem existed when he did not note the shortage of paper. Although he began the project, he did not interact thereafter. Father allowed himself to be symbolically brushed aside by his sons when the boys moved his teepee from its central position. His passivity was revealed as he failed to communicate on any level. He did not make contact through the art, nor physically, nor through any verbal interventions.

Mother acted helpless, exhibiting her dependency needs when she was unexpectedly left without her own piece of construction paper. It was her daughter who took care of her. In addition, she created a spiral, which was cut from the outside inward, indicating the possibility of depression and anger directed towards the self. Mother placed the symbolic rage directly in front of herself, again a clue that indicates bottled-up feelings.

Daughter responded to individual family members' needs, connecting to everyone. This was displayed by putting her cutout figure onto Father's teepee; making certain Mother was not neglected by sharing her own piece of paper; symbolically setting limits for her brother's acting-out Frankenstein play.

The *parental roles were reversed* since Father was passive and Mother dependent. Their teenager proved to be the *authority figure* when she asserted herself by using Mother's spiral to symbolically contain her brother's Frankensteins. In addition, the adolescent took the responsibility of bringing the family into a more cohesive unit when she utilized everyone's suggestions for the title. The daughter submerged her own needs, since all her gestures were either of support or of containment of the other participants.

The eight-year-old child displayed his aggressiveness when he quickly grabbed the paper, and was the first person to speak and make demands. His omnipotent fantasies were shown through his Frankenstein figure. When his parents did not communicate, he used his brother to take out his frustration. The boy's low frustration tolerance was viewed when he destroyed Frankenstein, after his sister attempted to contain it. Sibling rivalry was evident when both boys created similar images and fought for a central position and a larger space.

The six-year-old child's actions were similar to his brother, with the exception of self-destructive behavior since he did not tear up his cutout. It remained within Mother's spiral, as an indication of his willingness or feelings of relief at being metaphorically contained. When this boy was threatened by his brother's self-destructive act, he chose to withdraw (similar to his father), and did not participate in naming the title.

In the Grey case, divulging a great deal of information to the family was counterindicated. Basically, what was reviewed were the overt actions, that is, the parents' lack of authority; the boys' need for boundaries; the daughter's burden of carrying more responsibility than was appropriate for her age level. The family members were encouraged to discuss their emotional responses to the experience and to share the perceptions of the role that each person played.

Trial Task: Prognosis for Change

In cases where the therapist wishes to assess the prognosis for the family's ability to change, a mini-risk-taking technique is used. For the Grey family this risk focused on a shift away from "generational blurring." In an attempt to deal with the passive authority roles of the parents, the inappropriate parental role of the daughter, and the acting-out behavior of the boys, a directive was specifically designed. It included placing the parents in a position of control by setting limits for their younger children. This was handled by giving the family *symbolic containment* through the use of a single base provided by a tray. The art psychotherapist instructed the children *to point out on the tray the position and amount of space you wish to occupy;* then they were informed, *Your parents will help you make decisions that are fair. They will mark off each family member's territory with their felt markers.*

When the boys fought for the largest amount of space, the therapist supported Mr. and Mrs. Grey by encouraging them to *negotiate* the *appropriate* amount of territory for each family member. With their markers the parents designated each person's geographical place. The parents were thus placed in a position of authority, where they took an active part in dealing with the family situation.

To encourage insight and family exploration, a follow-up technique was introduced. Everyone was asked to *make something out of clay or other materials and place it in the space sectioned off for you by your parents. Your mother and father will make certain you will keep your clay sculpture within the boundaries of your own section.*

The family conformed to the directive with relatively little argument from the boys. When the task was finished, they related the meanings of their sculpture and the feelings that the experience elicited. The discussion that took place precipitated some family self-awareness. It also opened the way towards revealing personal information. For example, *Mr. Grey* said that the technique demanded some effort on his part. He confessed he had abdicated his authority role due to his wife's nagging a long time ago. However, upon introspection he realized it was simply easier to withdraw behind a newspaper at home than to enter into setting limits for the children.

Mrs. Grey admitted that the negotiating alliance she formed with her husband during the "tray exercise" gave her added confidence. She realized without a partner's support: she floundered, felt incompetent, depreciated herself, and abandoned her authority altogether. This insight led her to understand how these feelings evoked a great deal of unexpressed rage which she handled through withdrawal and depression.

The *daughter* claimed she experienced a sense of "relief" during the exercise. The parental/child role reversal was a burden on the adolescent. She related that when she tried to separate her younger siblings, she received undeserved verbal and physical abuse from the boys. The teenager expressed her delight in having her parents "take over for a change."

The *eight-year-old* son ventilated his anger towards the therapist. The boy belligerently told the author the tray exercise was "dumb and not fair." He wanted more room and also did not like the color of his plasticene (he had not verbalized his discontent about the color before). This son emphatically stated he did not like coming to art therapy. Even the trial shift in the family system was intolerable to the child. He was enraged with the therapist for diminishing his power by providing his parents with an authoritative tool.

In contrast, the *six-year-old* was pleased to have his father involved. He said, "Doing art with my Mommy and Daddy is okay." He didn't like having limited space but was happy that "Daddy was part of the game."

In this illustration of the Grey case, the therapist and the family were able to understand individual responses and emotions and their counterplay within the family system. Based on the trial art tasks, the prognosis for a change in the family system was a positive one.

Treatment Plans

The recommended treatment plans included an exploration of the following:

Father

1. Current role in the family;
2. Examining the emotions that were evoked while shifting himself to a place of authority;
3. His aloofness as a defense;

4. How an alliance with his wife would affect his marriage and the family system.

Mother

1. The need to relinquish her power to justify her poor self-image;
2. Anger towards her husband;
3. Children's acting-out behavior as an unconscious vicarious need;
4. The effects of gaining responsibility versus her own dependency needs;
5. The use of children to deflect possible marital conflict.

Daughter

1. Reason for becoming a parental figure;
2. The need to protect her mother;
3. Individuation as a focus for growth.

Eight-Year-Old Son

1. Aggressive acts to mask depression and/or anxiety;
2. Feelings of omnipotence and low self-esteem;
3. Low frustration tolerance;
4. Sibling rivalry,
5. Self-destructive behavior,
6. Understanding cause and effect.

Six-Year-Old Son

Issues are similar to the first four listed above for his brother.

SUMMARY

To assess the family system, the participants are involved in three art tasks: 1) team art that is made in silence; 2) the entire family working together, maintaining the nonverbal stance; 3) the entire family creating a single piece of artwork, with permission to speak to each other.

The family's participation in these projects provides the therapist with firsthand interactional information. Seventeen observational points are listed.

The techniques and the therapist's interventions are demonstrated through two case histories. The first is a conjoint session with a single parent and her son. The mother unconsciously revealed her sadistically destructive parenting. The second example encompasses an intact family with three children: two latency-age sons with acting-out behavior and the third an adolescent daughter. The art project exposed Father's passivity, Mother's lack of maturity, the boys' acting-out behavior due to nonexistent structure, and the daughter's parental role reversal.

Based upon the family system a corrective treatment plan is delineated.

RECOMMENDED READING

Ackerman, N. W., & Behrens, M. L. The family group and family: The practical application of family diagnosis. In J. H. Masserman & J. L. Moreno (Eds.), *Progress in Psychotherapy*, Vol. 3. New York: Grune & Stratton, 1959.

Anthony, E. J., & Bene, E. A Technique for the objective assessment of the child's family relationships. *J. Ment. Sci.*, 103, 541–555, 1957.

Bing, E. The conjoint family drawing. *Family Process*, 9, 193–194, 1970.

Blehar, M. C. & Reiss, D. Family styles of interacting. *Families Today*, I, 171–185, U.S. Dept. of Health, Education and Welfare.

Boss, P., & Greenberg, J. Family boundary ambiguity: A new variable in family stress theory. *Family Process*, 23(4), 535–547, 1984.

Brown, S. L. Clinical impressions of the impact of family group interviewing on child and adolescent psychiatric practice. *Journal of American Academy of Child Psychiatry*, 3(4), 688–696, 1964.

Brown, S. L. Family interviewing as a basis for clinical management. In C. Hofling and J. Lewis (Eds.), *The Family Evaluation and Treatment*. New York: Brunner/Mazel, 1983.

Burns, R. C., & Kaufman, S. H. *Actions, Styles and Symbols in Kinetic Family Drawings*. New York: Brunner/Mazel, 1972.

Cromwell, R. E., & Olsen, D. H. (Eds.). *Power in Families*. New York: Wiley, 1975.

Fisher, L. Dimensions of family assessment: A critical review. *Journal of Marriage and Family Counseling*, 2(4), 367–382, 1976.

Giddes, M., Medway, J. The symbolic drawing of family life space. *Family Process*, 6, 67–80, 1967.

Greenspoon, D. Multiple family group art therapy. *Art Therapy*, 3(2), 53–60, 1986.

Jacob, T., & Davis, J. Family interaction as a function of experimental task. *Family Process*, 12(4), 415–429, 1973.

Kwiatkowska, H. Y. Family art therapy. *Family Process*, 6, 37–55, 1967.

Landgarten, H. B. Initial family interview: Diagnostic techniques. *Clinical Art Therapy: A Comprehensive Guide*. New York: Brunner/Mazel, 1981, pp. 25–30.

Levick, M., & Herring, J. Family dynamics as seen through art therapy. *Art Psychotherapy*, 1(1), April 1983.

Machover, K. *Personality Projection in the Drawing of the Human Figure*. Springfield, IL: Charles C Thomas, 1949.

Mosher, L. R., & Kwiatkowski, H. Family art evaluation. *The Journal of Nervous and Mental Disease, 3,* 165–179, 1971.

Naumburg, M. *Dynamically Oriented Art Therapy: Its Principles and Practices.* New York: Grune and Stratton, 1966.

Rabin, A. J. *Assessment with Projective Techniques.* New York: Springer Publishing Co., 1981.

Reznikoff, M., & Reznikoff, H. R. The Family Drawing Test. *Clinical Psychology, 12,* 167–169, 1956.

Safilios-Rothschild, C. Study of family power structure: 1960–1969. *Journal of Marriage and the Family, 32,* 539–552, 1970.

Shearn, C. R. & Russel, K. R. The use of family drawing as a technique for studying Parent-Child Interaction. *Journal of Projective Technique and Personality Assessment, 33*(1), 35–44, 1969.

Sherr, C., & Hicks, H. Family drawings as a diagnostic and therapeutic technique. *Family Process, 12*(4), 439–461, 1973.

Szyrynski, V. A new technique to investigate family dynamics in child psychiatry. *Canadian Psychiatric Association Journal, 8,* 94–103, 1963.

Wadeson, H. Conjoint marital art therapy techniques. *Psychiatry, 35,* 89–98, 1972.

Williams, F. S. *Family Interviews for Diagnostic Evaluations in Child Psychiatry.* Paper presented to the American Orthopsychiatric Association. New York: Unpublished, 1967.

Wolfe, D. M. Power and authority in the family. In D. Cartwright (Ed.), *Studies in Social Power.* Ann Arbor, MI: University of Michigan, Institute for Social Research, 1959.

CHAPTER 3

Family Crisis Intervention for a Molested Child

INTRODUCTION

In the summer of 1985, the *Los Angeles Times* newspaper ran an article captioned TWENTY-TWO PERCENT IN SURVEY WERE CHILD ABUSE VICTIMS (Timnick, 1985). The reporter, Lois Timnick, related the results of a nationwide *Times* poll. The study was gathered from 2,627 people, both female and male adults. Responses revealed 22% of the pollees had experienced sexual abuse during their childhood; of this number 27% were women and 16% were men. The highest percentage of crimes were committed by friends and acquaintances (41%), with strangers next (27%), and a near equal number performed by relatives (23%).

Due to the lack of public education, the poll replies indicated that victims believed their molestation ordeal was a unique experience. They failed to realize that many individuals have suffered similar encounters.

Although professional literature contains many articles on the treatment of children who have been victimized by relatives or persons known to them, information on therapy for a child who has been molested by a *stranger* on a *one-time* basis is extremely sparse. For such cases, a family therapy crisis intervention model is the treatment of choice since the insult of the sexual assault affects all of the members. The abuse causes everyone in the family to be flooded with a myriad of emotions: rage towards the perpetrator, plus fear and anxiety over the unprotective and threatening environment. Coupled with these distressing feelings is the parents' guilt due to their preventative impotence.

An effective treatment approach for molested victims and their families is the clinical art therapy model. For this type of crisis intervention, concomitant meetings are vital. These include: individual therapy for the child, conjoint sessions for their parents, plus meetings for the family. Art tasks are specifically designed to focus directly and promptly upon the immediate problem. This author uses a psychodynamic here-and-now approach. For the child, latent material is dealt with through the metaphor, whereas the manifest indicators and goals are clearly stated through both the verbal and nonverbal modes.

Aside from the usual treatment benefits that psychotherapy in general has to offer, the art aspect offers two additional uniquely significant contributions. The first deals with the *courtroom trauma*; in many instances sexually abused children have illustrated the experience to be more damaging than the molestation itself. For this reason, this author engages the child in an educational experience, where she draws the courtroom scene, demonstrating the seating arrangements of the judge, the witnesses, and so forth. The youngster's familiarity with the legal setting tends to lower the anxiety about the "unknown" and lessens the psychic harm of appearing in court.

The second salient factor is the *child's own art*. This is admissible evidence for identifying the criminal offender. For instance, artwork often relates details of the molester's face, body, and clothing. Drawings also demonstrate information on the abuser's aberrant sexual behavior and discloses the site of the act.

Unfortunately, molested children are required to remember and relate details of their horrendous encounter, oftentimes long after the incident. Since the victim's own artwork is the visual documentation of the molestation, he or she can benefit from this recollective tool when accurate retrospection in the courtroom is required.

CASE ILLUSTRATION

Family art psychotherapy is described in this chapter as a crisis intervention model for a molested child. Therapy included individual, conjoint, and family sessions. The length of the brief treatment was six weeks.

PRECIPITATING EVENT

Eight-year-old Donnie Arbutus was temporarily kidnapped and molested by a stranger. The child's reactions were appropriately vulnerable and angry. His parents, enraged over the episode and concerned about the psychological effect on their son, contacted the author the day after the traumatic event took place.

The first meeting was a three-hour session divided into three parts: 1) conjoint meeting between Mother and Father; 2) individual session for Donnie; and 3) family therapy. Since much of the reporting was repeated by both the parents and the child during the various interviews, particulars about the events will not be reiterated herein to avoid redundancy.

SESSION ONE: PART I/*Conjoint Meeting: Mr. and Mrs. Arbutus*

During the conjoint session the art therapy format was eliminated. The parents, a psychologically sophisticated and well-adjusted couple, had a great deal of pertinent information to relate to the therapist. The art aspect would have prolonged the interview and added additional anxiety for Mr. and Mrs. Arbutus. Therefore it was deleted from the first part of the session.

The couple reported the following:

Donnie left school to walk the four blocks to his home. As a rule his next-door friend Johnny accompanied him. However, on that particular day Johnny did not attend school, and Donnie went home alone. Without anyone to talk to, the child resorted to collecting stones as he walked along. He was delighted to spot a particularly large and beautiful rock. Donnie stopped to figure out if he should come back later with his wagon because he wondered if it was too heavy for him to carry home.

As the child was examining the rock a young man stopped his sports car to ask Donnie the location of a certain street. Donnie, who had been taught not to talk to strangers, said he didn't know. Then, for some intuitive reason the boy decided not to linger but to return home as soon as possible.

The stranger drove his car at a slow pace, crawling alongside of Donnie. Although the man repeatedly asked the little boy questions, the child looked straight ahead, refusing to reply.

When Donnie was only a block away from his house, he told the stranger, "I'm nearly home. Ask my mother; she will tell you what you want to know." Evidently, when the driver heard how close the child was to home he decided to act fast. He immediately notified the boy to "hop in the car, I'll drive you home and then I'll ask your mother." Donnie calmly refused with a "no, thank you."

At that point the car was so close to the child it was practically on the sidewalk. Sensing danger, Donnie began to run but was blocked off by the swerve of the vehicle. The stranger opened the car door, reached out, grabbed and lifted the little boy off his feet, then quickly dumped him into the space behind the driver's seat. He warned Donnie to "keep still and to lay face down," with the threat of being "hurt" if he did not comply. Terribly frightened, the child cowered, hugging himself as a reaction to the danger which he knew was yet to come.

When the small sports car came to a "bumpy stop" Donnie realized he was in a nearby park where he often played. As the molester dragged the child out of the car, Donnie tried to look around for the exact location but the man pushed Donnie down to the ground where he sexually assaulted the child.

When the offender satisfied his desires, he returned Donnie to his neighborhood only a few blocks from home. (The child had not offered his parents any particular details of the sexual act itself.)

Mr. and Mrs. Arbutus reported their own feelings of rage and fear. They worried about their child's psychological reactions, wondering if the trauma would incur lifetime damage. The couple entertained the question of the role that the event might play in the future. As concerned and loving parents, they dreaded becoming overly protective. They realized they would worry about something terrible happening to their child once again, since "molestation" was now no longer a news item or a film scenario.

The Arbutus's reported that their son screamed and cried a number of times during the previous night as the trauma repeated itself in his dreams.

When the incident was reported to the police, Donnie himself offered the information. His parents struggled with the problems that could invade their lives if the police did find the molester. They believed it would be frightening for their son to identify the sex offender and then to have him appear in court. However, in spite of these anxiety-provoking considerations Mr. and Mrs. Arbutus were determined to have the molester punished and prevented from perpetrating such crimes onto other children. For this reason they decided to do what was essential to their moral code.

SESSION ONE: PART II/*Individual Meeting: Donnie*

When the second part of the session began, the author asked Donnie if he knew "why you are here to see me?" The child, who had been well prepared by his parents, stated, "To talk to you about what happened yesterday and to tell you about my feelings. You help people with problems feel better." Satisfied with the answer, the art therapist set paper, markers, plasticene, and some small toy props before the child, telling him, "You can do some art and talk to me at the same time." Without further instruction Donnie immediately seized the opportunity to draw and tell about *a car and a man grabbing me*. He explained the story about his walk home from school, about the man questioning him, and only briefly about the molestation itself. Several times he stressed, "It's too disgusting to talk about! It makes me sick to think about it. It's too disgusting, too disgusting to think about."

It was essential for Donnie to realize child molestation was not an experience he alone had undergone. It was also of the utmost importance to alleviate the child from suppressing details of the event. Therefore the author very gently informed the child, "In my work with other children your age who have undergone similar terrible experiences, they have told me how the man who kidnapped them put his penis in their mouths." Donnie's eyes opened up wide in amazement that the author knew about such incidents and also that other children had undergone experiences like his. With obvious relief he nodded in assent. The author continued on: "These little boys also told me that the stranger sometimes ejaculated in their mouths; that means a white liquid came out of their penis." The child looked the therapist directly in the eyes to check out her sincerity, and to acknowledge the truth of her statements. His gratitude was obviously displayed on his face.

To encourage Donnie's self-expression, the *plasticene was placed directly in front of him*. Without any instruction, the child picked up the pinkish color and rolled out a *large phallus*. Offering no interpretation, the clinician allowed the child to continue with his art task uninstructed. When he finished he noticed an *empty cigar* box, which he selected for the placement of his plasticene sculpture. He suddenly changed his mind, putting half of it into the box and half out. He looked at the phallic symbol, then said, "No, it doesn't fit—it's too big, I'll chop it off." He proceeded to slam the lid shut, thus chopping the piece in half. Symbolically, the cigar box acted as a castrating mouth and an unconscious means to punish the perpetrator. When he completed the art task he said, "That's that," and wiped his hands, trying to clean himself of the media and psychologically of the sexual assault that had been rendered upon his person.

Donnie was then questioned about the molester. Instead of giving a verbal answer, he drew a *red car, with a dented right front fender*. "What about the man?" the author asked. Again the child chose to respond nonverbally through a drawing that portrayed the figure of a *man with black hair* telling him to pull his pants down; although Donnie protested, the offender threateningly insisted (Figure 5). When asked about the age of the person in his picture, he said the man did not look as old as his father (who was 30) but was too old to go to high school (he could judge high school age as there was one situated at the end of his block). It seemed the molester was in his early twenties. Donnie feeling proud of his artwork boasted he could draw the picture that was on the "bad man's T-shirt." Encouraged to do so, he created a surf rider (Figure 6). In addition, Donnie made the "white and blue *jogging shoes* like the ones my friend Johnny has." Amazed at the child's uncanny observations, the author realized the pictures would be of help in case the child had to testify in court.

When Donnie was asked to portray his feelings towards the perpetrator, once again he did not need any instruction or encouragement. The picture was quickly poured onto the page as he portrayed the black-haired "disgusting *bad man.*" Donnie then picked up a red crayon and proceeded to "X" him out on the page.

Without a lead from the therapist, the child went on to say "I want the police to get him. I want them to find that man!!! I want to go to court to get even with him. I don't want him to do anything so disgusting to anyone else!" As he spoke, he drew a *finger pointing*, again unconsciously reproducing a phallic symbol (Figure 7). He said it was his own finger which would point out the criminal offender, adding, "That man did disgusting things, you know, and he kidnapped me too!!" He then quieted down as he drew a *house*, which he explained was his home, and only a few blocks from where he had been returned by "the bad man."

Some closure was needed for the Arbutus crisis intervention. Therefore, it seemed advisable to offer Donnie and his parents some time together.

SESSION ONE: PART III/*Family Meeting:*
All Members Present

The third part of the meeting required closure. Although the therapist did not have a "set plan," Donnie led the way. When his parents came into the room, the child immediately shared his artwork. First he showed his castrated phallic plasticene sculpture, without any insight into its meaning. Then he pointed to the drawing of the "disgusting thing that happened," adding, "and Mrs. Landgarten told me that she knows other kids who had bad mans do bad things to them. She even knows what the man did!!" As he boasted about the author's empathic knowledge, Mr. and Mrs. Arbutus looked relieved, suspecting the information would help their son feel less different than other children.

When Donnie finished talking about the artwork, the author notified the parents that the pictures of the dented fender, the T-shirt, and the

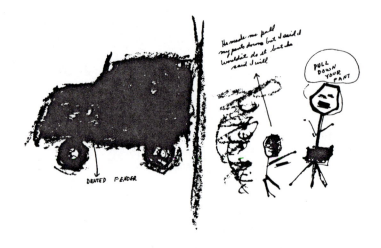

Figure 5. Molester's car has dented fender

Figure 6. Identifying T-shirt design

Figure 7. Pointing out offender

jogging shoes could be used in a courtroom testimony. Even the drawings that depicted the assaultive scene are valid evidence which could be submitted to the court.

Before the family left the art therapy session, the author gave Donnie a sketch pad and a box of crayons to take home, telling him to draw as many pictures as he wished with themes of his own choice. He was to bring the drawings when he came to the next session. These directions were given to help the child express himself, to encourage sublimation, and to serve as a transitional object since he had already established trust in the therapist.

A subsequent family appointment was set up for the next afternoon since Donnie would be going to the police station to view photographs of criminal offenders in the morning.

SESSION TWO/*Individual Meeting: Donnie*

When Donnie came for his second art therapy session three days later, he reported he had been to the police station and found the picture of the "bad man." He said, before he looked through the photos, that he told the police he remembered the assaulter very clearly and had even drawn pictures of him and his car.

Looking over the materials on the art therapy table the child selected the plasticene. Coincidently, the media that was hard served as a particularly therapeutic choice since it helped him ventilate his anger. As Donnie squeezed, banged, pulled, and pounded the plasticene, he provided himself with a cathartic experience. When the medium became soft enough to mold, Donnie again formed a *penis* which he attached to a toy *pig* prop. He stood it up on its hind legs and placed the protruding penis in the center of the pig's belly. "Yep," he said, "it's a pig with a big giant pecker" (Figure 8). The little boy then looked around the office and spotted some small toy soldiers. He became very involved in creating a *fortified trench behind which he placed his ammunition-laden soldiers.* Donnie laid them down on their bellies (unconsciously protecting their male organs) and engaged them in a one-way battle against the pig.

As the soldiers shot their bullets into the animal with its erected penis, Donnie kept repeating, "I'll shoot you, you pig, you ugly pig. I'll shoot you with your gigantic pecker, pecker. Pow, Pow, zap, zap. There, I'm going to kill you over and over again" (Figure 9). This scenario repeated itself for almost a half hour. Then Donnie suddenly looked as if he had used up enough energy on his play of the "good-guy soldiers and the ugly pig with the gigantic pecker." He turned to the author to say, "That's that. What do you want me to do now?"

Donnie was given paper and markers and was told he could *draw whatever he wished.* Nevertheless, when he related he wanted the author to give him an idea, she realized he was asking for needed structure after expressing his destructive fantasies. Therefore, she proceeded to draw a comic-strip-fashioned grid, informing Donnie that he was to *place sequential pictures into the squares depicting his experience in the police station that morning.*

The drawing showed the *"nice policeman" giving him candy. His parents sat nearby as a policeman showed him a "bunch of pictures."* The next scene portrayed him *detecting the molester.* The last picture was of the *policeman telling Donnie,* "You are a very smart and good little boy. Your mother and father must be very proud of you. I'm sorry you had such a terrible experience." Donnie continued to say, "Then Dad took us out for a hamburger and french fries and then we came here." Satisfied with his portrayal of the morning events, the child requested permission to get the sketchbook from his mother since he wanted to show the author the pictures he had drawn the previous evening. The sketch pad contained 16 pictures, all similar in content, with *Donnie in* one way or another *physically punishing the molester.* The majority of scenes were finished off by being *"Xed"* out or *scribbled over,* as an attempt to wipe out or to destroy the memory of the event.

A FEW DAYS LATER

Mrs. Arbutus phoned to report the molester had been picked up by the police. She was notified that Donnie's testimony in court would be especially respected because of his pictures of the red car with the dent-

Figure 8. Pig as a metaphor

Figure 9. Killing the perpetrator

ed fender, the surf-rider's T-shirt, and the jogging shoes. The police had discovered these objects at the criminal's home. In a short time Donnie would be required to appear in court.

SESSION THREE /*Family Meeting: All Members Present*

The author, who had seen the negative results of children who needed to testify in court, decided in the session one week later to acquaint the family with the environment of the courtroom. The therapist herself drew the judge behind his desk, the witness box where Donnie would sit, and so forth. Mr. and Mrs. Arbutus were invited to participate in making the picture of the courtroom. As Donnie asked questions, he was encouraged to join in by adding color to the project. The art psychotherapist withdrew as the family sat together drawing a mural, which would prepare them for Donnie's court testimony against the molester (Figure 10).

Mr. and Mrs. Arbutus were also encouraged to take their son on a trip to the courthouse, again as an attempt to lessen the surprise and trauma of the forthcoming experience.

SESSION FOUR/*Family Meeting: All Members Present*

When Donnie and his parents returned to see the author one month later, they brought along the original sketch pad which the therapist had given the child, plus several other drawing pads which Mrs. Arbutus had purchased for the purpose of self-expression. A large number of pictures depicted the *child's feelings* before and after the court situation.

The latest artwork displayed *a little boy playing in his yard, driving a bike,* and *watching television*. These creations, which matched Donnie's behavior, indicated a positive prognosis.

With the intelligent and caring help of his parents, Donnie had received the important and sensitive support which helped him continue his favorable self-image, handle a traumatic situation successfully, and express his feelings of rage through the creative process.

To bring closure to the crisis intervention, the author instructed the family to *make a single collage which shows your family during the time of the ordeal, your family now, and all of you in the future.* Before starting the project, the parents discussed the kind of magazine photos they would be looking for. As a group, they decided to find people or objects depicting anger, anxiety, or worry to express their *past* feeling; for the *now* pictures they wanted to show themselves leading a "normal life"; and in

Figure 10. Courtroom environment

the *future* they wished to find pictures signifying their family's pride and happiness.

The Arbutus family enjoyed making the collage. Their selections exemplified their emotions when they faced the fact of the molestation. A picture of *shaky hands* stood for their worry about Donnie and also their own anxiety (Figure 11). Their current picture, which was titled "normal life," showed *a family visiting Disneyland, going fishing, playing ball and eating a turkey dinner*. The future images were of *George Washington and the Statue of Liberty*. The first demonstrated their courage to be truthful and to testify in court against a child molester. They stated their satisfaction about the molester being sentenced and prevented from repeating criminal offenses against other children; therefore, the photo of the "Statue of Liberty represented justice" and their own "feelings of being liberated from the past event and a readiness to get on with their lives" (Figure 12).

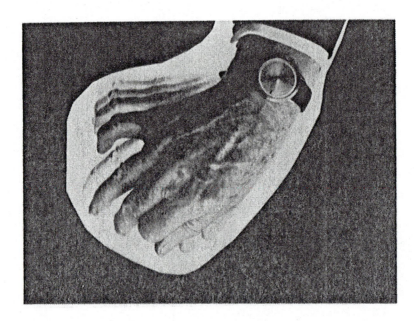

Figure 11. Past: worry and anxiety

FOLLOW-UP: SIX MONTHS, ONE YEAR, AND THREE YEARS LATER

Mrs. Arbutus phoned the art psychotherapist six months later requesting a follow-up art therapy session for Donnie. Although the child was doing extremely well, his parents believed an art therapy assessment would be valuable and reassuring. The author, evaluating Donnie and his artwork, found the boy had been alleviated of fear and guilt regarding his molestation. Responses to his sexuality and to male figures did not reflect any psychological distortions. Further treatment was counterindicated.

The one- and three-year follow-ups were made through phone calls on the part of the therapist. Mrs. Arbutus' reports showed Donnie to be progressing at a normal rate of development with no cause for concern.

Figure 12. Truth, justice, and liberated past

SUMMARY

A case history of art therapy crisis intervention for a molested five-year-old boy is described. The initial meeting, which took several hours, was held in three separate parts. The *first* section required the parents to relate the details of the incident. The *second* part was with Donnie individually where he created drawings of his experience. The use of plasticene followed for self-expression and to ventilate his rage. The child also formed images which offered clues for identifying the perpetrator. The entire family participated in the *third* segment. When Donnie chose to share his art with his parents, the family was notified that the graphics could be submitted as testimony. The child was given art materials to take home as a transitional object and to encourage the continuance of self-expression for cathartic purposes.

During the second appointment, Donnie continued the use of the media to symbolically castrate the molester. He was given structure through the serial fashion art as he portrayed his police station event. In the following family art psychotherapy session, Donnie and his parents were prepared for the court trauma. They had an opportunity to familiarize themselves with the environment, through drawings, to lower the child's anxiety while testifying.

During the last family meeting the artwork was examined to assess their working-through process and to bring closure to the crisis intervention treatment.

RECOMMENDED READING

Adams-Tucker, C. Proximate effects of sexual abuse in childhood: A report on 28 children. *American Journal of Psychiatry, 139,* 1252–1256, 1982.

Bender, L., & Grugett, A. E. A follow-up report on children who had an atypical sexual experience. *American Journal of Orthopsychiatry, 22,* 825–37, 1952.

Berliner, L., & Stevens, D. Harborview social workers advocate special techniques for child witness. *Response, 1*(2), December 1976.

Burgess, A. W., McCausland, M. P., & Wolbert, W. A. Children's drawings as indicators of sexual trauma. *Perspectives in Psychiatric Care, 19,* 50–58, 1981.

Burgess, A. W., Groth, A. N., Holmstrom, L., & *Sexual assault of children and adolescents.* Lexington, MA: D.C. Heath and Co., 1978.

Caplan, G. *Principles of Preventative Psychiatry.* New York: Basic Books, 1964.

DeFrancis, V. *Protecting the Child Victim of Sex Crimes.* Denver: The American Humane Association, Children's Division, 1966.

Ellerstein, N. S., & J.W. Canavan. Sexual abuse of boys. *American Journal of the Disadvantaged Child, 134,* 255–57, 1980.

Finkelhor, D. *Sexually Victimized Children.* New York: Free Press, 1979.

Kelley, S. J. The use of art therapy with sexually abused children. *Journal of Psychosocial Nursing and Mental Health Services,* 22(12), 12–18, 1984.

Koppitz, E. M. *Psychological Evaluation of Children's Human Figure Drawings.* New York: Grune & Stratton, 1968.

Landis, J. Experiences of 500 Children with adult sexual deviances. *Psychiatric Quarterly Supplement, 30,* 91–109, 1956.

Peters, J. J. Children who were victims of sexual assault and the psychology of offenders. *American Journal of Psychotherapy, 30,* 398–421, 1976.

Schultz, L. G. *The Sexual Victimology of Youth.* Springfield: Charles C Thomas, 1979.

Schwartz, B., Horowitz, J. M., & Sauzier, M. Severity of emotional distress among sexually abused preschool, school-age and adolescent children. *Hospital and Community Psychiatry, 36*(5), May 1985.

Stember, C. J. Art therapy: A new use in diagnosis and treatment of sexually abused children. *Sexual Abuse of Children, Selected Readings.* Washington: Government Printing Office, 1980, pp. 59–63.

Tilelli, J. A., Turek, D., & Jaffe, A. C. Sexual abuse of children: Clinical findings and implications for management. *New England Journal of Medicine, 302,* 319, 1980.

Weakland, J. H., Fisch, R., Watzlawick, P., & Bodin, A. Brief Therapy: Focused problem resolution. *Family Process, 13*(2), 148–168, 1974.

CHAPTER 4

The Family
in the Midst
of Divorce

INTRODUCTION

On July 15, 1985, the cover of *Newsweek* printed the photograph of a woman playing baseball with her two children. It had a huge title, "The Single Parent." This cover page included the statement, "By 1990 Half of All American Families May Be Headed by Only One Parent."

The accompanying article stated, "According to the Census Bureau statistics for 1984, single parents headed 25.7 percent of families with children under 18 in the United States . . . and approximately half of the children born in the 1980s will spend part of their childhood living with one parent."

Due to these circumstances, as of spring 1985, 33 states have authorized joint custody. In recent times many *binuclear families* (a term used to describe children who live in two households) find it beneficial to have both mothers and fathers involved in the child-rearing and decision making. With this type of arrangement, the offspring tend to be more secure since they view their parents as having equal authority.

Although *prevention* is always the treatment of choice, it is seldom practiced in divorce cases. Unfortunately, the clinician is usually contacted after a court appearance when the custody issues are still unresolved and the couple's negative feelings have escalated. Such situations place the child in a double bind laden with guilt and suffering. It is advantageous for family mediation to begin as early in the separation as possible. Whether the negotiations take place before or after a divorce, the clinician will act as the *child's advocate* and recommend arrangements that contribute to the child's well-being. Ideally, the joint custody contract is implemented while treatment continues.

The family art therapy approach to divorce emphasizes both the practical and emotional elements of a two-family system, and facilitates the child's adaptation to a new living style.

CASE ILLUSTRATION

This chapter demonstrates art psychotherapy for a family while the parents were in the midst of a divorce. Therapy meetings, on a weekly basis, encompassed one of the following: 1) the entire family; 2) either Mother *or* Father, plus the children; 3) Mother and Father in conjoint sessions. The length of treatment was three months.

PRECIPITATING EVENT

For several months six-year-old Patsy Maxella had repeated nightmares. She would awaken amidst sobs and screams, crying out to her mother for "help." In recent weeks Patsy's fears had exacerbated and her appetite diminished. Separation anxiety caused the child to balk at attending school. She was unhappy most of the time. During the initial phone call to the therapist, Mrs. Maxella focused on her daughter's problems. Although less concerned about her nine-year-old son Darren, she mentioned that his oppositional behavior was intolerable and that he bullied his sister unmercifully.

SESSION ONE/*Individual Meeting: Mrs. Maxella*

During the first appointment, Mrs. Maxella was seen alone. She reported the following family history:

After 15 years of marriage Mr. and Mrs. Maxella separated due to their divergent interests, value systems, and lifestyles. Although the couple attempted to be "friends," their relationship deteriorated when animosity was provoked through financial and legal matters. The children's living arrangements had become a major issue. From the various incidents related by Mrs. Maxella, it appeared as if both parents competed with each other as they vied for Patsy's and Darren's attention, in hopes of gaining the *favorite parent status*.

Both Mr. and Mrs. Maxella demanded a fuller share of their son's and daughter's time. In their current arrangement, Father picked up the children two or three times a week for dinner, and kept them in his apartment from Saturday morning to Sunday night. In spite of the couple's attempts to be fair to the children, Patsy and Darren were frequently placed in the position of reporting daily events and giving out information.

Darren's and Patsy's histories showed that their physical and cognitive milestones had been met during a normal course of development. Both children were bright and in "gifted programs" within the public school system and had a number of interests including art.

The family had experienced two traumatic losses in the last year, both the death of the maternal grandfather and the leave taking of the house-keeper, who had been an important figure in the children's lives.

Mrs. Maxella reported that Darren and Patsy had witnessed violent behavior between her husband and herself. For the most part, the abuse was verbal. However, they also saw their mother break dishes, slam doors, and on several occasions throw her husband's clothes outside. In addition, Mr. Maxella had punched his fists through doors and removed a part from the motor of his wife's car, rendering it nonfunctional.

The children still overheard their parents fighting on the telephone. It was not unusual for Mother or Father to hang up the receiver before the conversation was ended.

The "only area" in which Mr. and Mrs. Maxella controlled themselves was regarding their children. They both truly wished to do what was "best" for their son and daughter.

When the histories were completed, Mrs. Maxella was notified that a family art psychotherapy session was part of the evaluation. The author questioned if the children's father might be present at the session despite the marital dissolution. Since the Maxella parents were both very interested and involved with their children, they agreed to an art therapy family meeting.

SESSION TWO/*Family Meeting: All Members Present*

Nonverbal Team Drawing

After explaining the art therapy format and its purpose, the family was asked to *divide up into two teams*. Darren, who responded immediately, made the first choice when he selected his dad as a partner, leaving Patsy and her mother satisfied to become the other team.

Rules for the nonverbal duo drawing exercise were explained: 1) *a single piece of paper is shared*; 2) *each person selects a single color which is used throughout the project*; 3) *there is to be no communication either verbally or nonverbally*.

On the male team, Darren and his father worked cooperatively. They took turns as they created a *racing car on a speedway* (Figure 13). On the female team, Mother's glances silently urged her daughter to take the lead. Patsy began by drawing a *ghost* and her mother responded by changing the figure into a *real person*. During the next turn the child made a *circle* to which Mother added facial features (Figure 14).

Later when the teams were asked to *give titles to the artwork*, father and son each made a suggestion. The result was a combination of the two ideas and was named "Winner's Pace." In contrast the female team had difficulty choosing the title because Mother insisted upon "The Girls" and Patsy wanted "The Ghost," in spite of the additional ideas that were mentioned. The parent finally decided each person would select her own title. Patsy was satisfied to return to her original title, "The Ghost," while Mother added "And The Girls" in an obvious attempt to be friendly or connected to her child.

Dynamics. Alliances were formed through the power of Darren, who immediately selected his father. Without any discussion the family formed two teams—one of males, the other females.

The males worked cooperatively by taking turns; each person made his own image within the framework of a common theme. They enjoyed the task and were pleased with the results. Their title was formed in a similar manner, as each person's suggestion became a part of the name.

In contrast, the females' modus operandi was different, as Mother cued her daughter to begin. The child portrayed an imaginary figure, which Mother changed into an earthly one. After Patsy's second attempt, Mother again entered her child's space to form it into a concrete face. The interaction during the title selection showed both mother and daughter to be dissatisfied with their partner's ideas.

Patsy was determined to be autonomous, while her mother insisted upon injecting change and functioning as a duet. The impasse was dissolved only when Mother took the authority and declared individuality would be allowed. With this decision, Patsy grasped the opportunity to assert herself and to obliterate her Mother's alteration by giving it the title of a "Ghost." Mrs. Maxella, who seemed to understand her daughter's message, was still determined to connect to her daughter and had the final word when she added "And The Girls."

In order to observe the children's interaction with each parent, *the therapist shifted the teams* to mother-son and father-daughter. Again, a nonverbal duo drawing was requested.

Figure 13. Male team: cooperative

Figure 14. Female team: change to reality

Nonverbal Drawing: Mother and Son

Both participants began to draw simultaneously, each on their own side of the paper. Darren's picture showed a boy flexing his muscles. Mother made an abstract design. When she decided to color in the boy's shirt on her son's drawing, he shoved her hand away and belligerently colored onto her design. At one point she made an attempt to move his marker away. However, when Darren was insistent about drawing on her picture, she became frustrated and angry and decided to stop drawing altogether. With a smirk on his face Darren continued to draw on his mother's side of the page. When it came to writing the title, Mother, too upset to participate, withdrew. Darren, who looked as if he had won a victory, omnipotently named the picture "The Strongest Boy in the World" (Figure 15).

Nonverbal Drawing: Father and Daughter

Father looked at his daughter, allowing her to begin. She drew a house. Father added the chimney, door, walkway, and tree. Patsy placed curtains across the upstairs windows, then happily proceeded to fill in

Figure 15. Powerful son

details on the house. Father and daughter were pleased with the results and agreed on their title, "A Family House" (Figure 16).

Dynamics. In the *mother-and-son team* the authority struggle was evident from the beginning. Darren's picture of physical strength was a metaphor for his psychological power. Nonverbally he displayed his anger and a determination to get even (by coloring on her design). When Mother's attempts to utilize her authority were thwarted, she disengaged altogether, leaving her son to believe she was the weaker partner.

The *father-and-daughter team* began as Patsy was cued in to begin. The partners worked in concert obviously having a good time. The house project indicated the dyad's wish to have the family reunited.

Both children responded to their father in a friendly, joyful way and related to their mother with some difficulty. Patsy and Darren appeared to experience their mother as an intruder. In Patsy's case, Mrs. Maxella used her authority to implant changes which her daughter resented, while Darren's response to Mother was one of blatant hostility.

PARTICIPANTS' COMMENTS

A discussion of the participants' observations was opened by the author. Darren spoke up first, stating, "My Dad and I make a good team. We made a great picture." The therapist asked about Darren's observations regarding the picture he created with his mother. Without any hesitation he replied, "See the muscles? I'm stronger than her; she quit!" The attention was turned to Mrs. Maxella, who admitted, "I refuse to be invaded so I withdrew." The author then asked Darren, "What about Mother's attempt to add color to your drawing?" He was quick to reply, "I knew she would spoil it!" Without any anger in her voice Mrs. Maxella told her son, "Maybe I would have improved the picture." Although it was not stated as such, Darren heard his mother's statement as a put-down. He began to pout and got up to leave the room. In response Father placed his hand on his son's shoulder as he said to the therapist, "I'm sorry, my wife had a bad time with Darren. Guess he can't pull any of that tough stuff with me. Actually, I found it fun to draw with the kids. They are both very talented."

Patsy, who had been listening intently, agreed with her father, adding, "It was fun to draw. I wish our whole family could draw a picture together!" Looking at the author, she pleaded, "Could we do a picture together, please, please, can we?" The clinician puzzled aloud about the value of a family drawing at a time when Mom and Dad were getting divorced. Patsy voiced a wish, "Maybe we will be a whole family again."

Figure 16. Father-daughter duo drawing

The comment upset Mrs. Maxella. She firmly notified her child, "No Patsy, Daddy and I are *not going to get back together*. Mrs. Landgarten is going to help all of us while Dad and I are getting divorced." Facing reality was difficult for Patsy. The child buried her head in Father's lap to avoid eye contact and deny the painful situation. Mr. Maxella also looked away from his wife indicating the same desire to forget about the separation. Although sad, Mrs. Maxella was determined to deal with the marital dissolution.

Since the Maxellas were not a united family, nor was this a goal for treatment, the usual procedure (which requires the entire family to create two murals, one nonverbally, the other verbally) was deemed inappropriate.

The next appointment was set for five weeks later, since the children were going to camp for a month.

FAMILY SITUATION AS REPORTED BY MOTHER
IN TELEPHONE CALL

Mr. and Mr. Maxella were enraged with one another, as each believed he or she was being cheated out of a fair share of the estate. Verbal abuse had become a daily occurrence. When the children returned from camp, they overheard the fighting and frequently witnessed the deteriorating effect it had on their parents.

SESSION THREE/*Family Meeting: All Members Present*

To clarify the purpose of the treatment, the individual family members were told *to create three objects which show*: 1) what you *want* to happen in therapy, 2) what you *think* could happen here in the art therapy meeting, and 3) what you *believe* the outcome will be. They were given a choice of several media: collage, markers, and plasticene.

It was apparent Darren knew all his answers as he rapidly drew his *mother and dad getting back together*. He displayed them smiling and holding hands. Patsy's artwork, which also had her *parents as a happy couple*, included her *brother* and *herself* as well. Both children believed their single answer had a twofold meaning since it applied to both questions, "What do you want from treatment?" and "What could happen?" However, they differed when it came to drawing the *outcome*. Patsy again drew the family together. Her picture included her *cat* Mopsy, who had disappeared a few months ago (Figure 17). In contrast, Darren drew his *mother standing in the doorway* of their home on one side, while he drew a

Figure 17. Wish for united family

line down the center, with his *father standing alone* on the other side of the paper (Figure 18).

The content of the children's art poignantly portrayed the meaning. Mr. Maxella was saddened and remained silent as he looked at the pictures. However, his wife's reaction remained consistent as she told Patsy, "No, you must understand! Daddy and I are *getting divorced; we'll never live together again."* Although Mrs. Maxella's voice was kind, the child reacted as though her mother had struck her; Patsy skirted across the room to cower behind her father. Mr. Maxella tried to comfort his daughter, then claimed, "Mother is right, Honey. She is not angry but trying to have you believe what is actually happening." Darren's negative response to his sister was "Yeah, she (Patsy) always pretends." Father, disliking Darren's attack, defended his daughter, "No she doesn't, son. Now don't pick on your sister!"

To shift to the subject of separation, the author asked Patsy to tell why Mopsy the cat was included in the family drawing when it was mentioned she had "taken off." The child explained the picture represented her wish to have the animal home "so everyone would be together again." Realizing there would not be enough time to deal with Mopsy, the clinician told the family they would discuss this matter during another session. The symbolism of the cat, as an object of loss, was especially important for this family to deal with in light of the divorce and the work on separation.

Returning to the artwork, Father's drawings were examined next. He had created the *peace symbol* in plasticene three times. Mr. Maxella said, what he wanted from therapy, what he thought could happen, and what he believed the outcome to be was "a peaceable resolution for everyone concerned." He added he was aware of the burden that had been placed on the entire family due to the divorce.

Mrs. Maxella, touched by her husband's declaration, volunteered to explain her photo collage. It included a *surgeon,* which meant she *wanted* the therapist to "help the family through the trauma of divorce. I do not want the child to be left with scars" (Figure 19). Mrs. Maxella said she *believed* the family would manage to get through the difficult times and would experience more personal fulfillment in the future. For the *outcome* of treatment she drew a picture of the *art therapy office* explaining she was certain the therapist could mediate and recommend some workable arrangements (Figure 20).

As the session came to an end, the author declared ongoing therapy to be important. The following goals were outlined:

1. Aid the parents to proceed with the separation in a less rageful and painful way.

Figure 18. Acceptance of divorce

2. Help the children understand the reason for divorce.
3. Extricate Darren and Patsy from the vise of parental arguments and disagreements.
4. Make recommendations for a well-defined physical joint custody plan which could be submitted to the attorneys.
5. Assist the children in making the shift from a one family system to two separate family systems.

After listening to the therapist's statements, Darren gave the author a nasty look, Patsy appeared especially sad, and Mr. and Mrs. Maxella seemed grateful.

SESSION FOUR/*Family Meeting: All Members Present*

The family entered the room, seating themselves around the table with Mrs. Maxella on one end and Mr. Maxella and the children opposite her. Seeking to understand the dynamics behind the father-Darren-Patsy alli-

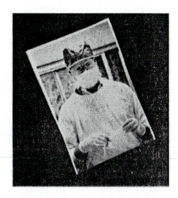

Figure 19. Aid for divorce trauma

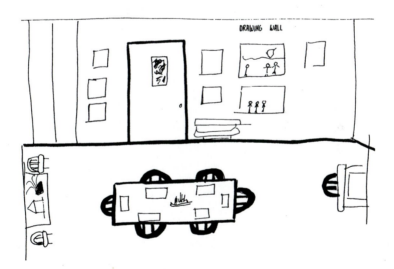

Figure 20. Therapist will mediate

ance, the members were given construction paper and told to *create something that shows what is going on in your family.*

Darren, who ventured to be the first to proceed, made a bold full-length drawing of his *mother* (including breasts and curvy hips). His major focus was on Mother's big mouth, which he described as her constant nagging. He said, "She is always saying 'Do this, do that'" (Figure 21). Although he had not represented his father, he added, "Dad never does that." The verbal message which Darren expressed was of primary importance to the session; however, the way in which he drew his mother and his choice of language indicated his Oedipal conflict.

Patsy looked reticent when she showed her plasticene sculpture of a *hamburger*, which she claimed stood for "McDonald's where Daddy

Figure 21. Mother nags

us to eat on Sunday. But Mommy was mad when we got home late" ...ure 22).

Mother willingly shared her artwork. She had cut out *several triangles* ...hich symbolized her children. The *arrows* which were coming out of ...e triangles were directed towards the oval shape which represented ...erself. She explained her construction portrayed *Mondays*, since that was the day the children came back home after a weekend with their father (Figure 23). Mrs. Maxella voiced her resentment towards the children's father for being a "good-time Charlie" on Saturday and Sunday, while she was stuck with the daily disciplinarian role.

Father, who had cut out a *punching bag*, said, "It represents Shelly who gets unnecessarily angry." He continued on to explain, "We got out of the movie late and it was impossible to have the children back home by seven o'clock. What is so awful about that?"

The art task provided an opportunity for the family to come to grips with the problem of the weekend father/children arrangement.

With the popularity of physical joint custody in California, the author has found it to be beneficial when greater equality regarding child care is arranged. However, before making such a plan, the parents must have time to think about such an alternative. Therefore, an art task was utilized to evoke the consideration for physical joint custody. The family was told to *use a number of sheets of paper depicting different ideas on the way in which Mother need not be bugging the children so much about daily chores.*

In response, *Mother's* visuals revolved around her husband's actions. Pointing to the drawing of a *book*, she claimed that instead of having a good time on weekends, he might help the children with their homework. She also showed a picture *of him fixing Darren's bike*. Mrs. Maxella revealed her idea for her husband Tom to live at the house on weekends while she went elsewhere. As Mr. Maxella listened, he appeared to be mulling the idea over in his mind.

A *series of squares which gradually changed into a circle* was created by *Father*. It focused on his wife "changing her attitude." He hinted at her jealousy because the children got along so well with him.

Darren, who agreed with the symbolic content of his father's pictures, proudly presented his own drawings of *two houses side by side*. They signified "Mom and Dad living next door to each other so Patsy and me could go in and out of both houses."

Patsy's sketches were compatible with those of her brother. While seemingly pleased with everyone's alternatives, she proudly showed her creation, "*Our house* where everyone lives together."

Mother did not respond to Patsy's fixed mind as she had in the previous session, for she was still involved with her own thoughts about

Figure 22. Father gives treats

Tom moving in on the weekends, believing it would make the children's lives less traumatic.

The Maxella's therapy time was over, curtailing any further discussion. The clinician requested a conjoint meeting with Mr. and Mrs. Maxella the following week.

Once again, as the family left the office, Mother hurried out of the building with Father close behind her and the fighting children the last to leave.

SESSION FIVE/*Conjoint Meeting: Mr. and Mrs. Maxella*

The session began with a review of the artwork of the previous meeting. While looking at Patsy's picture of the united household, Mr. and Mrs. Maxella were asked if getting together was a possibility. Mother answered with an emphatic "No," whereas father's lack of response, implied he still cared for his wife and would be open to considering a reconciliation. Nevertheless, the couple stated the divorce was taking place although the financial matters had lengthened the procedure; the lawyers were currently negotiating the settlement. Due to the definite forthcoming marriage dissolution, the clinician returned to Mrs. Maxella's picture of the previous session. It displayed her husband staying in their home on weekends. The therapist questioned the advisability of

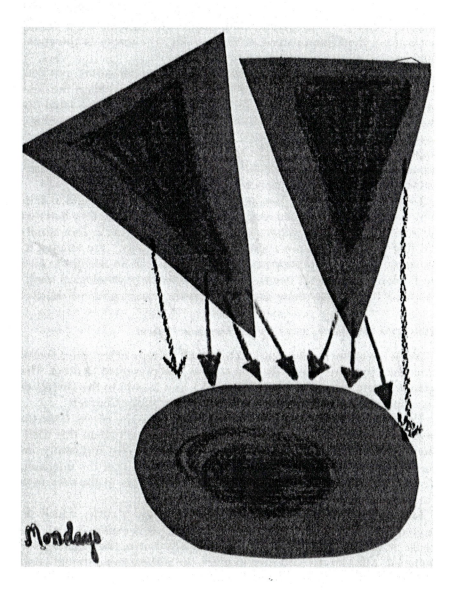

Figure 23. Angry Mondays

this arrangement, stating it would impede Patsy's perceptual reality of a permanent separation between her parents, particularly in light of her tendency towards denial. Having both parents in one house could only feed into the united family fantasy. The message of two separated parents, who live in two separate houses, with two separate lives, would not confuse the issue. Instead, it would clarify the reality of the situation.

The couple admitted Shelly Maxella's plan did contain certain practical advantages; however, they realized the psychological hazards of the double message—Daddy is here but he is not here. The author declared the difficulties might encompass not only the children but also themselves. Living in the house on a part-time basis would be an inhibiting adjustment factor for the entire family. Mourning the loss of their old life and adjusting to the unfamiliar would be a hardship, yet necessary for adaptation to the current circumstances.

It was essential for Mr. Maxella to establish his own household to help him form a new identity and for the children to understand they had two homes—one that was Mother's domain, the other Father's. Tom admitted that when he was not angry with his wife Shelly, "the longing to move back home often popped up." Nevertheless, in an attempt to give up his own dependency needs, he agreed with the psychological implications of two houses versus one, as well as the necessity to individuate.

SESSION SIX/*Family Meeting: All Members Present*

When the entire family returned to the art therapy office, the artwork from their previous family therapy session was presented to them. The graphics were placed in a particular order as a lead-in to the subject of the joint custody arrangements (see Addendum to this Chapter).

The first picture to be reviewed was Patsy's picture of *one home* for everyone to live in. The family was encouraged to talk about this wish. Both Mother and Father spoke to their daughter gently and firmly, informing her, a unified household was completely out of the question. They talked about receiving their final divorce papers in the very near future.

Father's drawing, with its design of *squares and a circle*, which required Mrs. Maxella to change her "attitude," was explored next. Because of the lapse of time since the picture was drawn, the meaning was softened. Mr. Maxella said he had given the picture some thought and felt he had been "unfair to Shelly." Since the mood of the members was less tense and angry than in the former meeting, the children did not challenge their father's statement.

The third piece of artwork that was reexamined was the mother's drawing of *Father in the yard*, symbolizing a plan for each parent to share one home, separately, in order to be with their son and daughter.

The children professed a positive attitude towards Mother's proposal. Pointing to the picture, Darren talked about it being similar to the past "with Dad right there at home." Patsy chimed in with her delight regarding "Daddy sleeping at home again." These gestures validated the therapist's opinion and offered the Maxella's proof of the wishful effect such an arrangement would have on the children. Both parents made it clear, a single household was definitely being ruled out! When Darren confronted Mother with "but you said we should last time and Daddy didn't say no," Mr. Maxella, in concert with Mrs. Maxella, said they had changed their minds and were disregarding the thought.

Darren was still angry when his picture was shown. He pouted as he fingered his drawing of two homes side by side. He was still determined to put in a pitch for his Mom and Dad to move next door to each other. Mr. Maxella's unconvincing smile, as he listened to his son's pleas, conveyed his own pain, even though he told his child *the idea was impossible*. The author supported the parents' statements that very close proximity was not a feasible plan. However, an apartment for Mr. Maxella located within the children's school district was desirable. It was explained that due to the California courts' encouragement for joint custodies, it had often proven successful for both parents to live within a few miles of each other. If Mr. and Mrs. Maxella could manage to live in the same neighborhood, it would smooth the children's transition. In that way, Darren and Patsy could continue neighborhood friendships during the week, the school situation would not be a hardship for either parent, and the children could maintain a level of continuity in their lives. To elaborate further, the following suggestions were offered: the children could stay in the mother's home four days a week including a Saturday. This would enable Mother to enjoy her children on a day when she did not need to get after them about preparing for school and doing homework. By the same token, Father, who worked on Saturdays, could have the children three days, starting on Sunday and ending with Tuesday. His shift would be away from the weekends only and would enable him to carry on normal daily responsibilities for his children.

Both Mr. and Mrs. Maxella were not completely certain about the recommendations. Mr. Maxella brought up several questions about the mechanics of making various arrangements, such as meals, baby sitting, and so forth, while Mrs. Maxella was not sure she wanted to give up the children for three days a week.

The therapist suggested the parents give the idea of shared physical custody additional thought. This plan could be discussed again in the future.

SESSION SEVEN/*Conjoint Meeting: Mr. and Mrs. Maxella*

Mr. and Mrs. Maxella addressed the plans for a joint physical custody. After a great deal of consideration, they believed the concept had many merits. The therapist was asked to draw up a detailed plan. Both had consulted their lawyers, who concurred with the benefits of a psychotherapist laying out a schedule. In the eyes of the court, the clinician served as the *child's advocate* and her recommendations would be highly respected by the judge. In addition, the presence of a clinician tended to lessen some of the anger that separated spouses usually ventilated and resulted in the children feeling guilty.

SESSION EIGHT/*Family Meeting: All Members Present*

To help the family members deal with the issue of loss it is important to mourn their former life in a household that included both parents and children. Working through metaphors or analogous situations is a helpful process. Therefore the family was given boxes of photo collage material. They were directed to *select two or three pictures of either people or animals whom you miss.*

Mrs. Maxella had selected a picture of an *old woman* who looked like her mother. She had been thinking about paying her a visit in Florida. Another photo was of a *man talking on the telephone.* Diverting away from the therapist's instructions, she identified the picture as her lawyer who had called that very morning (Figure 24). Mrs. Maxella announced the divorce would be finalized in a few weeks.

Resistant to dealing with loss/separation, *Father* ignored the therapist's directive completely. Instead, his collage showed a *headache* ad, relating the "hassle" that Shelly and he had been going through. He explained he was concerned about the difficulty in picking up the children and getting them home at the designated time. Another photo displayed a *man worrying, with dollar signs over his head.* Mr. Maxella said it signified the money thrown away on lawyer fees. A third picture portrayed *two smiling children,* which represented his son and daughter who, he claimed, were the only happiness in his life (Figure 25). The therapist asked the children how this made them feel. Without hesitation Patsy said it made her "feel good." It was Darren who paused, perhaps thinking about the hardship that so much responsibility carried.

Tom, sensing his son's discomfort, tried to relieve the children of their

Figure 24. Divorce soon finalized

burden by adding, "You know I didn't mean that. I like my work and I have good friends, but you kids know how much I love being with you." This incident gave Mr. Maxella the insight of how he innocently provoked guilt in the children. He realized he made it difficult for his son and daughter by making them feel they had to supply him with happiness.

Darren had followed the instructions about "loss" by selecting a magazine picture of a *man* who represented his "baseball coach" (Figure 26). He had been transferred to another school and the boy expressed his sorrow. Mr. and Mr. Maxella were surprised. They had no idea that Darren was emotionally attached to the coach.

Patsy realizing her turn was next, pointed to the image of an *airline hostess,* saying "the lady is pretty." Another photo was a *margarine ad with a person guessing ''butter.''* Although it was unconsciously selected by the child, the clinician puzzled whether the ad meant "things were not what they seem to be." This was tied together with Patsy's parents being legally separated yet still involved. The author pointed out that their circumstances were confusing and it was difficult to believe that divorce

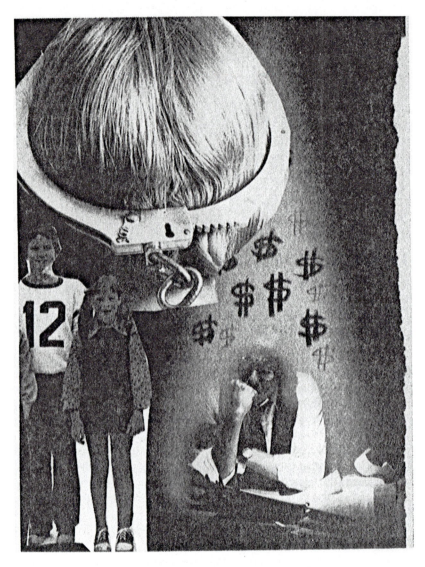

Figure 25. Problem and pleasure

spells out finality. *Patsy's* last picture was of a *child with a kitten*. She proclaimed "the girl in the picture was lucky to have a cat" (Figure 27). The therapist said she remembered she had promised Patsy they would talk about the loss of Mopsy and urged the family to speak about the cat. The conversation was mostly filled with facts about Patsy's involvement with the animal; she had been the main caretaker and often dressed the pet up, playing with her as she would with a doll. Most of the time Mopsy had slept in Patsy's room. Actually everyone had been very fond of the animal and missed her terribly.

To help the family deal with the disappearance and to relieve possible feelings of guilt, the family was told to *create art that was related to the cat's disappearance*.

Patsy made a plasticene figure of a *kitten* and *superimposed* it on a photo collage of a *man*. It symbolized someone stealing the cat. She voiced hope, "Mopsy will get away and come back home." When Darren's version portrayed the *pet roaming around lost and starving to death*, Mother

Figure 26. Misses baseball coach

Figure 27. Misses cat

and Father made eye contact which indicated they had a secret. Neither of them had done the artwork. When I asked them why they had not participated, Father began to make excuses. Mother, obviously upset, said she thought it was best to tell the children the truth. With tears in her eyes she elaborated, "Mopsy was actually killed by an automobile." Patsy hearing the bad news broke down and cried, whereas Darren displayed his anger towards Mother by trying to push her chair away.

Mr. Maxella protected his wife as Darren berated her with his rage. He informed his son, "Mother and I thought it would be better if we didn't tell you the facts. It seemed better to let you kids have some hope—I guess that was a mistake." Mother said she was sorry that she had not explained the situation when it happened. She acknowledged her realization that everyone would be better off with the true facts. When encouraged to elaborate on the event, Mrs. Maxella related the following:

> Before I went to work I called for Mopsy. When she didn't show up
> I looked outside but couldn't find her. I kept calling but she didn't

come. I had to go to work so I got into my car. As I went down our block I found Mopsy in the street, dead. Poor thing, she looked awful! I went home, got a carton, and put Mopsy in it. In fact, I remember selecting the nicest carton we had and I lined it with one of my good towels. After I put her in it I drove her over to the vet. I paid him to do whatever he had to do to have her cremated. Now I'm sorry I didn't tell you kids. We could have buried Mopsy's ashes in the yard next to the turtle.

Mrs. Maxella lovingly put her arms around Patsy as she finished her story, while Darren's Dad gently patted his son's back.

The clinician instructed the family to *create a mock funeral for Mopsy*. *Patsy* and her *father* molded a plasticene *cat*. Mr. Maxella selected a small box for a *coffin* and placed the sculpture inside of it. *Darren* drew a *cat* on the lid and *Mother* made plasticene *flowers* which she put on top of the coffin (Figure 28). Before the Maxellas left the office, the coffin was placed in a locked cabinet of the art therapy room.

Although Patsy was obviously sorrowful, she breathed a cathartic sigh on her way out of the office. The therapist responded with the interpretation that she felt relieved because she was able to put an end to something which had kept her unrealistically hopeful. Darren appeared less

Figure 28. Mock funeral

agitated, allowing himself to feel sad rather than angry. The parents also looked less pained since they had been honest and provided the children with an opportunity to mourn for Mopsy and to deal with the loss. This experience also represented hope for dealing with the termination of their marriage and the family's existence as a total unit.

SESSION NINE/*Family Meeting: All Members Present*

After the usual greetings and conversation on the feelings about Mopsy's mock funeral, the participants were asked to *show why the divorce had come about*.

A *clock* was constructed by *Mother*. She portrayed herself on one of the clock hands and her husband on the other, explaining they had gotten married at a very early age. In recent years each had developed their own interests and different ideas on what they wanted from life. Mrs. Maxella talked about her current involvement with upgrading women's job opportunities and expressed a desire to build an administrative career. She stated the clock meant "it's time to move on, since one hand is passing the other" (Figure 29).

Father's theme was similar, only he used *two different cars* for his metaphor. He said the *foreign* sports car was himself, since he was sleek and

Figure 29. Time to move on

generally liked to go at a fast pace, whereas his wife was similar to an *American* car, which was slower, more functional. She was interested in Women's Rights and was becoming upwardly mobile in her job. Mr. Maxella admitted that he was proud of his own success and that lately his wife had become very competitive with him.

Darren had listened intently when his parents explained their symbols for the reasons for the divorce. When it was his turn, he held up a picture of the *entire family with Mom and Dad wearing boxing gloves*. Although he refused to talk about his artwork, its meaning was obvious.

Patsy's picture showed *her parents having an argument at the dinner table with her brother and herself present*. Young children of divorced parents frequently believe they were the source of their parents' anger and the cause for separation. With this in mind the clinician asked Darren and Patsy to *portray the reasons for your parents' quarrels*. This was to be done in comic strip fashion (pointing out an example which another patient had put on the wall). Both children quickly began the art task. It seemed they needed little time for thought and had given the matter previous consideration.

When Darren finished, he shoved his graphic work into the center of the table, belligerently claiming, "I know my Mom and Dad fight a lot about me." He then shared a series of pictures which explored a particular incident. The first sequence depicted *him coming home from a cub scout meeting* and telling his parents, "I need a canteen for a hike." Another sequence showed Mother telling Dad, "I'm very busy for the next few days. You go buy it!"; and Father answering, "you've got more time than I do!" The rest of the series showed the *shouting escalating between his parents*. The last image portrayed *Mother and Father turning away from each other* "mad." Darren added, "Sometimes they would fight because I was mean to my sister or didn't want to go to bed on time!"

Mr. and Mrs. Maxella were shocked to hear Darren blaming himself for their arguments. It was now obvious their son had somehow blamed himself for their separation. They found it unbelievable. To lower Darren's anxiety for revealing himself, the author interjected, "In my experience, children whose parents are getting divorced often feel themselves partly responsible for the separation. This happens in spite of the reality of the circumstances." Facing Darren and Patsy directly, the author declared, "Children displeasing their parents in actuality *do not cause divorces*. Grown people separate because they do not get along and one or both parents decide that they would be better off if they were no longer married to their husband or their wife."

The therapist's focus was then redirected to Patsy and her picture of the family at the dinner table. When questioned about the cartoon strip, the child explained, Mother was telling her to "eat up your dinner." Patsy elucidated, although she "was full," her mother kept insisting. Her father finally yelled, "Let the kid alone!" Patsy reported, "Mommy and Daddy got into a big argument. It was my fault so she made me go to my room."

Picking up their cue from the therapist, the parents reiterated, "Arguments over you children are not the reason for our divorce." The clinician added, "Although disagreements over children do exist, when parents decide to separate it is due to problems *between the husband and wife.*" To verify this statement, Mrs. Maxella chimed in, "Mrs. Landgarten is right. Daddy and I have changed from the time we got married. You heard what I said when I drew my clock—Daddy and I want different things from life. That is the reason we are getting divorced!! You and Darren have nothing to do with all of this." Mr. Maxella concurred as he told the children, "Mother is right—you kids must never think our marriage problems have ever had anything to do with you, Patsy, or you, Darren. It was because of me and your Mom." The children glanced at each other indicating a weight had been lifted off of their shoulders since their self-blame had been mutually experienced.

As the family left the office, Mother could be seen affectionately holding Patsy's hand, while Father's arm around his son's shoulder was also offering love and comfort.

SESSION TEN/*Conjoint Session: Mr. and Mrs. Maxella*

Mr. and Mrs. Maxella reviewed the physical joint custody recommendations. (Refer to the Addendum at the end of this chapter.)

After a few minor alterations and discussion on the feasibilty of the plan, it was agreed upon. Father had already rented an apartment a few miles away from his former home. The author suggested the parents go over the plans with Darren and Patsy before they came to the family session. It would then be finalized and sent to the attorneys.

SESSION ELEVEN/*Family Session: All Members Present*

During the week, Mr. and Mrs. Maxella had talked to the children and shown them the physical custody plans. In fact, the children suggested a few changes which improved the arrangements. Mr. Maxella told the clinician that he and his wife and their attorneys wanted the custody plans reevaluated by the author each year for the next five years.

Except for the *yearly family visits*, the therapist notified her clients that the next session would be the *last family meeting* where both parents would be present. From this time on, the following schedule was recommended: 1) art therapy sessions for each single parent and children one time a month; 2) the art therapist's availability for additional meetings upon request; and 3) a family review with all members present at the end of six-month and 12-month periods.

SESSION TWELVE/*Family Meeting: All Members Present*

During the final "complete family" session, the author encouraged the participants to recapitulate the art therapy meetings and the joint custody plans. The structure for the future therapy and the therapist's role was repeated for the children.

The therapist gave Darren and Patsy a calendar. As they were given the schedule plans, they were told to "draw your mother on the days you will stay with her and your father on the days you will spend with him." The clinician xeroxed copies, enabling the children to keep a calendar in each of their homes.

As the family left the office, the children appeared to be on especially good terms with each other. At first, they were seen walking with their mother; then, dropping behind, they joined their father. This gesture seemed symbolic of the arrangements that had been laid out for their future.

THREE-MONTH FOLLOW-UP

SESSION THIRTEEN/*Single-Parent Family Meeting: Mother and Children*

To evaluate the family's reaction to their joint physical custody, the participants were asked in this follow-up session to *illustrate* the *good and bad parts of the current living arrangements*.

Darren, whose oppositional behavior had lessened, was quick to display the pros and cons of the subject. For the *positive* side of living in two homes, he *drew himself and his father together* (Figure 30). The boy looked pleased as he explained he spent far more time with his father in recent times than he ever had when his parents were married. He described more quality time with each parent separately, since he had either his mother or father alone with him. The *negative* aspect of the divided living arrangements was a lack of privacy at his Dad's home, because the apartment was "small."

Patsy was not as adaptable as her brother. She approached the task by

Figure 30. More time with Father

illustrating the *bad part* first. She spent a great deal of time on a collage of a *sad face*. It expressed her being lonesome for the missing parent (Figure 31). Nevertheless, she unenthusiastically managed to set forth the *good side*, "Daddy helping with homework" (which he had not done formerly).

A construction paper picture of *smooth ocean waves* demonstrated Mother's relaxed feelings since the divorce (Figure 32). The negative part was exemplified through the cutout of a *tear*. It depicted how sad she felt when the children stayed with their father (Figure 33).

To remind the children of the benefits of their parents' separation, the participants were told to *do a before and after divorce picture of your mother and father together*.

For the previous scene Patsy exhibited her *mother slamming her bedroom door while Father banged upon it*. In contrast, the current situation showed her *parents sitting down and making arrangements for a summer camp*.

Darren's picture was similar to his sister's. For the *present* time he created his *parents peacefully talking* about his sister and himself. He, too, had drawn them "quarreling" in the past.

Both children were anxious to see what their mother had made. They seemed to need concrete evidence of what she was experiencing. Mrs.

Maxella shared her abstract paper construct. It was a metaphor for her previous and current interaction with her ex-spouse. The *past* was represented by *two cutouts with jagged edges*. "Daddy and I were always at each other," she said, adding, "We were always prickly and angry and kept hurting one another" (Figure 34).

Mother was quick to switch over to her *current* construction paper design. She displayed *two rounded objects with only a few minor pointed edges*. Both were at a distance from each other. Mrs. Maxella told the children she and their father managed to keep their distance and were not so very angry any longer (Figure 35).

When all of the artwork was placed side by side, the children admitted

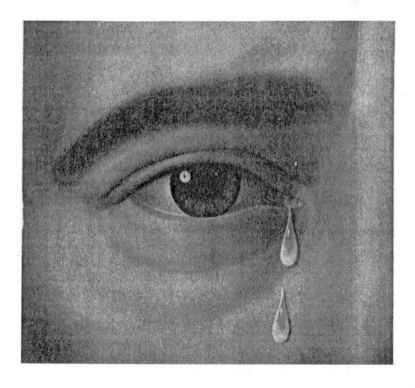

Figure 31. Lonesome for missing parent

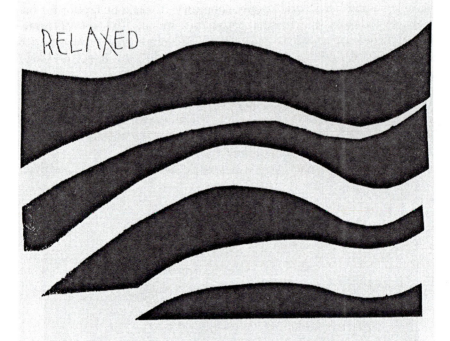

Figure 32. Mother relaxed

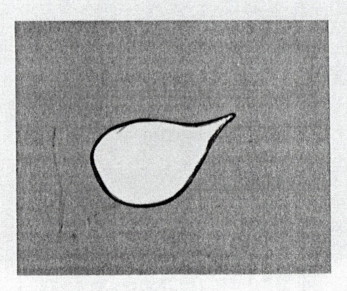

Figure 33. Sad without children

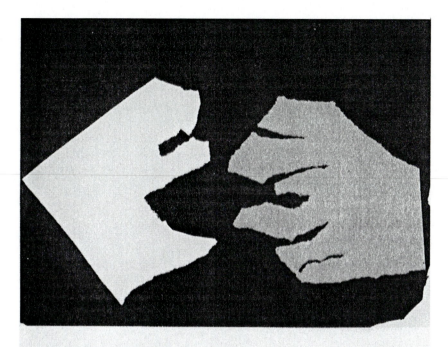

Figure 34. Previous interaction

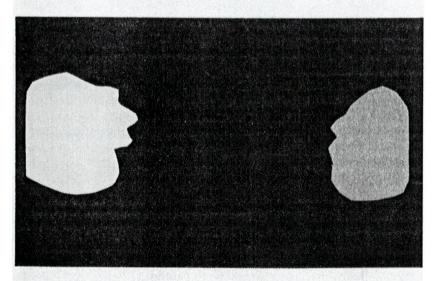

Figure 35. Anger lessened

they were adjusting to their new lifestyles. Patsy volunteered that her nightmares had ceased.

Before the family left the office, the therapist asked their permission to share the artwork with Father the following week. The children not only agreed, but said they looked forward to having their Dad do artwork on the same subject.

When the Maxellas left the office, it was interesting to note the pleasant way the children related to their mother. As each child held one of her hands, the author could hear them talking about their artwork as they walked away from the office.

SESSION FOURTEEN/*Single-Parent Family Meeting: Father and Children*

As soon as Mr. Maxella and the children stepped into the office the next week, Darren and Patsy pulled their father over to the wall that displayed the art from the former session. They both insisted that their father create art that showed his ideas on the *good and bad parts of the current joint custody schedule.*

Mr. Maxella invited his son and daughter to help him create the objects. The three of them joked and kidded each other during the process. They were enjoying their shared experience. Father used several media, including plasticene, to simulate: his *living room, a television set,* the *children,* and *himself.* He then placed all three figurative sculptures on the couch, stating, "I love having you kids around" (Figure 36). The bad part was represented by his *removing the plasticene figures of the children.*

The obvious message was that he watched television to keep himself from being lonely. After a brief discussion about the different ways the three Maxellas coped with sad feelings, Patsy asked the therapist for permission to use a large piece of paper. Apparently Father's admission of loneliness stirred up feelings of guilt. As a defense mechanism, she chose to divert the family away from dealing with their "sad" emotions. Patsy managed this abstraction by taking charge of an art task. She began by tracing around her hand and instructing her father and brother to do the same. When they finished, Patsy gave directions to "cut out the hand pictures." Obviously satisfied with herself, Patsy had a sudden rush of generosity as she turned to Darren, suggesting that he "take over."

Darren, delighted to have a turn to be the authority figure, pasted his hand cutout onto a colored piece of paper, then directed his sister and father to do likewise. Patsy asked the therapist to please pin up their

Figure 36. More time together

artwork as an example of the *"good art made by children who have divorced parents"* (Figure 37).

Before the Maxellas left the office, Father said he and his former wife still had great difficulty communicating with each other. There were still financial matters that kept their anger fanned. When Father was questioned about how this affected the children, he admitted it spoiled his mood and probably that of his former spouse.

Patsy and Darren were asked if they understood that their parents' moodiness was not related to them. Both children were very much aware of this factor; in fact, Patsy sometimes checked this out by asking, "Daddy, are you mad at me?" This clarification was given positive reinforcement. Father was also encouraged to notify his son and daughter that his "grumpy feelings" were not due to anything they had done.

Both children admitted being used to the two-household living arrangement. It had not interfered with school or neighborhood friendships.

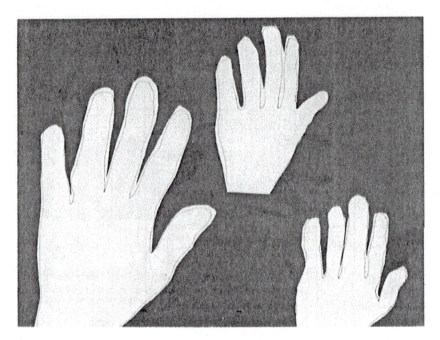

Figure 37. Good art by children whose parents are divorced

SUMMARY

Initially, the designated patient was six-year-old Patsy, who had re-peated nightmares. Early in treatment this symptom was identified with separation anxiety due to the parents' divorce. This trauma also pro-duced oppositional behavior on the part of nine-year-old brother Darren.

During the assessment phase, the family's art psychotherapy evalua-tion revealed the misunderstandings, anger, guilt, and other difficulties that related to the dissolution of the parents' marriage and the disruption of the family system.

Family art psychotherapy sessions were held with the following goals: 1) facilitate the parents to proceed with the divorce in a logical and less rageful fashion; 2) help the children understand the reasons for the divorce and to alleviate feelings of guilt; 3) make recommendations for joint physical custody arrangements; and 4) aid the children readjust from a one-family system to two separate family systems.

ADDENDUM: JOINT CUSTODY

The author has found it detrimental to place one parent in the position of the school routine authoritarian and the other as the "good-time" parent. Since it is usually the mother who keeps the children during the week, the children frequently see her as the ogre. In art therapy drawings the mother is often portrayed as a witch, or mean. In the family drawings her figure is overly exaggerated to symbolize her unbalanced power and responsibility. In cases where the parents have joint physical custody of the children, portraits tend to contain more realistic perceptions of her role.

On the other hand, since the father more frequently has his children on Saturdays and Sundays, this parent is shown in artwork as an agent of entertainment. Father's weekend activities require a great deal of energy and planning on his part and place him in an unrealistic role. This situation denies the father of a daily routine with his children since it strips him of the responsibilities that are gratifying and essential to maintaining his position of authority. It is important for the father to be present on school days; such times require problem solving and more meaningful interactions which are essential to the parent/child relationship. In testimony of these observations, children who see their father on weekends tend to depict him, in family drawings, as smaller than the mother and at the end of the picture or separated off from the page altogether. In contrast, in cases where the children's physical custody arrangements are more equitable, both parents appear to be more similar in size. In many instances the family picture changes with the children in the center and a parent on each end, thus indicating both the mother and the father as protective and equal authority figures.

It is important to have the custody arrangements detailed and clear. Specific dates and times are essential to facilitate the arrangements. A yearly calendar takes away surprises when it comes to holidays, birthdays, Mother's Day, Father's Day, vacations, and so on, and helps to smooth out the children's plans and expectations.

The arrangements must begin from the date of the recommendation and be laid out for at least one year. In many cases two- to five-year plans are presented.

Maxella Recommendations

The Maxella family's custody recommendations were as follows:

Children will be picked up at school by Mother at 3:30 p.m. on Wednesday and remain with her until Sunday morning at 9 a.m. Father will pick up the children on Sunday at 9 a.m. at their mother's home and will keep them until Wednesday morning when he takes them to school.

Each parent is responsible for the children on their designated days, including: getting them to school, after school arrangements, homework assignments, baby sitting arrangements, doctor's appointments, social arrangements, and so forth.

On Father's designated days, when the children are not in school, he is to take them to their mother's home on Wednesday morning between 8:00 a.m. and 8:45 a.m.

During Easter vacation the home schedule will remain intact. On Easter Sunday the children will be with their mother until 3 p.m. This will enable the children to go to church and have lunch with Mother. Father will pick up the children at 3 p.m.

Patsy's birthday falls on a Tuesday during the month of May. Father will celebrate with Patsy on Sunday. The following year, as the child's birthday falls on a mid-week night when she is to be with Mother again, Father is permitted to take both children out for dinner.

Darren's birthday is in June. This is on a Saturday when the children are with Mother. Father will celebrate with Darren on Sunday; therefore, the usual arrangements remain the same.

Children's birthdays, commencing next year, will be spent with Mother on all even numbered years, and with Father starting 1987 on uneven numbered years. Said birthdays will begin at 9:00 a.m. and will end 9:00 p.m. each of said days when they fall on weekends or holidays. On midweek birthdays, time with the designated parent will begin at 3 p.m. and end at 9 p.m. The parent with whom the children are spending the day will pick them up and return them.

The parents' birthdays and Mother's Day and Father's Day will be spent with the respective parent and will have priority over the usual routine. If these birthdays fall on a school day, the time limitation is from the end of the school day to 9:00 p.m. Children will be picked up and returned by said birthday parent or the parent whose day is being celebrated.

During summer vacation,

1) The *first two uninterrupted weeks* will be spent with Mother. This time will begin Monday morning at 9 a.m. when Mother will

pick them up and end on Sunday evening at 9:00 p.m. with Father picking up the children.
2) For the second two weeks the family will revert to the regular schedule for two weeks.
3) A two-week uninterrupted vacation will then take place with Father, starting on Sunday morning 9:00 a.m. and ending on Tuesday morning 9:00 a.m. with Mother getting the children.
4) For the rest of the vacation the children will revert to their normal routine. Camp arrangements will take place in lieu of the "normal routine."

During Christmas vacation the usual sleeping arrangements remain intact, except for Christmas Eve and Day. Both parents agree that the children will spend the Eve with Father. He will return the children by two o'clock the next afternoon on Christmas Day. As Christmas is on Tuesday (Father's time) Mother will bring the children back to Mr. Maxella anytime from 8:30 a.m. to 10:00 a.m. on Wednesday morning. This arrangement was preferred by both parents and shall continue the following year.

In regard to the New Year, Mother agrees to let Father take the children on a skiing trip, which will include New Year's Eve and Day. The following year the arrangement will be reversed and Mother will have the children for the New Year's holiday.

Maternal grandparents' birthdays and anniversaries will only be celebrated on Saturdays and paternal grandparents' birthdays and anniversaries on Sundays.

During vacation time (Easter, Summer, Christmas, plus single day holidays) each parent is required to make the necessary day-care arrangements. This will include the children being taken to various lessons and social activities.

The children may telephone their mother or father twice daily, providing a 15-minute limit is observed for each phone call.

Note to the Reader

Families vary in terms of the holidays that have special meanings for them. Therefore, the following dates should be given consideration: New Year's Day, birthdays of Lincoln/Washington/King, Ash Wednesday, Palm Sunday, Passover, Good Friday, Easter Sunday, Mother's Day, Memorial Day, Father's Day, Independence Day, Labor Day, Rosh Hashanah, Yom Kippur, Columbus Day, Halloween, Thanksgiving, Hanukah, Christmas Eve and Day. Religious holidays other than those mentioned may need to be included as well as birthdays, anniversaries, and other occasions that involve family members.

RECOMMENDED READING

Abarbanel, A. Shared parenting after separation and divorce: A study of joint custody. *American Journal of Orthopsychiatry, 49*(2), 320–330, 1979.

Ahrons, C. R. Divorce: Before, during and after. In H. I. McCubbin & C. R. Figley (Eds.), *Stress and the Family, Volume I: Coping with Normative Transitions.* New York: Brunner/Mazel, 1983, pp. 102–115.

Ahrons, C. R. The binuclear family: Two households, one family. *Alternative Lifestyles, 2,* 499–515, 1979.

Ahrons, C. R. Divorce: A crisis of family transition and change. *Family Relations, 29,* 533–540 1980(a).

Ahrons, C. R. Joint custody arrangements in the post-divorce family. *Journal of Divorce, 3,* 189–205, 1980(b).

Ahrons, C. R. Redefining the divorced family: A conceptual framework for post-divorce family system reorganization. *Social Work, 25,* 437–441, 1980(c).

Ahrons, C. R. The continuing co-parental relationship between divorced spouses. *American Journal of Orthopsychiatry, 5,* 415–428, 1981.

Benedek, E. P. Child custody laws: Their psychiatric implications. *American Journal of Psychiatry, 129*(3), 326–28, 1962.

Berg, G., & Kelly, R. The measured self-esteem of children from broken, rejected and accepted families. *Journal of Divorce, 2*(4), 363, 1979.

Bohannan, P. (Ed.). *Divorce and After.* New York: Anchor Books, 1971.

Britan, S. D. Effect of manipulation of children's affect on their family drawings. *Journal of Projective Techniques and Personality Assessment, 34,* 234–37, 1970.

Brown, E. A model of the divorce process. *Conciliation Courts Review, 14,* 1–11, 1976.

Brown, P., & Manela, R. Changing family roles: Women and divorce. *Journal of Divorce, 1,* 315–328, 1978.

Chang, P. N., & Dernard, A. S. Single-father caretakers: Demographic characteristics and adjustment processes. *American Journal of Orthopsychiatry, 52*(2), 236–243, 1982.

Derdeyn, A. P. Child custody consultation. *American Journal of Orthopsychiatry, 45*(5), 791–801, 1975.

Derdeyn, A. P. A consideration of legal issues in child custody contests. *Archives of General Psychiatry, 33*(2), 165–171, 1976.

Emery, R. Interparental conflicts and the children of discord and divorce. *Psychological Bulletin, 91,* 310–330, 1982.

Felner, R., & Farber, S. Social policy for child custody: A multidisciplinary framework. *American Journal of Orthopsychiatry, 50,* 341–347, 1980.

Foster, H., & Freed, D. Joint custody: A viable alternative. *Trial Magazine, 15,* 26–31, 1979.

Galper, M. *Co-Parenting.* Philadelphia: Running Press, 1978.

Gasser, R., & Taylor, C. Role adjustment of single-parent fathers with dependent children. *The Family Coordinator, 25,* 397–401, 1976.

Goldman, J., & Coone, J. Family therapy after divorce: developing a strategy. *Family Process, 16*(3), 357–62, 1977.

Goldstein, J., Freud, A., & Solnit, A. *Beyond the Best Interests of the Child.* New York: The Free Press, 1973.

Greif, J. B. Fathers, children, and joint custody. *American Journal of Orthopsychiatry, 49*(2), 311–330, 1979.

Grote, D., & Weinstein, J. Joint custody: A viable and ideal alternative. *Journal of Divorce, 1,* 43–53, 1977.

Hess, R., & Camara, K. Post-divorce family relationships as mediating factors in the consequences of divorce for children. *Journal of Social Issues, 35,* 79–96, 1979.

Hetherington, E. Divorce: A child's perspective. *American Psychologist, 34,* 851–858, 1979a.

Hetherington, E. Family interaction and social, emotional and cognitive development of children following divorce. In V. Vaughn & T. Brazelton (Eds.), *The Family: Setting Priorities.* New York: Science and Medicine, 1979b.

Hetherington, E., Cox, M., & Cox, R. The aftermath of divorce. In J. Stevens & M. Mathews (Eds.), *Mother/Child/Father/Child Relationships.* Washington, D.C.: National Association for the Education of Young Children, 1978.

Hetherington, E., Cox, M., & Cox, R. Play and social interaction in children following divorce. *Journal of Social Issues, 35,* 26–49, 1979.

Irving, H. H., Benjamin, M., & Trocme, N. Shared parenting: An empirical analysis utilizing a large data base. *Family Process, 23*(4), 561–570, 1984.

Kalter, N. Children of divorce in an outpatient psychiatric population. *American Journal of Orthopsychiatry, 47,* 40–51, 1977.

Kalter, N., & Renbar, J. The significance of a child's age at the time of divorce. *American Journal of Orthopsychiatry, 51*(1), 58–100, 1981.

Kelly, J. Visiting after divorce: Research findings and clinical implications. In L. Abt & R. Stuart (Eds.), *Children of Separation and Divorce.* New York: Van Nostrand Reinhold, 1981.

Kelly, J., & Wallerstein, J. The effects of parental divorce: Experiences of the child in early latency. *American Journal of Orthopsychiatry, 46*(1), 20–32, 1976.

Kelly, J., & Wallerstein, J. Brief interventions with children in divorcing families. *American Journal of Orthopsychiatry, 47*(1), 23–39, 1977a.

Kelly, J., & Wallerstein, J. Part-time parent, part-time child: Visiting after divorce. *Journal of Clinical Child Psychology, 6*(2), 51–54, 1977b.

Keshet, H., & Rosenthal, K. Fathering after marital separation. *Social Work, 23*(1), 11–19, 1978.

Magrab, P. For the sake of the children: A review of the psychological effects of divorce. *Journal of Divorce, 1,* 233–245, 1978.

McDermott, J. F. Divorce and its psychiatric sequelae in children. *Archives of General Psychiatry, 23*(11), 421–517, 1970.

Roman, M., & Haddad, W. *The Disposable Parent: The Case for Joint Custody.* New York: Holt, Rinehart and Winston, 1978.

Rosen, R. Some crucial issues concerning children of divorce. *Journal of Divorce, 3,* 19–25, 1979.

Steinman, S. The experience of children in a joint custody arrangement: A report of the study. *American Journal of Orthopsychiatry, 51*(3), 403–414, 1981.

Wallerstein, J. S., & Kelly, J. B. The effects of parental divorce: Experiences of the child in later latency. In J. Skolnick & A. Skolnick (Eds.), *Family in Transition: II.* Boston: Little, Brown, 1977.

Wallerstein, J. S., & Kelly, J. B. Divorce and children. In J. D. Noshpitz et al. (Eds.), *Basic Handbook of Child Psychiatry, IV.* New York: Basic Books, 1979.

Wallerstein, J. S., & Kelly, J. B. *Surviving the breakup: How children and parents cope with divorce.* New York: Basic Books, 1980.

Wallerstein, J. S., & Kelly, J. B. California's children of divorce. *Psychology Today, 13,* 67–76, 1980.

Westman, J. Effect of divorce on children's personality development. *Medical Aspects of Human Sexuality, 6,* 38–55, 1972.

Williams, F. S. Children of divorce: Detectives, diplomats or despots? *Marriage and Divorce, I.* New York: Abraxas Communications Publishing Co., 1974.

Williams, F. S. What can judges do to ameliorate the effects of divorce on parents and children? *Family Laws News, 6*(1), 1–8, 1982–83.

Woolley, P. *The Custody Handbook.* New York: Summit Books, 1979.

CHAPTER 5

Therapy for a Family with an Encopretic Child: Long-term Treatment

INTRODUCTION

Encopresis or chronic fecal incontinence is a psychological disorder with a physical manifestation. This dysfunction tends to weaken the ego since the self-image is debased and thus places stress on the child's psychosocial development. It most frequently occurs in boys of latency age. The child's soiling tends to engender frustration, anger, and guilt in the mother; disgust and disappointment in the father; embarrassment in the siblings; and self-mortification in the encopretic child.

This author's practice has shown consistent features in family members where encopresis exists. For example, the mother, in her determination to toilet train her son, becomes overly involved and enmeshed with this child, seemingly unable to disengage and maintain objectivity. Mother's self-blame exacerbates the preoccupation with her boy's bowel movements. The personality of the mother is usually overtly friendly and warm. The fathers, who appear to be solid and caring individuals, are not readily available to their children because of their long and/or unusual working hours. They are highly motivated to succeed because of their desire to give their children a good education and material comforts. The younger siblings are generally attractive in several ways and appeal to their parents because they are trouble free and have accomplished the milestone of controlling their bowel movements at the appropriate age.

In the author's experience the encopretic boys have a good appearance, are generally clean, have positive peer relationships, participate in sports, and excel in one or several academic subjects. If and when oppositional behaviors are exhibited, they are directed towards the mothers. Relationships with fathers appear to be good, yet the children are resentful of the limited time they spend together.

The mothers and fathers of encopretics appreciate many of their children's qualities. Yet, due to the humiliation that soiling brings, the boys place themselves in the vulnerable position of the "scapegoat."

Although family styles vary in their verbal interchange, they all display a poor communication system. Clarity is lacking and it is not unusual to detect messages that are veiled over, at times through humor.

The content and style of the family art tasks exhibit the following characteristics:

1. It is Mother's artwork that reflects a "free spirit" style. It is individualistic, loose, and lacking structure. Her contributions are placed in many directions.
2. Father gives the construct a solid foundation. His objects are representational with well-defined parameters.
3. The younger siblings place themselves in a center position, occupying a large space.
4. The patient is initially withholding and assertive later on. Their symbols are frequently connected to Mother's contributions.

While working with the encopretic child, the author has found a multifaceted art therapy approach to be effective. During the initial session, the family is notified that treatment for this particular problem is often successful, providing the encopretic member wants to cease this soiling behavior. A self-management program and the parents' positive reinforcement plan are mentioned. Again, the possibility for the encopretic child to accomplish his goal is commented upon. This statement is purposely repeated to *instill the family with a positive mind set*. This author believes a *hopeful* outlook is an influencing factor in treatment success.

In addition to the family meetings, concomitant individual art therapy for the encopretic child takes place. Its emphasis is twofold: one is to focus on the self-management procedure, and the second is to foster an atmosphere for self-expression. In the art therapy office, symbolic bowel movements are created and discussed. This gesture, which grants nonjudgmental permission to explore the issue, is a major contributing factor in forming the therapeutic alliance. The author has found encopretic boys to be withholding of their inner emotions and conflicts. For this reason, it is vital to aid the ventilation of hidden feelings through the safety of the metaphor.

The content of the art is a resource for discovering psychological clues to past traumas and the source of the child's behavior. Whether or not insight is pursued, specific art tasks are designed to act as a reinforcing device for autonomy, self-control, and increased self-esteem.

The entire family benefits from the treatment of the problem on encopresis, for they gain an awareness of family dynamics plus more effective communication skills and interaction.

CASE ILLUSTRATION

This case history illustrates long-term family treatment. The reader will follow a complete, session-by-session description of the art psychotherapy modality in process. The encopretic problem is dealt with in weekly family or conjoint meetings, which are reported and numbered herein. Included each week were concomitant individual appointments with the designated patient. Only highlights of the child's individual treatment are related in this chapter.

PRECIPITATING EVENT

Mrs. Sontag's frustration over her son's encopretic problem had turned to feelings of hopelessness and despair. She was furious with nine-year-old Peter for his refusal to conform to a toilet-trained routine.

During her initial phone call to the author, Mrs. Sontag, verging on hysteria, reported the following:

> Today I just couldn't stand it any longer when I threw those urine-soaked sheets into the washing machine! In the mornings my house literally reeks of bathroom smells. I think both of my boys will never stop peeing in bed. And if that's not upsetting enough, what is far worse is my hands and knees routine. Every day I have to look under Peter's bed for his B.M.-soiled jockey shorts. He has a habit of throwing his smelly underwear out of sight. It's become a game of hide-and-seek, with him hiding and me seeking. *I feel like such a failure. Imagine, a kid that age still making bowel movements in his pants like a year-old child*!! I was so upset today that I didn't even go to work and that's very bad. I really hope you can help Peter with this problem.

The therapist made a conjoint appointment with Mr. and Mrs. Sontag. The focus would be on gathering the designated patient's developmental history. The initial session, which is held conjointly, is especially important since it gives the parents a chance to have the therapist to themselves and to ventilate their concerns privately. Without this visit, parents are more likely to terminate the assessment or treatment phase of therapy prematurely because they feel the therapist has not respected their role as parents. This first visit with Mother and Father tends to aid the positive transference.

SESSION ONE/*Conjoint Meeting: Mother and Father*

When the therapist first met Mr. and Mrs. Sontag, the contrast in each spouse's affect was striking. Mr. Sontag was a cool, quiet, soft-spoken man, with a bland facial expression. His wife's appearance was the antithesis, with her warmth, friendliness, rapid speech, and obvious nervous energy. She displayed a wide range of emotions as she talked about herself and her family.

Both John Sontag and his wife, Laurie, were 35 years old. At the ages of 21 they became engaged and were married a year later. They believed their 13-year-old marriage to be successful, although in recent months Peter's encopretic behavior had caused stress and friction in their relationship.

John was a post office employee. He considered his night shift working hours, from 10 o'clock in the evening until 5 o'clock in the morning, to be advantageous since that gave him a great deal of time to spend with his sons. The couple agreed they had managed to adjust their daily lives to his work hours.

Laurie had maintained her career as a college administrative assistant throughout her marriage. Her position, which was part-time, increased her self-esteem and the family's income.

Both parents talked about their children—Peter, nine, and Mikie, seven,—as "terrific kids." They described their presenting complaint as the problem with Peter's soiling, because in all other respects he was an "extremely compliant child who never gets angry." Aside from the encopresis he was a near perfect boy—friendly, popular in school, a high achiever academically, and excellent in sports.

Encopretic Background

Bowel training started at the age of two. When Peter was three years old, Mrs. Sontag complained to the pediatrician about his lack of toilet use for defecation. Although the doctor advised Mrs. Sontag to stop her stress on the child's bowel movement behavior, she found herself unable to do so due to pressure from family and friends.

When Peter began kindergarten he soiled several times a week while he was in school. After a discussion with the teacher, it was decided Peter would bring a change of clothes. In first grade the same procedure was followed. During second grade, a new situation occurred when Peter's large stature outsized his classmates' and his teacher selected him as the "strong arm student." His job was to separate fighting children. Mrs. Sontag claimed her son's authority and responsibility had a detrimental effect on him. It was at that particular time when his soiling frequency changed to a daily occurrence both in the classroom and at home.

During a teachers' conference, the instructor agreed to make an exception to the school's toilet rule, which allowed its use only at designated times. This plan had successful results. Fortunately, it was agreed that Peter would be permitted to go to the lavatory "as needed" rather than at the appointed class time. The child had this same teacher during the third grade and he continued going to the toilet whenever a bowel movement was necessary. During those two years, although soiling did not happen in school, it continued to be a daily occurrence when he was at home.

Peter had recently begun the fourth grade. Mother said she had decided not to inform the new teacher about the situation. Her friends had advised her against it, hoping to avoid giving her son a reputation among the teachers and students. Nevertheless, Mrs. Sontag had found Peter with feces-filled pants when she picked him up at school several times the previous week. She also reported her son's most recent soiling episode, which happened during a baseball game. When he was confronted with the incident, Peter denied it was noticeable to other children, claiming, "No one can smell the B.M."

In recent years the Sontags had had numerous conversations with their pediatrician after medical checkups. The doctor informed them that the nightly enuretic behavior and Peter's encopresis were not physically oriented. He told the parents, "Not to worry. The bed wetting and soiling will be outgrown!"

In spite of the doctor's opinions, Mrs. Sontag still wished that the author's assessment would point to an organic malfunction rather than a psychological problem. However, her husband openly disagreed; he was certain Peter's soiling was a manipulative, attention-getting device. Yet he gave another message when he reported his own father and brothers lacked nocturnal bladder control until their mid-adolescence. Mrs. Sontag, who heard this as new information, said this news relieved some of her guilt since Peter's problems may have a genetic component. It also fed into her fantasy as she repeated her wish for a "logical explanation" for her son's behavior.

When the Sontags spoke about Mikie, they said he was more assertive and less agreeable than his brother. Mrs. Sontag emphasized that when it came to toilet training her younger child, she handled it differently, mainly ignoring all the unsolicited advice. She allowed Mikie to dictate his own timing for bowel control, stressing that the second time around she did not set herself up for a power struggle. Mrs. Sontag proudly boasted Mikie completed the appropriate use of the toilet at the age of three.

As the meeting came to an end, a family art psychotherapy appointment was made for the following week.

Just as the couple began to leave the office, Mrs. Sontag told the therapist she was familiar with the literature on encopresis. As an informed person, she claimed the biggest mistake was the large amount of pressure she exerted on Peter's toilet performance when he was too young. As she walked out her last words were, "I'm a blunderer and a failure mother."

SESSION TWO/*Family Meeting: All Members Present*

Impressions of Peter and Mikie

Peter and Mikie resembled one another. Both boys looked older than their ages. One might guess nine-year-old Peter to be 11 and seven-year-old Mikie to be about nine. They were tall, broad-shouldered, and chunky in build. They looked like two child-sized football players. Their appearances were neat and scrubbed. The only thing that was not in place was their straight blond hair, which hung down on their foreheads. Peter was polite and reserved, tending to be a responder rather than an initiator of conversation. Although he said he really liked art "a lot", his affect was flat, showing little enthusiasm even when claiming to be "glad."

Mikie was also polite but more enthusiastic and outgoing than his brother. He asked many questions about the artwork displayed in the office. This child tended to answer questions that were put forth to the family in general.

After the preliminaries, the family related their reason for seeking therapeutic help. Acknowledging their purpose, the author gave a brief explanation of the family art psychotherapy approach and its benefits.

The first instruction that was given to the family was the *selection of different colored markers, one for each person*. Mikie went first, picking out red; Mother, who was second, chose green; Peter followed with black; and Father, who went last, decided on orange.

The next step, which points to family alliances, required the Sontags to *divide up into two teams*. The procedure began as Peter nodded to his mother, signaling his desire to be on the team with her. When she agreed, Father and Mikie looked pleased to form their own dyad.

Nonverbal Team Art Task

The family was given the dual nonverbal drawing instructions, whereby each couple shared a *single* piece of paper. They were told to *create a picture without talking or signaling to one another. After the picture is completed you may talk to each other about the title.*

Mother and Peter team. Peter drew on the far left of the page making a *house with another house attached to it* (at times, a sign of symbiosis). Mother's contribution was *hearts and flowers*. Even when the pair was allowed to speak to one another, the silence was still maintained. Each wrote a title on their side of the page.

Peter named his art "A Double House," while Mother called her drawing "Hearts and Flowers." Both pictures were synonymous with the creator's affect. The child avoided the inclusion of figures and emotions, while Mother's warmth and affection were visually expressed.

Father and Mikie team. Each partner drew on his own side of the page. Mikie made *a boy playing baseball* and Father had created *a letter-separating machine*. When the pictures were finished they discussed various ideas for the title. The final decision was for each partner to label their own art. Mikie called his, "Practicing Baseball" and Father's title, equally practical, was "The Letter-Separating Machine."

Family Verbal Art Task

Due to the limitation of time the nonverbal family art technique was eliminated. Therefore, given the family verbal art task, everyone was led to a large mural-size paper which was tacked onto the wall. The directive stated the *entire family is to do a drawing together. This time you are allowed to speak to one another.*

Father started by asking his family, "What shall we draw?" Mikie immediately made his suggestion of "the park." Mr. Sontag agreed as he stepped back, cuing Mikie in to begin drawing his idea. The child, obviously pleased, walked over to the center of the page. He took a long time to create a large elaborate *tree*. Mother, watching her youngest son take up a great deal of space and center stage, too, began to giggle. She nervously mumbled, "I'd had better hurry up to get my marks on the page," as she joined Mikie and drew a *large sun* and a *flower*. Father followed her. His first move was to *improve his wife's sun*, then he continued on to enhance Mikie's tree by *filling in the leaves and trunk*.

Mrs. Sontag became very absorbed in her own creative process and continued to draw with exuberance. She made waves, which went across the entire top of the page, and a design which encompassed all four sides of the page.

The entire family was actively involved except for Peter, who stood aside waiting to be invited to participate (as Mikie was). Finally, when he realized that he could be left out altogether, Peter walked over to the picture to draw a *faintly lined mountain* and a small-sized, hard-lined *scribble* which he connected to his mother's waves, saying it was "a tornado."

When Mother paused long enough to notice what the other members had done, she made a *larger copy of Mikie's tree*. Then she placed a *figure on top of Peter's mountain*. The boy responded positively to his mother's attention by adding skis onto her person.

After the family decided the mural was completed, Mikie, without saying anything, managed to slip in an extra turn to color in his mother's flower.

Father stepped back to look over the family's artwork. When he noticed his lack of contact with Peter, he seemed compelled to offer an explanation. Mr. Sontag claimed *his son's black color* did not go well with *his own orange* marker. This comment came across as a rebuke regarding Peter's poor choice. The author silently noted Father had selected his color *after* Peter.

Since Mikie was the first person to suggest the title, he asked his father's permission to write "The Park" on the page. After Mr. Sontag consented, the younger child placed it in bold print onto the mural (Figure 38).

Leadership Roles

In order to understand the participants' perceptions of the family members roles, they were asked, "Who was the leader?" Peter saw the dynamics realistically, as he replied, "It was Mikie." He reasoned, his brother's suggestion of the "park" was carried out; Mikie was the first person to draw and also the person who wrote the title. The rest of the family saw the role of leader differently. Father believed it was his wife since she did "the most drawing." Mother's opinion was to the contrary, stating her husband was the leader because he took charge and "directed" the picture. Mikie agreed with her but he was unable to offer his own explanation as to the reason.

THE PARK

Figure 38. Family mural

After the family finished expressing their thoughts about the leadership role, the therapist took over the responsibility of voicing her observations. This gesture established her active role as the family therapist and gave the family a chance to learn about their interactions. When the family dynamics feedback is given, tact and sensitivity are essential. The therapist's manner and choice of words, such as "boss," "leader," and "authority," must be selected to suit the individual family. With some participants humor is productive, while with others a serious tone is more understandable and appropriate.

The author began to share her observations with the Sontags by stating, "What is witnessed in the art task is usually analogous to the interactions at home." Peter's perception of the leader was then confirmed, adding that Mikie was not only the person to begin the mural, but also the one to end it (by filling in his mother's flower). Pointing to the mural, Mikie's color was seen to have a central position and took up a large amount of space. Therefore, a guess was put out that this child functioned in the same way at home.

Peter's actions were addressed next. The therapist noted he waited so long to be invited to participate that he was almost left out completely.

Another guess was made about his anger, which was directed towards Mother. To eliminate seeing the therapist as a magical person, the family was directed to look at the picture, showing how her assumption was based on the "tornado which he placed on top of his Mom's waves." The interpretation caused Peter to give the clinician a knowing look. As a child who did not verbalize his angry feelings, he experienced catharsis by having his nonverbal symbols correctly analyzed. The therapist proceeded to recapitulate. She pointed out that when Mother connected to Peter by drawing a figure on his mountain, he responded positively by adding the skis onto it.

Again the author reiterated that these patterns were probably acted out at home. To help the family relate to an abstract statement, it is concretized through a fantasized example. This therapist proposed that perhaps when the family had time together it was Mikie who tended to make the suggestions, because Peter waited to be asked for his ideas, and therefore never took the opportunity to voice them. Maybe this was how he tested his parents, and if they didn't come through for him, he expressed his rage in a nonverbal way. For example, maybe he wouldn't pick up his things as Mother instructed. The parents, agreeing with the therapist's insight, offered their own examples of how Peter managed "to get even."

Mother's green lines on the picture were observed next. They took up a great deal of space and went in all directions. At this juncture everyone, including Mother, laughed. Continuing on in a light manner, the clinician suggested, "Mom is all over the place at home. Maybe she does this at home by wanting to know what goes on everywhere. Perhaps she checks the rooms and is the person who manages to do a lot. It also seems she likes to do her own thing." Once again the family looked to the author to acknowledge the exactness of her assumptions.

Father's participation through the color black was examined last. The author claimed he was the person who "fixed things up" and liked "to add the finishing touches." This opinion was derived from his gestures to "improve" his wife's sun and by "enhancing Mikie's tree." Since Mr. Sontag had already pointed out his own avoidance of Peter when he claimed it was due to their noncomplimentary colors, the metaphor was used to suggest, "Father likes things to fit or go well together. If something is not to his liking, he probably tends to avoid it." An example might be that if "he has a disagreement with one of you he won't yell or make you talk about it. He probably walks away or reads a paper or does something by himself." Both Mrs. Sontag and Peter acknowledged the truth in this statement, relating similar illustrations in a good-natured way.

As the session came to an end, the family was obviously impressed with the art therapy approach. Everyone, with the exception of Mikie, seemed pleased with the insight that they had gleaned.

Family Dynamics

Although a great deal of the family dynamics were displayed, the author withheld information that would have been overloading or too confrontive during the assessment phase of art psychotherapy. The inappropriate timing of premature interpretations can be particularly detrimental in family work. For this reason the *observations noted, but not verbalized*, are listed below:

1. *Peter's* hostility displayed by the tornado symbol might correlate to his soiling, as a device to get even with his parents, for not receiving as much attention as his brother.
2. *Peter* avoided making contact with his father or brother, due to his feeling rejected by Father and to sibling rivalry with Mikie.
3. *Peter's* way of testing his father (and possibly Mother) is self-destructive, since it can remove him from family involvement.
4. *Mother* displayed a looseness through her drawing style, lack of structure, and narcissistic involvement.
5. *Mother* avoided contact with Mikie. Her only response to him was the competitive gesture of making an enlarged copy of his tree.
6. *Mother's* and Mikie's drawing styles were similar. It was age-appropriate for a seven-year-old; yet it indicated a lack of maturity on Mother's part.
7. *Father* communicated a "not good enough" message by making his wife's sun "better."
8. *Father*, who selected his color after Peter, unconsciously picked out a marker that was not synergistic with his son.
9. *Father* began the mural with a gesture of structure by asking for thematic ideas. However, after he cued in Mikie to start, he withdrew his authority and did not offer any further direction.
10. *Mikie* inappropriately has the leadership role in the family.

Individual Meeting: Assessment of Peter

In addition to the family art psychotherapy sessions, individual meetings with Peter were held. At the first individual session (which took place the same week as the first family session), one of the standard requests was a colored drawing of the *House-Tree-Person*, a part of a projective test (Buck, 1970). The child eliminated colors when he chose the black marker for his drawing. In his picture of the house, only a single window was included. When asked, "What room was behind that window?", Peter replied·that it was "the bathroom," possibly an indication of the emphasis on toilet training and his withholding behavior.

When Peter was questioned about the picture of the *tree*, he claimed it was "a five-year-old boy tree," divulging a younger self-perception. In reference to "the best thing that could happen to the tree," Peter said, "If it could grow more loose." This statement seemed to symbolize the child's wish to overcome his withholding anal fixation. With further questioning,"what would be the worst thing that happened to the tree?", Peter replied, "It got chopped down by a strong, big person," a reference to his castration anxiety. Although the author has heard many replies that stated, "the tree got chopped down," the perpetrator is seldom designated.

As the therapist proceeded to the drawing of the *person*, Peter related it to "a man, 37 years old" (close to Father's age), claiming,"He is a happy person." When asked for further information about the man, Peter said, "The man works in the post office." Both of these statements signified his identification with Father. The therapist stated, "I know this is a happy man, but can you tell me what makes him angry sometimes?" The only reply, which was repeated several times, was "I dunno." This may have indicated father's own passive aggressive behavior (Figure 39).

In addition to the House-Tree-Person drawings, Peter was told to create *three wishes*. For the *first wish*, he sketched a *toy shop* which he wanted

Figure 39. House-Tree-Person

to own. However, he was mainly involved with the *second wish*, demonstrating a *thousand dollar bill* plus a *mansion*. He declared the money would enable him to "buy a mansion with four bedrooms and five bathrooms." The picture displayed a two-story house. The four upstairs windows, which were visible in the drawing, were identified as "my bedroom and my bathroom," and on the floor below, "my mother's bedroom and bathroom." In spite of the fact that the back side of the picture could not be seen in the sketch, he explained that the mansion also contained bathrooms and bedrooms for both his father and brother.

The parental room separation, as well as the visual emphasis on the sleeping and toilet quarters for both mother and himself, is evidence of the child's oedipal conflict. The graphics also offer hints to obsessive thoughts around bodily functions and probable masturbation. These are revealed through the attention to "private rooms," with the exclusion of all others, such as kitchen, and dining, living and family rooms.

Still another insight is gained through Peter's *third wish*, which exhibited a *cross* and *the gates of heaven*, as the child exposes his wish "never to die" (Figure 40). It is possible his concern around death is related to feelings of guilt and punishment.

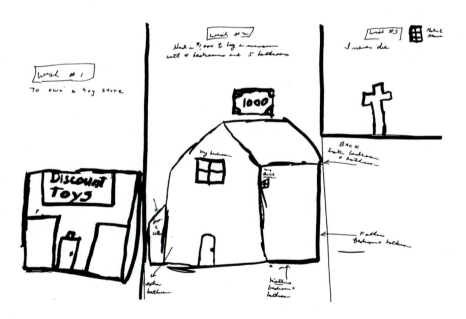

Figure 40. Three wishes

Although projective tests are not definitive, they do lend valuable clues to the patient's perceptions and fantasies.

Individual Meeting: Assessment of Peter

The assessment session (which took place the same week as the second family session), began with an offer to *make whatever you wish; that is, pick your own subject and select your art materials.*

Peter used a lead pencil at first to draw a picture of a *male and female* from the movie *Star Wars*. He then colored in the forms very carefully. When he was asked to present a dialogue between the two figures, he made every effort to print the words as perfectly as possible. One of the males in the story "was young and liked the ladie warier (sic) a whole lot. He was taking her away from the older cheef (sic). The older cheef was mad but he new (sic) he was beat out and gave up. The ladie warier was happy to go with the young cheef." This story of Peter's was classic, revealing his unresolved Oedipal conflict.

As an additional warm-up technique and as a means for evaluating his relationship to the therapist, the *nonverbal dual drawing directive* was given. Both Peter and the clinician engaged themselves in creating a picture together.

At first Peter watched the author a great deal. He seemed to be appraising the rules of the game. Initially he took a distance stance; as the drawing progressed, a number of passive–aggressive graphic gestures were made. These were exhibited when the therapist drew designs on her own part of the page and Peter changed them. This was repeated numerous times as he placed himself in the center of the forms. The child was obviously pleased about the amount of control he exerted over the picture.

After the first two exercises, Peter was asked about his bowel movements. The clinician questioned the frequency, textural consistency, and size of his feces. Peter reported he moved his bowels twice a day, the texture "was not too soft or too hard" and the size was "this big," displaying about a four-inch span.

To show Peter that his problem could be explored in a nonprejudicial, nondemanding, and unemotional environment, the author asked the child to *use the plasticene to create the usual size of your feces.* He selected the brown-colored plasticene and rolled it between his hands until he was satisfied that the size and shape were correct. As Peter's affect was flat, it was difficult to detect any embarrassment, anger, or other feelings, as the model *bowel movement* was being made. The therapist questioned if he had to strain himself while making a bowel movement (she wondered if constipation was related to the encopretic problem.) Peter explained it was not necessary to strain since he could easily defecate at will.

As the session was coming to an end, Peter was instructed to *get a box from a shelf and place your plasticene feces in it, then close the lid.* Following instructions, he put his metaphoric sculpture into a container. He was told, he could take the box out any time he wanted, if he wished to look inside or take it out. Peter was very interested in what the author said. He watched closely as the box was put on a shelf. Afterwards as he viewed the art therapy table, he saw pieces of plasticene and felt markers in disarray. The author was encouraged about a positive prognosis when Peter symbolically straightened up the supplies and announced, "I'll clean up before I leave." Although time was up for Peter, the child tried to linger on as an attempt to stretch out his cathartic experience.

SESSION THREE/*Family Meeting: All Members Present*

Family Drawings

While the Sontag family was waiting for their session to begin, each member was given pencil and paper and instructed to *draw your family.* The individual pictures, which read from left to right, are as follows:

Peter drew his Father first, then Mikie, Mother, and himself last. The most significant factor in the drawing is the hands; Peter, his brother, and his father are all depicted with no hands. The lack of hands on the males may represent Peter's perception of psychological helplessness. Mother's hands, which are well proportioned and clearly defined, may correlate to his seeing her as a more powerful or active person or, in cases of encopresis, her involvement with her son's soiling process.

In addition, all the males wore jeans with the flies well defined. This appears related to Peter's encopretic and masturbatory behavior (Figure 41).

Father drew himself first, then Mikie, his wife, and Peter last. Peter is oversized, with hands that are placed in his jeans pockets, wearing a cowboy hat and boots. Peter's hidden hands may have bearing on the encopresis, since Father and Mikie, also wearing jeans and boots, are hatless, with hands in view and well-defined. Mother was drawn the same size as Mikie, appearing as a curly-headed little girl with faint sketchy hands showing her to be immature and helpless (Figure 42).

Mother placed Peter first, herself closely next to him, with Mikie and Father drawn at a distance. Mother and Peter are equally oversized with their bodies touching each other. Mikie, on her left side, is closer to Father than herself. Mrs. Sontag emphasized her own feminine figure

FATHER MILIE BROTHER MOTHER ME

Figure 41. Peter's family drawing

ME PATHER MILIE WIFE PETER

Figure 42. Father's family drawing

and facial features, indicating her narcissism. Her hands, which are large, suggest her self-perception as an outgoing and open person. The dress with buttons from top to bottom reveals her dependency needs. Peter is drawn with an emphasis on his pants fly and a large belt buckle, which signified his Mother's perceptions of his dependence and somatic preoccupation (Machover, 1949). He is handless, again implying helplessness, perhaps in regard to toilet-training. Mikie is also wearing jeans with the fly and hands lacking, suggestive of enuresis. Mrs. Sontag created her husband on the edge of the page taller than herself, with hands that are held out perceiving him as an open, competent person. Everyone is presented as wide-eyed and smiling, similar to compensatory wishes frequently drawn by children (Figure 43).

Mikie drew his family according to height: Father, Mother, Peter, himself. Everyone was dressed alike in pants and shirts with mitt-like hands. A smile was on everyone's face (Figure 44).

During the session, the family was told to *create your earliest memory*. As

Figure 43. Mother's family drawing

FATHER   MOTHER   PETER   "HE" MIKIE

Figure 44. Mikie's family drawing

the most significant artwork was made by Peter, only his results will be reported here.

In spite of having a full set of colored markers and oil pastels available, Peter asked if he could use a pencil. Using the lead pencil and a large size 14' x 20' piece of paper, he proceeded to make a *sketch of a small fish*. It was weakly drawn and about one inch in length (Figure 45). Peter told the following story about the picture:

> When I was four years old my fish died. I came home from school and I found him floating in the water and I felt kinda upset. I wondered how he died. I ran to my Mom and asked her what to do with it. She said, "Wait until your father comes home." I just went out and played basketball. I felt sorta okay and sorta not. When my Dad came home he flushed the dead fish down the toilet. Then we just forgot about the whole thing. Even now when the fish die I wait for my Dad to come home and I ask him what to do. He tells me to "flush them down the toilet"; then I do it.

After hearing the explanation of Peter's picture, Mr. Sontag remembered the incident although he did not see any special significance to his son's story.

The author connected Peter's fish story to his fear of death, revealed in his wish "never to die," along with his refusal to make bowel movements in the toilet. The child's association to flushing down his feces seemed to be identified with the fear of the loss of self. This interpretive correlation was not addressed during this session because of premature timing.

The next family art task was a *free choice*. Again only Peter's artwork will be reviewed since it held the greatest significance.

The boy modeled a bird who had a beard. Turning to his mother he asked her to record the following story:

> There was a bearded bird. A rocket ship flew over his head and a man in a parachute fell out. The bird feels sorta dumb because he is the only one of the birds that has a beard and everyone teases him; it makes him shy. The man from the rocket fell in the ocean; he almost drowned. It was scary. The Griffith observatory was trying to find the man from the rocket, but the beard bird got in the way. They felt angry at him because he got in the way of a testing thing. (Figure 46)

When his puzzled parents asked for the meaning of the sculpture, Peter said, "It doesn't mean anything! It's only a story!" The author believed the content to be revealing although it was apparent that its symbolic content eluded the family. The art therapist used a part of the story to mention, "One of the characters in the story is the bearded bird

Figure 45. Dead fish flushed down toilet

Figure 46. The odd bird

who gets teased and it makes him shy." No one picked up on its connection to Peter. To the author, it appeared to be a metaphor for his fear of being teased by his peers for his encopretic behavior. The phallic beard of the bird was an upward displacement for Peter's bowel movement, since the form was identical to the plasticene feces which he had previously created. A similarly related shape was the fish from Peter's earliest memory. The image of the rocket is yet another repetition of the phallic symbol.

In Peter's tale he claims, "The man who fell out of the rocket into the water almost drowning." This statement reverted to his unconscious fear of toilet training and the loss of self. The Griffith observatory in the story can be equated with the therapist who is watching Peter draw and speak. In contrast, the reference to "testing thing" indicates the child is fearful of what his artwork might reveal.

SESSION FOUR/*Conjoint Meeting: Father and Peter*

To examine the relationship between father and son a conjoint session took place. When the pair came into the office, they sat themselves at a corner of the art therapy table. Father placed himself at the head with his son on his right side. After exchanging the usual greetings the couple was told to *create a picture together selecting your own topic and media.*

With the holidays coming up Mr. Sontag and his son decided to draw and cut out construction paper images relating to Christmas. Drawing sideways to accommodate his father, Peter made a *black house*. As Mr. Sontag cut out his *Christmas tree*, he kept asking his son a number of questions. He was friendly and tried to get his child involved on a verbal level. However, Peter's answers were always very brief, and he never initiated any of the conversation.

Father, reacting to Peter's passivity, kidded him, saying, "Son, you are not enthusiastic." He sounded more serious when he added, "You are falling down on the job." In spite of his placid expression, Mr. Sontag was upset and discontinued the artwork. Father's cessation made Peter laugh, sensing himself in a position of power because of his own passivity. The parent ignored the laughter as he looked over the artwork. When he noticed Peter had cut out a *house* which did not have any windows or doors, he became involved again as he filled in the *missing features* and added a *base line* and a *reindeer*. Although Father did not verbally demand his son's participation, his glances communicated a pressureful message.

Peter took a long time before he finally conceded and paid attention to his father's desires for a joint effort. He cooperated by cutting out *grass* for their picture, in a very slow and compulsive fashion. He managed to cover the entire width of the page as he carefully cut each blade the same height. When he was finished with the grass, he added *Christmas lights* to the tree, making certain they were very evenly distanced between one another. Viewing the picture, Father commented, "Packages are missing, son"; then he himself cut and pasted the *gift boxes* onto the project. He continued on to ask his son many questions and to make a number of suggestions. His conscious efforts to keep his child engaged were obvious. After the picture was completely finished, Peter, unsolicited, announced the title, "Here comes Santa Claus," then proceeded to write it down before his father had a chance to comment.

SESSION FIVE/*Conjoint Meeting: Mother and Peter*

In this evaluation session, the mother-son relationship was examined. The two participants were instructed to *create a picture together without speaking to one another.*

The outcome showed two separate images on a single page. Each person drew on their own side of the page. Peter created a *drum with drumsticks* while Mother made a picture showing *herself at work*.

The second instruction was for *the two of you make another picture together but this time you are to talk to each other.*

Mrs. Sontag began by asking her child, "Shall we do the picture together?" Peter shook his head "No." Nevertheless, for no apparent reason she gave him a hug, then smiled as she drew her own picture of a *pink Christmas tree*. She titled it, "A heartfelt tree." Peter viewed his mother's picture, then made a *blue tree*, half the size of his mother's, naming it, "A baby tree."

Peter appeared to be threatened by his mother's overt display of emotions. Although he responded by selecting a cool unemotional color, he identified with the young tree. The dual drawing process exhibited Mrs. Sontag's affection and the infantilizing effect it had upon her son.

SESSION SIX/*Family Meeting: All Members Present*

To warm up the group for personal family discussions, the following directive was given. *Each person is to create a series of scenes (comic strip fashion) which reported some home events since your last visit.*

When the project was finished, a request was made for volunteers to share their work. *Peter* went first showing his graphics, which displayed *himself batting the baseball and winning the game*. Mikie portrayed himself bringing home a note from his teacher, which stated he had performed exceptionally well in school. *Mother* had waited impatiently to share her artwork. The pictures displayed *the boys at breakfast* with "Peter as a good boy because he had washed up nicely and eaten up all his breakfast." On the other hand, "Mikie had fussed, refused to clean himself up or eat." He demanded "to go out and play!" Another scene portrayed *Mikie crying* as he declared, "I hate cereal." The next picture showed *herself making pancakes* to please her younger son.

While reviewing her artwork, Mrs. Sontag questioned the value of doing the "busy work part of the therapy session" (referring to the art tasks). It looked as though she was considering leaving the table when she spotted a *toy bath tub* prop. Mrs. Sontag lifted it up, examined it, then placed it down in front of herself. She proceeded to use the plasticene to model a *child* which she set into the tub. Mrs. Sontag vehemently explained she remembered becoming frustrated and angry over an incident which happened last Sunday. She said that, as the family was getting ready to go visiting relatives, she filled the tub with warm water for the boys' baths. Although Mikie was to wash up first, Peter convinced his mother to let him take a quick bath since he was actually clean. He told her that when he was finished he would leave the warm water in the tub for his brother to wash up in. Mother agreed, believing everyone would be ready sooner if she followed Peter's suggestion.

Mrs. Sontag burst out in rageful tears as she reported the rest of the story: "When I went into the bathroom to wipe Peter off, I saw that he had *messed* himself up and the tub water, too. That kid had actually shit in the tub! Yes, shit in the water that Mikie was supposed to use! I couldn't believe it. The nerve of him. How ugly and gross." The author asked, "What happened next?" "Well," she replied, "I took a wash cloth and washed up Peter's buttocks. Then I dried him up and, of course, I bawled him out. Since all that fuss took so much time, there was no time left for Mikie to take his bath. Imagine him making a B.M. in the tub!"

After Mrs. Sontag quieted down both she and her husband sat depressed while the boys, embarrassed, looked around the room to avoid any eye contact. There was a long silence as the parents stared at Mother's artwork. Mrs. Sontag, thinking about the past event, admitted she had gained insight. Her home-scene pictures made some sense when viewed in connection with her bathroom sculpture. She could see "how Peter's disgusting behavior was a way of getting even with me and Mikie." She realized her older son was jealous of all the attention his younger brother received from her that morning during breakfast.

This was a major awareness. It pointed out how Peter, instead of communicating his anger through words, used passive–aggressive means.

Mikie's negative behavior during breakfast was also brought into focus. He had gained his mother's attention while Peter's positive behavior had gone unrewarded. Yet, when Peter acted inappropriately, Mother became actively involved with him. I explained how some people preferred to get negative attention rather than none. The boys listened attentively as Mr. and Mrs. Sontag discussed this issue with the therapist. The parents offered assurance that they would become more aware of this dynamic in the future. They planned to employ positive reinforcement for the behavior that deserved attention and reward.

Mr. Sontag, still absorbed in his thoughts about Peter's psychological motivations for expressing anger through encopretric behavior, was the next person to share the artwork. He had depicted *Peter and himself playing ball*, explaining how he helped his son become a better baseball pitcher. His wife threw out the remark, "John, you are too hard on Peter; you are a good father and you do spend a lot of time with him, but you are never satisfied with his ball playing." At first Father defended himself by claiming, "I only want to help Peter because I know he'll be happier if he is a better player. I wish my father had helped me when I was a kid." Mrs. Sontag retorted, "But Peter isn't you! His father spends time with him! Your father didn't!" Mr. Sontag took in his wife's statement. After mulling over the interactions between his son and himself, he turned to Peter to say, "Maybe Mother is right . . . do you think I'm too hard on you?" When his son shrugged his shoulders unknowingly, Mr. Sontag said, "I'm beginning to think that you get even *on me, too,* by shitting in your pants." "On you?" the author questioned. "Well, not on me but I see how Peter acts —placid and pleasant, but he shows his anger by shitting in his pants."

Mrs. Sontag, trying to understand the soiling situation, announced, "I believe he's getting even with both of us." She then turned to the therapist to direct her remarks: "I'm beginning to think that we give Peter a lot of power because whenever he soils himself, my husband and I say, 'What did I do wrong?'"

Peter was surprised to hear his parents express themselves so openly and honestly about their personal lives. The interaction being exhibited was contrary to the usual family style. Peter, who listened intently to every word, appeared frightened by the display of emotions. On the other hand, Mikie, who was bored with the attention his brother was receiving, resorted to playing with the plasticene.

To help the children understand alternatives for gaining positive attention, the boys were told to *draw ways you can get good attention from your dad.*

Peter's artwork was drawn in a sequence. It portrayed him: 1) *doing well in baseball;* 2) *getting top grades in school;* and 3) *cleaning up his Dad's car.*

After explaining the pictorial series, Peter was instructed to *draw the conversation you wish you could have with your Dad by writing in bubbles what each person would be saying.*

With a big grin on his face, Peter said "I gotcha," then proceeded to draw himself and his father in a dialogue: "Dad, I want you to do more things with me" and his father answered, "Son, I'm going to go to the park with you this Sunday and we will play ball together."

The parents instructed Peter to be more open verbally about his needs instead of soiling to gain attention. The author puzzled aloud about the advantages that "very young children may have." Peter volunteered an answer, saying "They're like my puppy. They only play and don't have to do anything." After acknowledging his thoughts, the child was told to create *the good things to being more grown up.*

Peter combined collage and drawing to portray himself *playing baseball, using a computer, going to the toy shop with a friend, walking to school alone,* and *going camping.* After sharing his artwork, he asked permission to tack his pictures up on the wall. As Peter did this, the therapist silently wondered if this act was the child's way of making a greater commitment to give up his infantile actions.

Mikie's response to the directive about getting "good attention from your Dad," showed him: 1) *cleaning up his room;* 2) *playing ball "good";* 3) *going to bed on time;* and 4) *"being nice."* Mikie, wishing to have his equal time to talk about his artwork, spoke about the puppy—how he was helping to feed, wash, and brush the dog. Triggering off from Peter's responses, Mikie said that when he was more grown up he, too, could play baseball and use a computer and go to the toy shop with a friend; and he would also go camping like Peter was going to. The rest of the family laughed, enjoying Mikie's wish to have the same advantages as his brother.

Although bringing about the family's awareness regarding their dynamics is essential for clinical effectiveness with the encopretic patient, *management* is one of the major elements of treatment. Therefore, the Sontags were notified that management procedures would be addressed in the near future.

SESSION SEVEN/*Conjoint Meeting: Mother and Father*

The most important part of the meeting with Mr. and Mrs. Sontag was informing Peter's mother she was not to wash her son's buttocks, dry him off after a bath, or change his underpants. It was explained this type of contact provided the child with unnecessary stimulation and served to infantilize him. Also, the message that Mother conveyed to Peter was "You are a baby and Mommy must take care of you—wipe you up, wash your bottom, and change your underpants." From now on, they were to inform their child *his behavior was going to change. He was to have the responsibility for being in charge of his body from now on.* He was to keep clean and take care of his clothes. Mother was to tell Peter that she would no longer treat him as a baby since he was a nine-year-old and *truly capable of greater self-care and responsibility.*

Although offering information is unusual in art psychotherapy, it is vital to the behavioral approach. Skills for dealing with the encopretic problem are necessary for the parents, since such skills give the couple a definite program for helping their child. Of equal importance is the mind-set that they will be instrumental in changing their child's behavior. The psychological weight of thinking in positive terms is one of the greatest influences in curing encopresis. The author believes the attitudinal shift is facilitated by the *therapist's conviction that encopresis, which is not organic, will come to an end.*

SESSION EIGHT/*Family Meeting: All Members Present*

To gain further understanding of the Sontag family's dynamics a variety of media was placed before them along with the directive to *create an art project together.*

Father, remembering his lack of leadership in the past, made certain to select the construction paper. Both parents decided to establish their authority in the eyes of the children. After a brief discussion between Mr. and Mrs. Sontag, they notified the boys that the family would *create a house together*. Everyone was assigned a task, which was willingly carried out. When the structure was completed, Mr. Sontag picked up the *toy toilet, sink,* and *bathtub props* and placed them inside the construction paper house. With Father's permission, Peter continued on to create a *bike rack*, with a *boy* nearby, and Mikie also formed a *figure*. Mother, believing the boys had made representations of themselves, decided to create a *figure of herself*.

It was Mikie who began the play action by taking his little figure and zooming it around the house. Peter followed by putting his figure next to the bike rack. Mother, witnessing this gesture, proclaimed, "Oh, that's where you soil your pants at home, near the bike rack." Father was surprised to hear this information. Although Peter glanced sideways at his mother, his affect did not reveal his feelings.

Mother continued to explain that Peter soiled his pants almost every day at three o'clock—about a half hour after returning home from school. The author took this lead to establish a toilet schedule for Peter. She told him to *draw two clocks, one that is set at 7:30, the other at 3:00* (Figure 47). To keep Mikie involved also, his instructions were to *draw two clocks: one showing the time you wake up and the other the time you go to bed.* The parents were directed to *create a calendar for the months of March and April.*

Figure 47. Toilet schedule

After the artwork was completed, Peter was instructed to sit on the toilet for five minutes, two or possibly three times a day. Pointing to his picture, the therapist set the daily routine for 7:30 in the morning, before going to school, and for 3 o'clock, when he returned. If he did not make a bowel movement either time, he was to sit down on the toilet again after dinner.

Mr. and Mrs. Sontag were told they could help Peter by reminding him for one week only. At the end of that time he was to take full responsibility for remembering the schedule. When Mikie asked what part he was to play in the family plan, he was told to ask his brother. Peter, obviously pleased with the therapist for providing a master plan to cure his problem, benevolently told his brother that tomorrow Mikie could remind him at the 7:30 morning time "because," he proudly said, "next week I'll be on my own!"

Before leaving the office, Peter asked the author if he could take his clock drawings home. The rule of keeping all the artwork in the office was reiterated; however, Peter and Mikie were given paper and crayons to take with them. Peter was encouraged to repeat his drawings at home. Such extra artwork would serve the double purpose of reinforcement for the schedule and as a transitional object.

SESSION NINE/*Conjoint Meeting: Mother and Father*

Peter was sick in bed with the flu. Rather than cancel the appointment or have the parents and Mikie appear without Peter, the therapist set up a session for Mr. and Mrs. Sontag. They entered the office in a good mood, reporting that Peter had stayed *free from soiling* a few times at the beginning of the week but then reverted back to soiling again. When asked how had they responded to Peter in light of his accomplishment, Father declared, "We didn't want to make a fuss over what any three-year-old could do."

The parents were notified that it was essential for Peter to receive positive reinforcement to keep him motivated. They were instructed to praise their son any time he gained control over his bowel movements. The clinician reminded them that Peter had formerly received attention for negative behavior. Now it was necessary to *ignore the negative* and to *stress the positive*. They were to give him credit for any successful attempts to master his problem. Emphasis was placed on acknowledging his initial victories. In simple language the author reiterated, "In the future, when Peter stays clean you are to tell him how proud you are of him that he has managed to be responsible for making B.M. in the toilet." They were told to have Peter continue to sit on the toilet for 5 to 10 minutes each day at 7:30 a.m., 3 p.m., and if need be, after dinner.

Mrs. Sontag mentioned that the mutual family drawing was most insightful and helpful to her in understanding where changes must be made. She reported her attempts to avoid immersing herself in her "own thing" and to improve lines of communication.

To examine the couple's communication style when the children were not present, they were instructed *to create something together.*

Without consulting with each other about the theme, a colored construction paper *house* was built in tandem. They selected toy props to decorate the interior. At one point Mrs. Sontag picked up a toy washing machine, stating it was necessary for her husband to create a service porch since the washing machine was the most important appliance in the house. When the author questioned Mrs. Sontag about the reason for the washing machine's importance, she replied, "'Cause of all the smelly clothes. Every day I use that machine . . . I have to pull those pee-soaked sheets off the kids' beds. I told you how I get down on my hands and knees to look for Peter's wringing-wet pajamas and his B.M.-soiled jockey shorts. Can you imagine the kind of daily laundry I have to wash?" She began to cry as she reminded herself how angry and guilty the situation made her feel. Mr. Sontag, trying to comfort his wife, reached out to pat her hand.

The therapist again reminded the couple to give Peter positive reinforcement for making bowel movements in the toilet each day that he succeeded. In addition, from now on Peter was to be instructed to place his own wet or soiled clothes and sheets into the washing machine by himself. He would also have the job of replacing the bed with clean sheets. A reminder not to clean Peter's anus, buttocks, and/or penis was made, with the repeated reference to Peter's responsibility for cleaning his own body. (The redundancy of the words was intentional as an "imprint" influence.)

Remembering the parent's style of communication, they were told they must refrain from hinting at instructions by asking their children questions. If they wanted the children to perform a task, they were to make the message clear and straight. For example, they were not to ask Peter, "Would you towel yourself dry?" Instead they were to say, "Towel yourself dry."

Individual Meeting: Peter

When Peter came into the art therapy office he noticed that the family's mural (drawn several weeks previously) was still tacked on the drawing wall. After his greeting, he walked over to the picture, thoughtfully surveying it. Peter was silent for a few minutes then turned to the therapist to announce he had made B.M. on the toilet a number of times since his last visit. The child reported he had experienced the need to make a bowel movement when he was on the toilet both at 7:30 a.m. and 3 p.m. He notified the therapist, "I expelled one large piece each time." I responded by telling him it was wonderful that he could manage to go on the toilet for his bowel movements instead of soiling his pants. To reinforce his success he was told to "draw yourself making a B.M. on the toilet."

Peter's approach to the artwork was enthusiastic. With satisfaction he titled it, "Me On The Toilet." It was interesting to find he had omitted the word "making" as an indication of his resistance to giving up control. The author asked Peter, "What is missing in the picture?" He puzzled for a while. When it appeared he was unable to figure it out, he was reminded the picture was to portray him *making* a bowel movement. Peter lit up as he said, "I get it—I left out the B.M. It only showed me sitting, not making." Then on the left side of the page he colored a large bowel movement, this time labeling it correctly (Figure 48).

Figure 48. Bowel movement

Individual Meeting: Peter

During the following session Peter requested to review all of the art-work which he had produced by himself, as well as the family's productions. When the author went to the cabinet to take the work out, Peter mentioned it was a good idea for her to keep it so he could look things over. As he reviewed the art, he remembered the conversations that accompanied them. The child paid special attention to the plasticene feces which were kept in the box. Peter completed the perusal with satisfaction.

Returning to the art materials, he chose the plasticene to make a *watch*, which showed the time to be *nine o'clock*. Without being prompted he said it meant that last night he went to bed at nine o'clock, stayed there for five minutes, then got up to make a bowel movement on the toilet. Peter was told it was wonderful that he could manage a movement at times other than 7:30 and 3:00 because this allowed him greater freedom and validated his control over his body.

Individual Meetings Report

As Peter began to see the author as trustworthy, his attitude began to change. His affect was labile and he became friendly, making jokes and showing his warm feelings.

For several weeks Peter and the author were engaged in a number of mutually created projects. They included several rules; if Peter needed help he was required to communicate this clearly by saying, "I need help." If he was feeling frustrated or angry he should voice his emotions out loud. In this way, the author explained, she would understand his needs and feelings and by working this way their art project would turn out to be more rewarding.

Although Peter learned to express himself through the artwork, his range did not include anger or fear. This was of particular significance since these repressed emotions are often a salient encopretic dynamic. For this reason Peter was offered an opportunity to express rageful and aggressive fantasies. His metaphoric characters took on the guise of jet bombers, sharks, and dragons. On rare occasions when people were included, they took on the role of victims. The most popular themes revolved around Oedipal conflicts and castration anxiety. When the family saw Peter's artwork they failed to understand the underlying meaning, yet they were very impressed with the quality of his product.

An example of the child's Oedipal theme is seen in his sculpture titled "King Arthur's Castle" (Figure 49A). This is the story that was dictated to the therapist:

Figure 49A. King Arthur's castle

Once upon a time there was a fierce dragon (Figure 49B). He wanted to destroy the castle and the guards; he doesn't like the guards and the King 'cause they want to hurt the dragon with their big strong swords.

The dragon sneaks in and attacks at night. Then he puts the castle on fire by blowing smoke out of his mouth.

Then King Arthur who is in bed with Queen Guinevere wakes up. She calls the guards. Then the dragon escapes by sneaking out the way he came in. Then the whole Castle burns down.

King Arthur's money got burnt so then he couldn't get a new castle. The Queen went to live with the dragon. They lived happy together for the rest of their life.

The author, believing it was important for Peter to express his aggression in a nonthreatening way, invented the game WIPE OUT. The child and clinician drew on a single sheet of paper. Each had their own color. As the therapist drew, Peter was encouraged to scribble over her part. The gestures were accelerated as he scurried around to keep up his wiping out pace to the author's graphic speed. This interaction was always fun and brought the feeling of power to the child. Peter was told, "Wiping someone out in art is good, but in everyday life it is not good" (Figure 50).

SESSION TEN/*Conjoint Meeting: All Members Present*

In the Sontag family where Peter and his father masked angry feelings and Mother needed to master greater control, specific teams and techniques were devised. The father and son team was told to *form one dyad*, with instructions to *pick out five pictures of angry people from the photo collage box*, whereas the mother and Mikie team was told to *select only three pictures of people who are doing something specific. Both teams are to paste your pictures onto your own sheet of newsprint paper. When finished, fantasize what each person in the photograph is thinking, saying, and wishes they could say. Write these answers on the page.*

After several such assignments, the author began to interpret the statements of the characters in the artwork as similar to the participants' own feelings. These techniques had role-playing benefits as well as insight work. It led the way to understanding Peter's behavior in regards to *cause* and *effect*, that is, what situations evoked rage but were veiled in his affect and verbal communication.

SESSION ELEVEN/*Conjoint Meeting: Peter and Father*

A conjoint session with Peter and his father took place when Mrs. Sontag and Mikie had to attend a special meeting at school. As they entered the office the pair looked upset. When asked, "What's the trou-

Figure 49B. Fierce dragon

Figure 50. Wipe out

ble?" Peter looked away, as he sat himself down at the table and began to scribble on a piece of paper. When Mr. Sontag was seated, he explained his disappointment in Peter. The child had made many requests for permission to walk home from school unescorted. Peter was finally granted his wish and managed just fine for a week; then one day, instead of going directly home, he stopped to play with a friend.

The Sontags were very worried when Peter came home later than usual. Believing their son had abused his privilege, they punished him by rescinding permission to walk home by himself. Mr. Sontag went on to explain he believed there was a direct correlation between their punishment and Peter's regressive subsequent soiling episode that particular week. Because of Peter's blank expression it was difficult to understand what he thought about his father's claim. When Mr. Sontag was asked if Peter had understood that abusing his privilege carried a punishment, he answered, "No." Although Peter looked upon the author as an ally, he stubbornly resisted any discussion, in spite of her encouragement to speak his mind.

The therapist slipped a piece of paper in front of the boy, suggesting he create *a future plan, one that might prevent difficulties in the future.*

Peter thought for a while; then, still silent, he drew *two figures* labeled ME and DAD. In a bubble he wrote his father saying, "Now son, you did not come right home. That was bad. Do not do it again. If you don't come right home again, you won't be able to watch television for a week and you can't have any dessert for a week." Above himself he wrote a reply, "OK, Dad, I am sorry. I did not know you would worry. I will not do it again."

The picture triggered off a conversation between father and son. They dealt with the prevention of similar misunderstandings in the future. Utilizing the incident for interpretation, the therapist told Peter, "It seems when your parents give you more grown-up privileges, like walking home from school alone, they expect more grown-up behavior on your part. I think *your pants soiling is your way of having a silent temper tantrum.*"

The author referred to the first family drawing when the Sontags failed to communicate. He was reminded that *if he did not speak up, then no one knew what he was feeling*. Since everyone had recently realized the need to express themselves, it was particularly important to speak up, to be clear, and not to expect other people to mind read.

The clinician told Peter, "If you were angry with your Dad for punishing you when you believed it wasn't deserved, then you need to talk to him about it. Soiling your pants won't solve disagreements. I know it's hard to change and to express your feelings openly, but I think you'll find it has more advantages and will help you feel better about yourself."

Mr. Sontag was empathic with his son, as he explained he himself was trying hard to behave differently. He had hoped Peter would feel free to voice his opinion, especially in light of the fact that he had never punished him physically. Mr. Sontag told his son, "You have nothing to fear," adding, "Only good things could happen by talking. Negotiations are always possible if we'd all tell what's on our minds. From now on if you are going to be punished for your misbehavior you'll know about it in advance, what it'll be, and how long it will last."

Peter and his father looked relieved because they believed an important understanding had been established between them.

SESSION TWELVE/*Conjoint Meeting: Mother and Father*

During the conjoint meeting, the author referred to the previous session when Mr. Sontag told his son he could speak his mind without fearing any repercussions (especially physical abuse). The clinician related that many children did not fear physical abuse as much as being punished through their parents' withdrawal of love. To help the Sontags understand their son's noncommittal way of dealing with dissatisfactions, they were informed about Peter's defense mechanisms. The therapist explained that he did not reveal himself since he perceived it as a way of keeping things safe and on an even keel. Although unexpressed the therapist also saw this defense as a struggle to maintain the family homeostasis. Once again the Sontags were encouraged to give clear messages which stated their expectations. If any rewards or punishments were to be included, it should be made certain that the children were told the reasons. The parents were also warned that *when Peter did feel safe enough to express his thoughts and emotions they might not always like what they heard.* It would probably make their lives harder since more issues would have to be dealt with. The couple acknowledged the author's statements; however, they claimed that if the soiling which was guilt-provoking and a social embarrassment would cease, it would all be worth the consequences.

SESSION THIRTEEN/*Family Meeting: All Members Present*

Although it had been a long time since Mr. and Mrs. Sontag had made their construction paper house, Mikie suddenly became very interested in it. When he asked the therapist if he could work on this house, the decision was turned over to his parents. Mr. and Mrs. Sontag suggested they work along with Mikie while Peter, who wished to create his own work, was allowed to do so.

Peter used the plasticene to model *himself with a smile on his face.* He pressed the figure onto construction paper where he continued to draw a *one-week calendar.* Knowing exactly what he wanted to do, the child took some *gold stars* and pasted *one on each day of the week.* When Peter was asked to talk about the artwork, he explained there had been no soiling incidents for the entire week (Figure 51). The author must admit at that point, it was not only Peter who was proud and hopeful, but she too shared that feeling for it indicated a very positive prognosis toward complete cessation of the encopretic problem.

SESSION FOURTEEN/*Family Meeting: All Members Present*

Before the family seated themselves, Mr. and Mrs. Sontag reported their pride in Peter's progress; he had defecated in the toilet most of the week. They also stated everyone was "getting along better." To support their gains, they were given a task *to draw what makes your family get along better.*

Father drew *Peter on the toilet, Mother* portrayed the *boys putting their wet*

Figure 51. Success; no soiling

pajamas and sheets in the toilet, Peter drew his *father helping him fix his bike,* and *Mikie* showed *Peter helping with his stamp collection.* The Sontags talked about the changes that were taking place in their family. Feeling in a particularly good mood, they themselves decided to *do another family mural together,* which they titled in advance "Super-Boys." It portrayed Peter and Mikie dressed up as Superman running around in the yard, while Mom was in the kitchen and Dad was fixing his car.

SESSION FIFTEEN/*Family Meeting: Mother, Father, and Peter*

The art therapy session consisted of Peter and his parents since Mikie was invited to a party and was unable to attend. The family was told to *decide what all of you are going to make.* Peter suggested that his mother and father work together while he did his "own thing." The author saw this as a positive gesture towards working through the Oedipal conflict, as it symbolized Peter's attempt to separate himself out and see his parents as a couple.

Peter drew his *mother and father smiling.* The interesting facet is the way in which Peter had drawn his parents. In the past he had always made small-sized figures in a weak and sketchy style; however, this drawing was done with conviction and the figures of his parents had the appearance of substance. Peter was instructed to *write down what is being said by your parents in the art.* In bubbles above his father, he stated, "I'm proud of you son," and Mother is saying, "Good!" The Sontags were pleased to read this message. Later on, Peter titled it "Happy Parents Because I Don't Do a B.M. Anymore" (Figure 52).

HAPPY PARENTS BECAUSE I
DON'T DO A B.M. ANYMORE

Figure 52. Parents happy

As the family was leaving the office, Mr. Sontag told the therapist how very pleased he and his family were with the management instructions and their son's results.

SESSION SIXTEEN THROUGH TWENTY/*Family Meetings: All Members Present*

In sessions sixteen, seventeen, eighteen, and nineteen, which are not reported here, the issue of Peter's encopresis was not mentioned. Those art therapy meetings dealt with daily decisions and problems. The emphasis was placed on open communication.

During the twentieth meeting, the family triumphantly reported that Peter had *discontinued his soiling altogether.* He made a daily bowel movement at home, at approximately four o'clock.

The author suggested a *family project on the theme of the reason you are coming to art therapy NOW.* The family decided everyone would make their own picture, then the four pictures would be pasted onto one large page. When the individual artwork was finished, *Mother* volunteered to share her picture first. The drawing revealed the *boys wetting their beds at night.* It was titled "More Help." *Father* realized he had created a *similar theme* which was titled, "Going on to the Next Problem." *Peter's* drawing showed *Mikie playing with his toys* and the picture was named, "My Brother Is a Pest." *Mikie's* picture was a *complaint,* "my brother never wants to play with me." He requested his mother to write down, "Peter Is Mean to Me."

The family was led into talking about Peter's and Mikie's complaints and solutions to these problems. After several suggestions were made, the Sontags appropriately decided to solve these problems at home. Attention was then turned to Mother's and Father's artwork, which stated they desired "more help" and "going on to the next problem."

The family agreed to work on Peter's bed-wetting problem next. The author, feeling omnipotent, enthusiastically notified the Sontags, "Next week you will be given an *enuretic self-management plan.*"

Individual Meeting: Peter

With Peter's consent to work on the problem of enuresis, the child was instructed to set his alarm for two o'clock at night to awaken him to go to the toilet. Without instruction, Peter proceeded to draw a *picture of the alarm clock set at 2 o'clock in the morning.* The therapist agreed it was a very fine idea to graphically depict his future plans.

Peter was told to try to get up at 2 o'clock to see if that was the best time. In case he was already wet, he was to set the clock to an earlier time the following night. Peter was excited about tackling his "last problem," which kept him back from going on overnight campouts with his friends.

SESSION TWENTY-ONE/*Family Meeting: All Members Present*

Peter spoke to the author as the family was entering the room. He reported how he had to change the alarm several times because he did not hear when it rang. His big complaint was that if he did not stay partly awake he could not hear the alarm. It was suggested that the Sontags change to another alarm clock which rang louder and would awaken Peter.

When the participants were involved in creating their own individual sculptures, Peter took great care with the *bed* he was forming. The author was struck by the fact that the sculpture, similar to Peter's own bed, had a *water mattress* on it. In the past, this author paid little attention to the type of beds upon which enuretic patients slept, having treated many children before the "water" bed was marketed. However, at this particular time she considered the question about the effect of the undulating, warm water bed on the enuretic patient. She believed it was possible for the soothing motion to be similar to the intrauterine experience. Also, the comfort of the warm water bed (even when wet) could continue to lull the child into sleep and thus encourage enuretic behavior.

The author wondered if a regular mattress, which caused some discomfort, would strengthen the motivation to stop the bed-wetting. When this question was put before Mr. and Mrs. Sontag, they asked for time to think about this idea before investing money in a new mattress.

SESSION TWENTY-TWO/*Family Meeting: All Members Present*

The family took control of the session from the beginning of the meeting. They decided to *create a mutual family sculpture* around the theme of *what we did last week*. The artwork showed the *family cleaning out the boys' bedroom*, "getting rid of the baby toys," a task that the Sontags admitted was long overdue. The therapist interpreted the parents' activities as a way of helping the children to grow up and to leave their babyish ways behind them. It was pointed out this act was congruent with the work on bowel and bladder control.

This particular piece of art, which was aesthetically outstanding, gave the family a way to show off their creative talent and, of greater importance, their adaptive style of working together both at home and in the therapy.

SESSION TWENTY-THREE/*Family Meeting: All Members Present*

When the therapist told Mr. Sontag to begin the session, he notified the family, *we will involve ourselves in making a mural together.* As Mikie hastened to walk up to the drawing wall, Peter made a point to get there first. Father encouraged communication by saying, "Let's talk about the way we will approach this mural. Peter, do you have a suggestion?" Peter, who was caught unaware, looked upset as he responded with a mere shrug. Mother, concerned about her son's feelings because he was put on the spot, began to intervene. However, Father asserted himself by telling Peter, "If you want to go first then you'd better let me know."

Peter responded by declaring, "I want to go first this time." "That's fine," Mr. Sontag replied. 'Now let's talk about the entire procedure. Should we take turns, all draw at once, or what?" Peter claimed that if *he* were allowed to *begin*, he would take the opportunity *to section off the paper into four spaces; one for each member of the family.* When everyone agreed it was a good way to proceed, Peter divided the page. In his own space he began by writing the title "My Room," continuing on to draw a picture of *himself lying in bed, with the alarm clock on a shelf nearby.* He later explained, "The alarm clock went off and now it's time for me to get up and go to the bathroom to go urinate" (Figure 53).

After seeing his brother's picture, Mikie made a drawing of himself in bed. He said it represented his very own plan to also start using the toilet at night instead of bed-wetting.

Peter and Mikie were instructed to create *artwork that showed what usually happened at night.* Peter portrayed himself wetting the bed, and Mikie, copying his brother, repeated the scene. After the boys finished sharing their artwork, the entire family turned to fix their gazes on the

Figure 53. Enuretic plan

author. Their positive transference and complete faith in this author's abilities to help them once again elicited her feelings of omnipotence (which was later to be regretted). With a great deal of confidence, several rules were laid out:

1. The children are to be responsible for placing their wet bed sheets and pajamas into the washing machine.
2. Urination is to take place before bedtime.
3. The alarm clock is to be set an hour before bed-wetting usually takes place.
4. A reward system is to be established at home.

Mr. and Mrs. Sontag's pictures of smiling-faced figures reflected their pleasure with the boys' determination to end their bed-wetting problem.

Individual Meeting: Peter

The art therapy meeting began when Peter decided to create one of his favorite themes of a *jet plane*. As he molded the plasticene, he dictated the following: "This time I want it to fly *right*. No diving, no fighting. This is going to be a *night flight. The pilot is a winner.*" Peter asked if the therapist would join him in the art project, although he would continue to be the leader. At one point the sculpture became a complicated problem-solving task. When Peter, determined to somehow keep a jet suspended, was unable to accomplish such a task, the therapist purposely held back from making suggestions since it was beneficial for Peter to speak out and ask for aid.

When he finally asked for help he was told to select a paper carton. The top was cut off and the box was turned on the side to create a stage effect. Peter was told to tie a string around the plane and to attach it to the outside top of the box. This approach enabled the jet to float in mid-air. Peter, excited with the effect, could hardly wait to decorate the environment. He pasted black paper on the background for the night sky, and using white oil pastels, drew stars onto the background (Figure 54).

When the artwork was completed, the author pointed out the similarity between the jet pilot who had a successful night trip and Peter's wish to manage the trip to the bathroom. Peter let out a gleeful chuckle when he realized the way art expressed his inner desires.

The process of Peter's environmental sculpture project proved to be a fine experience as a model for communication. The therapist reviewed the boy's actions during the session. The way he had asked and answered questions directly and in general let his needs be known.

Figure 54. Night flight pilot is a winner

Sensing his own increase in self-esteem, the child asked the therapist if she would appoint him the leader during the next family project. Peter was told to consider voicing this desire during the art therapy meeting rather than being dependent on the clinician's invitation. Before he left the office, Peter informed the therapist he was seriously thinking about asserting himself in the next family therapy session.

SESSION TWENTY-FOUR/*Family Meeting: All Members Present*

When the Sontags came to the office, Peter, filled with pride, showed his environmental jet sculpture to his family. Somehow it seemed to give him the courage to present his wish to be in the role of leader. His father, open to the idea, said, "Sure, son, it's OK with me." Looking to his mother, Peter awaited a reply but before she could answer, his brother intervened, "Daddy is a good leader, he has good ideas."

Mother, diverted by Mikie's sabotaging act, failed to answer Peter immediately. Although Peter was disappointed, his facial expression did not reflect his emotions. When he sat down, Mother took this gesture to mean Father was going to be the leader and asked her husband to begin the artwork. As Mr. Sontag was about to start, the therapist decided to prevent the family from reverting to their former mode of functioning.

Therefore, the author intruded upon the family system by telling them to "stop and recap what is happening."

Mr. Sontag reported Peter had wished to direct a family art project to which he had agreed. However, after Mikie got jealous of Peter for wanting to be in charge, Father changed his mind. He realized he did not want his younger son to feel badly. In retrospect, he knew he should have kept his word and dealt with Mikie's feelings afterwards.

Father mentioned that his wife *misunderstood* Peter's gesture, although he knew his son felt hurt and defeated. Mother, realizing her husband was right, turned to Peter to apologize. She claimed she was not trying to protect Mikie but if Peter didn't express himself verbally she simply did not understand what he was thinking. She ended by telling her husband she was impressed with his ability to understand the family dynamics.

Mikie did not like what he had just heard. He denied his disruption of Peter's desire as a diversive action. Whining, Mikie insisted he was "not jealous" of his brother, but his "daddy always makes up good art stuff."

Peter was relieved by his father's assessment of the situation. He felt understood by him and gained comfort from the family's awareness of Mikie's jealousy and the influence that he wielded.

The family was encouraged to replay the situation, starting with Father's agreement to have Peter as a leader. However, this time they were to begin with a fresh start, taking it to the correct conclusion with Peter leading the family through the art project.

Henceforth, Peter decided on a "farm scene," designating each person's contributions. When the task was completed, the entire family was satisfied with the results, both artistically and psychodynamically.

SESSION TWENTY-FIVE/*Family Meeting: All Members Present*

To indicate their increasing autonomy, the family, without any invitation from the author, decided to make a colored-paper construction. The children were asked for input regarding the theme. Peter said he wished to make a new construction which was similar to the one his parents had worked on some time ago. Mikie consented and Father claimed it was a "great idea."

Father made the *base* and the *walls* out of a cardboard box. *Mother* added *windows* and *doors* out of plasticene, pressing them onto the carton. *Peter* created *himself in bed with the alarm clock showing one o'clock. Mikie* copied his brother, making *himself in bed with a checkered blanket.*

When Peter asked his mother to please make the toilet and sink, Mrs. Sontag, who was about to follow her son's suggestions, remembered the long-past discussion about being less involved with Peter's body. For this reason she suggested that Peter make the toilet himself since that was the problem he was still working on. Mrs. Sontag announced "the kitch-en" was the room she would create. Father volunteered to make the garage. Mikie was unsure of his part, and asked what he should do. Peter, feeling kindly towards his brother, said he could help him make the toilet and sink (perhaps because this was their shared problem).

When the project was completed, Peter said he would like the family to dictate to the author the meaning of their input (similar to the techniques that the author utilized during his individual art therapy sessions). Everyone was agreeable to this format. Peter, watching the art therapist very closely, dictated the following information: "Saturday night I heard the alarm clock. I woke up, then I got up and I went to the bathroom. I feel happy." He went on to point out, "this shows me in bed and the alarm going off" (Figure 55). The author asked the family if they had known that Peter felt happy. They all claimed a lack of awareness, yet they were not at all surprised to hear about these positive emotions.

Mikie was anxious to tell his story next: "When the alarm went off, I got up too and went to the toilet!! My bed was dry!!"

Mother smiled at her sons, then turned to the therapist to record, "Sunday morning was wonderful. The beds were dry and I made the kids their favorite breakfast—eggs, pancakes and bacon."

Father's vignette followed, "The house is a happier place. Peter's behaving in a more grown up way and we're all more open with each other. We are all happier these days."

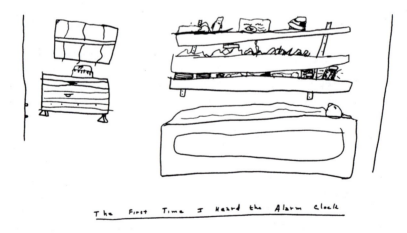

The First Time I Heard the Alarm Clock

Figure 55. Awoke to urinate

When I asked the family to title the artwork, Peter wanted to name it "The First Time I Heard the Alarm Clock." Mikie said "me too" should be added to the title. Mother suggested "The First Time Peter and Mikie Heard the Alarm Clock." When everyone agreed it was a good name, Father instructed his eldest son to write the first six words and Mikie the last six.

Aside from the content of the project, the process was reviewed. The problem-solving task had included everyone. Decision-making and self-expression was an integral part of the experience and a model for future interaction.

SESSION TWENTY-SIX/*Family Meeting: All Members Present*

Two weeks later (after the meeting reported above), *Peter's* self-appointed artwork portrayed him *soiling his pants* several times in one week. *Father*, for his free choice, drew *himself working on a new evening shift* from five in the evening until midnight, while *Mother* made an *abstract* picture of her "upset" feelings about not having John home at dinner time. *Mikie* drew his *mother* "being mean."

The therapist asked the family to focus on the way Dad's new hours affected them. Peter, who had been doodling while the family was talking, volunteered to analyze his own scribble, saying it meant he was "mad at Dad for not being home more." Father told Peter he wished he would have said this to him in the first place rather than resort to soiling.

Mikie acted disgusted with his big brother. He managed to gain his parents' attention by talking about Mother's "meanness." Mrs. Sontag admitted she had been in bad humor and apologized to her sons for displacing her frustration onto them. Throwing up his hands in despair, Mr. Sontag said he was being blamed for something beyond his control and he himself resented the switch in hours. Nevertheless, he intended to adjust to the new schedule and hoped the family would follow suit.

It was unusual for Mr. Sontag to talk about his personal unhappiness. Sharing it with his family showed him to be more human, a person with his own vulnerable feelings.

Comments

Peter's loss of time with his father was painful since their relationship had strengthened in recent months. Therefore, this author realized Peter's recent soiling episode was his regressive way of exhibiting his anger towards his father. It also dawned on the therapist that a *clinical error had been made* by beginning the program for enuresis so quickly after Peter's success with the encopresis. The father's change in work hours had merely added to the child's stress, for there had not been sufficient time for Peter's bowel toilet training to be fully integrated.

The author admitted being inflated because of the early success of treatment, especially in light of the psychiatric literature which predicted negative prognosis for children with a profile similar to Peter's. Considering the misjudgment, it was important to reprieve the mistaken timing for working on Peter's enuresis.

Therefore, this art therapist apologized to the Sontags for the clinical error in prematurely initiating the program for enuresis. It was suggested, Peter's bowel regression was probably due to the pressure of getting up at night to urinate, in addition to adjusting to Father's working hours. Since a confession about an unwise decision was made, Peter feeling understood, looked relieved as he voiced his affirmation. Therefore, the family was notified that the current nightly self-management plan would be delayed until Peter himself let it be known he was fully ready to stay dry at night.

Mr. and Mrs. Sontag appreciated the therapist's honesty. With conviction, they declared their confidence in Peter's ability to stop soiling altogether and agreed to discontinue the emphasis on bed-wetting until their child *requested* such help.

SESSIONS TWENTY-SEVEN THROUGH THIRTY-ONE/
Family Meetings: All Members Present

The Sontags missed two weekly meetings due to the therapist's vacation. Upon their return they reported that a great deal of "good things" had happened. The boys got *new mattresses* and they were managing to *keep dry most nights.*

It was unclear whether the results were reflected in one or all of the following: 1) a desire to keep a new mattress dry; 2) the lack of the "suggestive" water motion; and/or 3) the therapist's implanted equation of a nonwater mattress with a dry bed. Regardless, the family was feeling very good about the results.

The rest of the "good news" was about Peter's bowel self-management. He had not soiled in the past several weeks.

This family meeting, as well as the next few, revolved around problem-solving and productive communication and interaction.

Individual Meeting: Peter

During an individual art therapy session with Peter, he asked me to open up the cabinet where I kept his plasticene feces in the box. He carefully took the box out, took off the lid, and lifted out the symbolic bowel movements. Slowly revolving the sculpture, he gave it a thorough inspection. With a look of determination, Peter got himself a very large piece of paper and drew a picture of *himself sitting on the toilet*. He chatted away cheerfully as he drew, telling the author he had his "problem beat forever!" When he finished the picture he *picked up the plasticene bowel movement and pressed it into the picture of the toilet upon which he proudly sat* (Figure 56).

The image was extremely innovative and creative. This author sincerely admired the artwork as well as its symbolic meaning. Peter, who worked hard on self-management, had currently conquered the encopresis for the longest length of time thus far. Although it was possible for Peter's bowel habit to lapse again in the future, in the author's experience a child who makes a concrete and spontaneous commitment through the art frequently parallels it in life by stopping the encopretic or enuretic behavior altogether. When Peter put the finishing touches onto his artwork, his increased self-esteem was obvious.

Figure 56. Problem beat forever

SESSION THIRTY-TWO/*Family Meeting: All Members Present*

As the family meeting began, Peter looked the author in the eyes and announced he was *not going to do the artwork*. In spite of his positive transference he had the need to test the author, possibly because termination was in sight. Deciding to be in control, Peter looked for my reaction to his resistance. Mr. and Mrs. Sontag became upset, seeing Peter's actions as an impolite way of dealing with Mrs. Landgarten. However, the therapist interpreted the resistance as a way of individuating and allowed his withdrawal.

The rest of the family continued the session using the art therapy modality as Peter *spoke* but would *not draw*. It was helpful to Mr. and Mrs. Sontag to observe the interaction between their son and the therapist. They saw how their son's reactions need not be taken personally and an objective distance had a beneficial result.

It was interesting to note Peter's resistance was not displayed again in future sessions.

SESSION THIRTY-THREE/*Family Meeting: All Members Present*

When the family meeting began, the Sontags were disgruntled over a previous argument. They wanted to explain the situation and to have the therapist lead them through a solution. To further the family's autonomy, the therapist placed the problem-solving back into their own hands. With this in mind, everyone decided to *work individually at first; then they would paste all the artwork onto a single piece of paper.*

Father led by gluing his photo up first, which he stated stood for his "complaint" about his wife "talking on the phone too much." *Mother* said her picture belonged next to her husband's since she had "a bone to pick" with him. The collage portrayed her agitation because his working hours made their home life difficult. She felt totally responsible for the boys with no time for herself. *Peter*, taking a turn, claimed his artwork was directed towards his "anger" with his Mom because she made him "empty the trash and clean up the garage." *Mikie* said his picture needed to be placed next to Peter's because it meant his brother messed up their bedroom.

The concrete visual statements of everyone's dissatisfactions with one another called for a discussion of the complaints and resolutions that would improve the situations. After a heated and productive conversation, they looked to the therapist to act as an negotiator. Once again, the author placed the responsibility back on the family, reminding them they could manage by themselves, and chose to remain inactive for the rest of the session.

TERMINATING PHASE OF TREATMENT

SESSION THIRTY-FOUR/*Family Meeting: All Members Present*

As a way of comparing family gains, the Sontags were instructed to *create a drawing together without speaking*. (This technique was identical to that used in the family's first meeting.)

It was Peter who asserted himself and began the picture by making a *fully-leafed tree*. His *mother* went next to add *apples*. *Father*, too, enhanced Peter's structure as he *colored in the trunk* and placed a *house* next to the tree. Mother responded to her husband's drawing by inserting a *door* and *windows*, then added *flowers shaped as hearts*. In turn, Father enhanced his wife's flowers by putting *grass* nearby.

During the entire process, Mikie stood by watchfully. He was assessing the moment when his contribution would have the greatest impact. When he believed the time arrived, he added *two full-sized bushes*, taking up almost a third of the page. Both parents got involved with Mikie's symbols simultaneously, each choosing a bush to color in. Nevertheless, when the family began to speak about naming the mural, it was Peter who made the very last mark by adding a *spider* onto the top of the picture. Before anyone had a chance to make any suggestions for the title, he alone wrote down, "Us On Our Nature Walk" (Figure 57).

Figure 57. Family mural

SESSION THIRTY-FIVE/*Family Meeting: All Members Present*

To continue comparing gains, the family was given directives which were the same as those in the initial session: *divide into teams and proceed with the nonverbal dyadic drawings.*

Since the family had gradually undergone a series of changes, it was not surprising to observe a shift in alliance to Father/Peter and Mother/ Mikie. The duo drawings portrayed Father and his older son taking turns in drawing a *baseball field*, while Mother and the younger son took turns in drawing *food on a table.*

The second comparative task was to *make a family mural together; this time you may speak to each other.*

For the mural, contrary to the *family's first verbal art task*, there was a good deal of discussion and planning before Father encouraged the boys to "get started." The Sontags decided to portray their upcoming vacation. *Peter* started by drawing an *airplane*, while *Mikie* put in the *sky and sun*. *Father* made his *parents' home in Montana* and *Mother* added the *grandparents waiting on the porch for their guests.*

The family was very invested in the project, injecting humor as they worked.

The title, "Our Summer Vacation," was easily agreed upon. Peter suggested Mikie write "Our Summer" since he himself could spell "vacation" and Mikie could not.

Dynamics

Graphic contact among various members was demonstrated by the following gestures:

1. *Mother*, when she placed the grandparent figures onto the house which her husband made;
2. *Father*, who printed TWA on Peter's plane;
3. *Mikie*, by drawing the sky and clouds which touched his brother's plane;
4. *Peter* alone did not make any contact in the mural suggesting his autonomy.

The author brought forth the first picture created by the family as a means for comparison. The Sontags were encouraged to talk about the contrasts in the two murals.

Mother remembered the first family drawing when she had hurried to draw before Mikie filled the entire page. She was also mindful of her husband improving her sun, which illustrated his nonverbal means of implying she was inadequate. Mrs. Sontag embarrassedly laughed, when she pointed out the fact that her lines had been literally "all over" the whole picture. She insightfully added she must have been nervous and not very controlled when they began therapy.

Father recalled how he had allowed Mikie to take charge when the child took the central position and used the greatest amount of space. Reviewing the first and last murals, he mentioned the vast improvement in family communication. Nevertheless, Father became sad when he saw his lack of contact with Peter, on the original picture.

Peter spoke up to remind his family that they had almost left him out altogether during the initial session. However, his father corrected the child when he stated, "You almost left yourself out." He laughingly continued, "That wouldn't happen nowadays." Although unaware of the meaning of the tornado, Peter pointed it out. When the therapist interpreted the symbol as an expression of anger during that particular session, he was able to recall the feeling that had been stirred up in that meeting.

Mikie claimed he remembered very little about the first artwork except he believed he had enjoyed working along with everyone.

The family appreciated the opportunity to compare the murals since it helped them recall the past and to realize their current growth.

SESSION THIRTY-SIX/*Family Meeting: All Members Present*

A few weeks later, Peter brought up the question of termination. For him the end of art therapy validated the cessation of his problems. After the family addressed this issue, they agreed they would stop coming for treatment when they felt more secure about maintaining the status quo. They wanted more time to prove that Peter's use of the toilet was an established pattern and a natural event, which no longer required any special thought on his part.

Mr. and Mrs. Sontag commented on how Peter conveyed his feelings far more than in the past, as well as the positive changes that the entire family had undergone. Once again, they referred to the differences in the process between their first and final nonverbal family drawings as a reflection of their interaction.

Mikie was questioned about his opinion since his central position had been shifted. He admitted he did not like his brother being bossy. As an example he said, "Like when he named the 'Nature Walk' picture without letting me say what I wanted." Mikie continued on, "But I used to be ashamed of Peter shitting in his pants. Guys at school used to tease me that Peter was a baby. I'm glad he stopped!" The family was taken back by this statement since Mikie had never expressed his embarrassment in the past. He went on to say he was also "glad Peter's smelly pants doesn't stink up our room anymore."

SESSION THIRTY-SEVEN/*Family Meeting: All Members Present*

The family was told to create *free choice artwork*. Peter decided on a collage to display an array of images, which were unconsciously chosen. All of the pictures exhibited a *person alone* in various environments: in the *house, walking outdoors*, and *playing ball*. When the interpretation was made concerning his feeling of loneliness, Peter agreed. The therapist wondered aloud if it reflected his feeling about the issue of termination. Peter, as well as the rest of his family, denied this thought, saying they realized the end of treatment was in sight and they "couldn't come to therapy forever." To help them deal with the emotions related to termination they were told to do a *drawing about the feelings behind the idea of ending treatment*. The results exhibited the family's determination to block the subject with artwork that veered away from the topic.

SESSION THIRTY-EIGHT/*Conjoint Meeting: Mother and Father*

The boys went with the rest of the school children to a special event. During the conjoint session Mr. and Mrs. Sontag were instructed to *create an object which expresses something about your relationship to one another.*

Mrs. Sontag painted an *abstract picture* which represented "a good marriage" (Figure 58). However, she did include a dark area which she said stood for Peter, who was causing her and her husband anxiety and anger. *Mr. Sontag* cut out a *construction paper sheet of music* (Figure 59). He explained the collage as symbolizing their harmonious relationship. Nevertheless, he added, "What my wife said is true—things would be great if it wasn't for Peter." The clinician was surprised to hear this discontent, since the Sontags' family life had improved considerably. When the author asked for clarification about these puzzling complaints, Mrs. Sontag related their concerns: "Peter might soil his pants again," and "he is tattling in school on other children, arguing and disagreeing with us at home, bullying Mikie and demanding to have his bedroom painted, and nagging to go to school unattended. He wants to go to sleep late, and insists on selecting his own school clothes."

Mr. Sontag also added a list of complaints: "Peter is not finishing homework, he is acting up in school, he isn't doing as well as he could in baseball, he's sassing back, he's not doing his chores on time, and he is hitting Mikie. Besides all that, he has to be reminded about practicing his guitar."

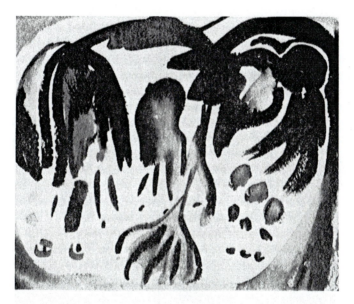

Figure 58. A good marriage and concern over son

Figure 59. Harmonious relationship

Mr. and Mrs. Sontag began to talk about the ways in which Peter was changing. They claimed he was no longer a quiet polite child, but frequently demanding and disagreed much of the time. The child "suddenly seems to have an opinion on everything." They found him annoying and aggravating. Mr. Sontag made it clear "we don't like it and won't stand for it." His wife added, "I see in him a decline, he's a good candidate for drugs." Obviously worried, Mr. Sontag claimed he was "upset about Peter's future." He felt he "no longer had any control over his child."

Heed was paid to their concerns, although all of this information came without any warning in previous meetings. It seemed odd that in one week's time so many concerns had become full-blown. The shift in family structure was evidently a threat to Mr. and Mrs. Sontag. Peter's acting-out behaviors were attempts towards individuation which apparently were difficult for his parents to accept. Autonomy was seen as a decline, which evoked anxiety in Peter's mother and father.

It was evident the issue of the child suddenly becoming a candidate for drugs was some sort of projection. The Sontags were questioned if their older son reminded them of someone they knew. They immediately admitted a neighborhood boy had been reported as an alcohol abuser: "He had always been a nice boy like Peter who was good in school, in sports, and had a lot of friends just like Peter! And his parents were very nice middle-class church-going people just like us."

Peter's parents were warned about projecting their fears of what had happened to their neighbor's boy onto their son. They were told Peter was a person in his own right; he was not to be mixed up in their minds with other people. It was unfair and dangerous to displace their anxiety over their neighbor's child onto Peter. The theory of self-fulfilling prophecy was explained.

The Sontags were redirected to their complaints about Peter, discussing them one at a time. First, Peter's soiling: the therapist reminded Mrs. Sontag that occasional regressive incidents were possible. However, Mrs. Sontag was encouraged to speak about her thoughts around "things being too good to be true" (she had used this phrase a number of times in the past). The second dissatisfaction, which both parents related, was Peter's occasional refusal to do all of his homework. The author pointed out Peter's need to test out what the results would be. If their son got graded down, perhaps he would return to doing all of his homework again. The author wondered if it would be worth seeing what would happen if they left him alone. The third point was in reference to Peter's tattling on other children in school. It seemed that Mr. and Mrs. Sontag might check out the whole story to see if Peter's actions were appropriate. The fourth complaint about Peter not doing as well as he could in baseball, led to a discussion on the meaning behind being the "best ball player." The question arose whether this desire was based on Father's wish fulfillment or on Peter's own ability or need. The fifth criticism, in regard to Peter's acting like a bully (at home), raised the question of whether this type of action was a way of asserting himself or whether it was possible that his being bossy towards Mikie was the usual type of power which older brothers often exert.

The author suggested that as the Sontags examine the change in Peter's behavior, they should remember that change had been necessary. However, it was understandable how Peter's self-assertion was difficult for them. They were told role changes and a shift in the family system caused many new adjustments and accommodations on the part of all the members.

Before Mr. and Mrs. Sontag left the office, the therapist interpreted their sudden complaints about Peter as a way of denying termination.

SESSION THIRTY-NINE/*Family Meeting: Mother, Father, and Peter*

During the terminating phase the emphasis was placed on bringing closure to family issues and on preparing to separate from the therapist. Attending to the first item, the author instructed the family to *make individual artwork which tells your family something you want to be known. You can select a media of your choice.*

Father chose to work with a photo collage. His image was a *composite of facial features from various individuals*. It represented his feelings of "pride in my family for getting it together" (Figure 60).

Mikie also utilized a magazine picture to portray a *woman with blond hair* (similar to the author's) which he pasted on the clinic's notepaper. He added the sketch of a *dress* which matched the therapist's outfit. Mikie said his picture meant he "wanted to see the therapist by *himself*" (Figure 61).

Mother had formed a plasticene sculpture of an *apple*. She claimed it represented "the wholesome attitude that our family has towards each other." Remembering it was a time of termination, she shoved the object towards the therapist saying, "It also is an apple for the teacher" (Figure 62).

Before *Peter* got started on his artwork, he made sure he used a media which was different from that of the other family members (an indication of his individuating attempts). He selected water colors to convey the *more grown-up advantages* his parents had recently bestowed upon him.

The author wondered about Mikie's request to see the therapist alone.

It may have been precipitated by any or a combination of the following reasons: a reluctance to terminate due to the positive transference, a family need to have some member with a problem, or a competitive wish to get what his brother had received, that is, individual treatment.

Before stating an opinion, the therapist asked the family to respond to Mikie's collage. The first person to answer was Peter. He stated, "It's OK with me. Maybe Mikie has a problem you can help him with!" Mr. and Mrs. Sontag were taken by surprise. Father said he would like to hear why Mikie wanted individual treatment, while Mother told Mikie it was fine with her, once Peter's therapy was finished.

To clarify Mikie's reasons for his request he was told to *make artwork which shows why you want to see me by yourself.*

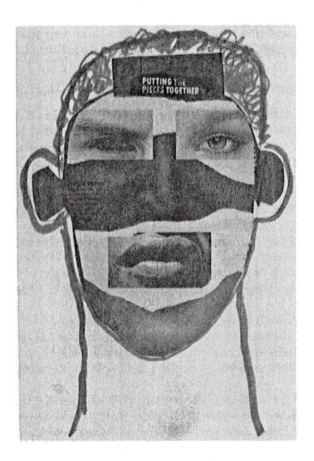

Figure 60. Getting it together

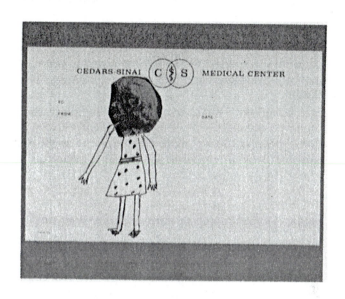

Figure 61. Wants to see therapist alone

Figure 62. Healthy family attitude

Mikie's pictures portrayed his family, yet he said, "It's to help me with my problems." Since he was unable to focus on an issue for self-improvement, the clinician interpreted his request as a way to receive the therapist's attention and art materials that he did not have to share with the rest of the family.

When Mikie agreed with the interpretation, his request was denied. If the author believed the child was in need of treatment, a recommendation would have been made for another therapist to work with him. It was important for Peter to continue seeing the clinician as *his* special person.

TERMINATION OF INDIVIDUAL TREATMENT FOR PETER

During his final month of therapy, Peter's free-choice drawings showed him *playing baseball* (Figure 63). He also portrayed himself on *camping trips* with friends, *overnight sleep-outs* at his peers' homes, and participation in *activities with his father* and brother. The child stated the pictures of "sleep-aways" could not have happened if his soiling problem had persisted. The art products equated Peter's self-management success and involvements that brought him pleasure.

Pictorial images revealed the physical and emotional involvement with his mother had appropriately lessened and his identification with his father had increased. Although Peter still enjoyed drawing "wipe out" with the author, its frequency lessened and "cooperative" graphics were requested more often.

During Peter's terminating session, he arranged all of his plasticene sculptures in a row, numbering each separately from the first to his final work. He asked the therapist if she would take snapshots of these creations and send them to him. The author agreed to the request, for the photo would serve as proof of his psychological gains as well as an inducement to continue his creative and self-expressive process.

SESSIONS FORTY THROUGH FORTY-TWO/*Family Meetings: All Members Present*

During the last few art psychotherapy sessions, the family resisted the art tasks. This was interpreted in several ways: a metaphoric gesture towards severing the connection with the therapist; proof they could deal with feelings solely on a verbal level; and a way of exhibiting the family's full authority without any dependency on their therapist. In

Figure 63. Increased self-esteem

spite of the Sontags' art resistance, as they readied themselves for their final good-byes they looked around the office, seeking out their own family's artwork and the symbolic messages that still spoke out to them.

SUMMARY

The successful treatment for nine-year-old Peter with an encopretic disorder was twofold: family art therapy, which included management plans, plus concomitant individual treatment for the designated patient. Although stress was placed on symptom removal, an insight orientation was simultaneously employed.

The family system was assessed and attention to readjustments were implemented. Mother's infantalizing messages to Peter were stopped, Father's awareness and communication skills were improved, and younger brother Mikie had to shift his central position in order to share it with Peter.

Creativity led the way to Peter's self-exploration. He gained the ability to relate through the art and to express his emotions. The tasks enabled the boy to become more assertive and to give up his passive-aggressive tendencies. Work on autonomy lessened his Oedipal conflict, dependency upon Mother, and withholding defenses.

The entire family became more psychologically attuned and dealt with each other with greater clarity and openness.

REFERENCES

Buck, J. *The House-Tree Person Technique,* revised manual. Los Angeles: Western Psychological Services, 1970.
Machover, K. *Personality Projection in the Drawing of the Human Figure.* Springfield, IL: Charles C Thomas, 1949.

RECOMMENDED READING

Alexander, F. *Psychosomatic Medicine: Its Principles and Application.* New York: Norton, 1950.
Amsterdam, B. Chronic encopresis: A system-based psychodynamic approach. *Child Psychiatry Human Development, 9*(3), 137–44, 1979.
Andolphi, M. A. Structural approach to a family with an encopretic child. *Journal of Marriage and Family Counseling, 4*(1), 25–29, 1978.
Anthony, J. E. An experimental approach to the psychopathology of childhood:

Encopresis. In S. I. Harrison & J. F. McDermott (Eds.), *Childhood Psychopathology*. New York: International Universities Press, 1972, pp. 618–625.

Baird, M. Characteristic interaction patterns in families of encopretic children. *Bulletin of the Menninger Clinic, 38*(2), 144–53, 1974.

Bemporad, J. R., Pfeifer, C. M., & Gibbs, L. Characteristics of encopretic patients and their families. *Journal of the American Academy of Child Psychiatry, 10*(2), 272–92, 1971.

Bemporad, J. R., Kresch, R., Asnes, R., & Wilson, A. Chronic neurotic encopresis as a paradigm of a multifactorial psychiatric disorder. *The Journal of Nervous and Mental Disease, 166,* 472–479, 1978.

Blechman, E. A. Home-based treatment of childhood encopresis. In C. E. Schaefer (Ed.), *Therapies for Psychosomatic Disorders in Children*. San Francisco: Jossey-Bass, 1979.

Bornstein, P. H., Sturm, C. A., Retzlaff, P. D., Kirby, K. L., & Chong, H. Paradoxical instruction in the treatment of encopresis and chronic constipation: An experimental analysis. *Behavioral Therapy and Experimental Psychiatry, 12*(2), 167–170, 1981.

Caplan, G. *Principles of Preventive Psychiatry*. New York: Basic Books, 1964.

Davis, H., Mitchell, W. S., & Marks, F. A Behavioural programme for the modification of encopresis. *Child Care Health Development, 2*(5), 273–82, 1976.

Doleys, D. M., Weiler, D., & Pegram, V. Special disorders of childhood: Enuresis, encopresis and sleep disorders. *Psychopathology in Childhood*. In J. R. Lochenmeyer & M. S. Gibbs (Eds.), New York: Gardner Press, 1982, pp. 90–97.

Easson, W. M. Encopresis: Psychogenic soiling. *Canadian Medical Association Journal, 82,* 624, 1960.

Esinan, A. Nocturnal enuresis: Some current concepts. *Journal of the American Academy of Child Psychiatry, 16,* 150–58, 1977.

Fritz, G. K., & Armbrust, J. Enuresis and encopresis. *Psychiatric Clinics of North America, 5*(2), 283–296, 1982.

Halpern, W. I. The treatment of encopretic children. *Journal of the American Academy of Child Psychiatry, 16*(3), 478–99, 1977.

Hoag, J. M., Norriss, N. G., Himeno, E. T., & Jacobs, J. The encopretic child and his family. *Journal of the American Academy of Child Psychiatry, 10,* 242–56, 1971.

Hulse, W. C. Childhood conflict expressed through family drawings. *Journal of Projective Techniques, 16,* 66–79, 1952.

Kessler, J. W. *Psychopathology of Childhood*. Englewood Cliffs, NJ: Prentice Hall, 1966.

Kisch, E. Functional encopresis: Psychiatric inpatient treatment. *American Journal of Psychotherapy, 38*(2), 264–71, 1984.

Landman, G. B., Levine, M. D., & Rappaport, L. A study of treatment resistance among children referred for encopresis. *Clinical Pediatrics, 23*(8), 449–52, 1984.

Levine, M. D. Children with encopresis: A descriptive analysis. *Pediatrics, 56*(3), 412–6, 1975.

Levine, M. D. Encopresis: Its potentiation, evaluation and alleviation. *Pediatric Clinics of North America, 29*(2), 315–30, 1982.

Levine, M. D., & Bakow, H. Children with encopresis: A study of treatment outcome. *Pediatrics, 58*(6), 845–52, 1976.

Margolies R., & Gilstein, K. W. A systems approach to the treatment of chronic encopresis. *Int. J. Psychiatry in Medicine, 13*(2), 141–52, 1983–84.

Pinkerton, P. The psychosomatic approach in child psychiatry. In J. C. Howells

(Ed.), *Modern Perspectives in Child Psychiatry*. New York: Brunner/Mazel, 1965, pp. 306–333.

Schaengold, M. The relationship between father-absence and encopresis. *Child Welfare, 56*(6), 386–94, 1977.

Seymour, F. The treatment of encopresis using behavior modification. *Australian Paediatric Journal, 12*(4), 326–9, 1976.

Shearn, P. R., & Russell, K. R. Use of the family drawing as a technique for studying parent-child interaction. *Journal of Projective Techniques, 33*, 35–44, 1969.

Whitehead, N. Childhood encopresis: A clinical psychologist's approach. *Health Visit, 56*(9), 335–336, 1983.

Wolters, W. H. The influence of environmental factors on encopretic children. *Acta Paedopsychiatrica, 43*(4), 159–72, 1978.

Wolters, W. H., & Wauters, E. A. A study of somatopsychic vulnerability in encopretic children. *Psychotherapy and Psychosomatics, 26*(1), 27–34, 1975.

Wright, L., & Walker, C. E. Treatment of the child with psychogenic encopresis. An effective program of therapy. *Clinical Pediatrics, 16*(11), 1042–5, 1977.

Wright, L., & Walker, C. E. Case histories and shorter communications: A simple behavioral treatment program for psychogenic encopresis. *Behavior Research and Therapy, 16*(3), 209–12, 1978.

CHAPTER 6

A Single-Parent Household: Issues of Abandonment and Masked Depression

INTRODUCTION

All single-parent households are stressed by the emotional impact of separation. With the roles and structure in a state of chaotic flux, both the parent and his/her offspring are in a search for a new functional system to settle their discomfort. This realignment is particularly difficult since the humiliation of abandonment damages both the individual and the family ego.

Aside from the complexity of adjusting to a new lifestyle, the emotional aspects are a serious matter for all concerned. The feelings of anger, which are identified with loss, through death or divorce, are amplified when a parent/spouse has willfully chosen to physically leave the family without notice. In these cases, the work of mourning that loss requires is sometimes clouded over, and depression may be masked on an unconscious level.

This chapter describes a mother with three of her children who, abandoned by the husband/father, handled their rejection and loss by resorting to various defense mechanisms. Each member displayed his/her own unique malfunctioning way of coping with the situation: mother, by withdrawing from the authority role; the eldest offspring, an adolescent, by utilizing acting-out behavior; the middle child of latency age, by sporadically exhibiting bizarre conduct as he ran round the house in a frenzied fashion, unable to cease at will and experiencing repeated nightmares; the youngest, also latency age, by becoming socially reticent and a selective mute. Symptom removal took place within a relatively short

151

period of time. The abandoned family's dynamics and case management factors for each individual are examined in this chapter, as well as the prophylactic and failure issues.

CASE ILLUSTRATION

The Akima family presented in this case example received art psychotherapy for a period of three months. The eight-month-old baby was included in the first family session only, then was excluded from the rest of the family meetings.

PRECIPITATING EVENT

Mrs. Akima's initial phone call was one of desperation. Her husband had abandoned their four children and herself several months previously. She reported being extremely anxious and that she lacked the ability to control her family. Although the author did not question Mrs. Akima about suicide, the latter volunteered that she would not commit suicide, although the thought definitely existed. She began to cry as she declared, "I'm at the end of my rope," claiming her chaotic household made life unbearable for the children as well as for herself. Her major concern was related to the eldest child, Hugh, whom she believed alluded to suicide that very morning by stating "I feel like driving the car off a cliff." Between sobs, Mrs. Akima related the ongoing war between herself and this particular son. Hugh's verbal abuse had escalated to frightening and intolerable proportions. The boy, who had been a high academic achiever in the past, was currently performing poorly. His lack of motivation and hatred of school caused a battle every morning as he rebelled against attendance. She also reported Hugh was incessantly "bossing and hitting" the two younger children who reacted with resentment and anger.

SESSION ONE/*Individual Meeting: Mrs. Akima*

The next day the therapist saw Mrs. Akima to gather additional information. Focusing on her children, Mrs. Akima began with her older son Hugh, who was 16 years old. She reported he had always been among the outstanding students and was surprised when the principal had recently called to report an academic slump. When Mother confronted Hugh, he said he had been telling her all along that the teachers were "rotten" and the coursework "terrible," and "I can't stand the kids at that school."

The arguments between Mother and this son were never-ending. Mrs. Akima also complained of Hugh's relationship with his younger siblings which had altered drastically since her husband had left home. In the past, he had been tender and caring towards Sissie and Jimmy. However, in recent times he was incessantly "on their case." It was only towards his six-month-old baby sister, Alena, that Hugh showed his affection.

When the therapist brought up Hugh's suicidal ideation, Mother said she realized she had overreacted to her son's reference to "running the car off the cliff," adding, "But I'm glad I did because it finally got me to come for therapy."

Although Hugh's problems took priority, Mrs. Akima was also concerned about Sissie, her eight-year-old daughter, whose behavior had become increasingly withdrawn. For several months the child rarely spoke at home, conveying important thoughts only through notes which she left in her mother's bedroom.

An equally distressing problem was 10-year-old Jimmy's symptoms of stress. These were revealed through nail biting, repeated nightmares, and hyperactive behavior.

When the therapist questioned Mrs. Akima about her own suicidal ideation, she said a plan was never set. Although thoughts of "never waking up" had occurred as an escape mechanism, the love and commitment to her children were paramount and would prevent such an act.

Family History

During the initial interview the following information was included:

Mr. Akima had been unusually attached to his wife, yet emotionally unavailable to the children. The desertion was a complete surprise to his family since they had been totally unaware of his discontent. Without notice he had abruptly left home to live in Hawaii. During the six months of his absence Mr. Akima visited his family on only two occasions. He failed to write letters, and when he phoned his wife, he did not request to speak to the children. The entire family had never talked about the abandonment because they colluded to avoid dealing with the separation and loss. Mrs. Akima notified her children they must handle Father's leaving as a *secret*. They were warned not to reveal the desertion to anyone, neither friends nor relatives. This was done out of feelings of shame plus Mother's wish that her husband would soon return.

SESSION TWO/*Family Meeting: All Members Present*

When this author went to the waiting room to get the Akimas, she saw an extremely attractive Asian family. Mother, Hugh, Sissie, and the baby had straight black hair, high cheekbones, beautifully shaped mouths, and straight noses. Their lovely complexions were complemented by their brightly colored clothes. Jimmy, equally attractive, had less delicate features and an impish quality about his personality. This group is best described as "The beautiful-people family."

Sixteen-year-old Hugh carried himself like a self-confident athlete. When his mother talked to him, he bristled with obvious irritation. Sissie, the eight-year-old, was the slight-built family member. She sat slumped down in the chair, looking scared as she furtively watched the interaction between Mother and Hugh. The baby, who was seated on the couch next to Mother, was happily playing with a toy, while 10-year-old Jimmy nervously walked in and out of the waiting room. The boy sat himself next to Mother for a moment, jumped up to get a magazine, and put it down after a mere glance. Soon afterwards Jimmy got up to look through the window for a minute, then sat down near Mother again. A few seconds later, he got up to walk around, making it obvious that standing still was a difficult task.

It was evident that in addition to the assessment the Akimas would need to have "crisis intervention" to bind them over during their time of stress. For this reason a two-hour (doubletime) session was set for this first family meeting.

When all the members were asked how they felt about coming for help, their responses varied. Hugh bluntly announced his anger, implying therapy was for "people who had something *wrong* with *them.*" Then, glancing at Mother, he indicated the wrong was with her not with him. Sissie's reactions were the opposite, as she sat frozen with a petrified expression on her face. She withdrew, verbally shrinking down into the chair, almost disappearing under the art therapy table. In contrast to his siblings, Jimmy voiced a positive response, "Because," he replied, "maybe you (Mrs. Landgarten) could help me from being nervous!" With everyone taking turns with their answers, Mrs. Akima, in spite of fear and anxiety, felt obliged to state an opinion. She timidly related that a friend who was a social worker had urged her to seek treatment. She added, "everything is so terrible that coming to therapy is my only hope for the family."

It was obvious Hugh and Sissie were perturbed with their mother's attitude that a "shrink" could help them. They perceived the therapist as an "intruder." This impression was validated by the author, who admitted she was an intruder. She continued on to inform them that since everyone in the family was rightfully angry, they could probably use an outsider, especially one who was an expert in working with families who had lived through circumstances similar to theirs. The Akimas were told, "When a family has been abandoned, everyone feels miserable, rejected, rageful, and scared. As a matter of fact, the oldest child usually feels overloaded with responsibility, while some children withdraw and hardly talk, and others have nightmares, or begin to do poorly in school; some even begin to get themselves in trouble." The art psychotherapist went on to declare, "The rejected husbands or wives react in different ways, but most often they have a hard time keeping themselves together and running the family with a strong hand." The Akimas appeared more relaxed as they sensed their own feelings had been touched upon by the clinician.

The author proceeded to explain the art psychotherapy approach as a tool for understanding their family and the way they functioned as a unit.

Nonverbal Team Art Task

The first instructions required the family to *divide up into two teams*. The instructions for the nonverbal drawings were given.

The members had a great deal of difficulty in creating two teams. Everyone stressed individuality without a willingness to form an alliance. Finally, due to the seating arrangement, Mother and Hugh became one team, with Sissie and Jimmy as the other.

Mother and Hugh team. Without looking at her son, Mother immediately became involved in the art task. Her drawing, which took up three-quarters of the page, had large *arrows directed towards her partner*. When Hugh hesitated, she proceeded to draw a *brick wall*, indicating her wish to cut him off and to keep him out of her space. When Hugh did participate, he kept within the remaining quarter of the page, sketching a *surfer on a big wave*, while Mother diligently watched him to make sure he stayed out of her portion.

When Hugh completed his artwork, Mrs. Akima continued on to draw a *girl standing with her hands on her hips* shouting swear words. Later on, when she explained her artwork, Mrs. Akima angrily added exclamation points to the sketch to emphasize her dissatisfaction. Her facial expressions were extremely labile, as she inappropriately escalated a lack of verbal control (Figure 64).

Figure 64. Hugh and Mother team

Jimmy and Sissie team. It was Sissie who split the page into two parts. On her half she drew a *person* with emphasis on the face. Later, when the family was given permission to speak, she said the body represented "a strange person." Since "the person" had the same color hair and dress as her mother, it appeared the child was depicting her feelings about this parent.

Jimmy hid his part of the picture with his arm while he drew, trying to keep its contents a secret. He portrayed a *spaceship "dropping bombs on a person."* At a later time, when Jimmy spoke to his mother and failed to get a response, he returned to this drawing to scribble out the person. Although the child did not confront his parent verbally, his symbolic gesture indicated his frustration and rage (Figure 65).

Nonverbal Family Art Task

When the instructions for the *family's nonverbal mural* were given, Mother chose to go first. She made *scribbles*, which were loosely drawn, and appeared unwilling to give up her turn. The children, obviously frightened by her regressive actions, responded with a determination to make something concrete out of the scribble. Hugh immediately changed a part of it into a *house,* with Sissie entering into the picture by placing a *sun* in the corner. Jimmy responded to Mother's loose demean-

or by displacing his anger onto his sister, by attacking Sissie's sun with a cluster of *spaceships*. In spite of Jimmy's actions, Mother smiled. However, Hugh, recognizing his brother's destructive aggression, ran graphic interference by drawing a line, separating Jimmy from Sissie. He then proceeded to improve the entire picture.

Verbal Family Art Task

The next step in the diagnostic interview was the *family mural*. The Akimas were informed that during this exercise "you can speak to one another."

It was Jimmy who asked the other family members, "What should we draw?" Before anyone had a chance to reply, Mother again began to *scribble* on the paper. Then turning to Jimmy, she said, "Here's you with a microphone." Looking puzzled, the child asked, "What do you mean?" Ignoring Jimmy's need for clarification, Mother continued to scrawl, as she claimed, "I feel like drawing a big mess." Upset by his parent's lack of control, he questioned, "Why'd you do that?" Since an answer was not forthcoming, Hugh moved up to the mural to change Mother's graphic mess by altering it into a *mountain* and *house*. He was un-

Figure 65. Jimmy and Sissie team

doubtedly lending his parent a sense of reality. Jimmy, comforted by his big brother's action, turned to him and said, "It's good you could make the picture into something real." Then both Jimmy and Sissie added their own *strokes to the mountain*, to reinforce its physical existence.

When Jimmy stepped back to view the mural, he voiced a new idea about adding a "bank" to the picture. He loudly declared, "And there will be money in it." As he became involved with the sketch, his mother interrupted to say, "It should be blown up." The children, who were taken aback by Mrs. Akima's symbolically destructive remark, chose to ignore their parent's statement.

The family, gazing at the mural, spent a few minutes contemplating their creation. When Mother realized her initial scribble had been changed into a reality-oriented shape, she responded appropriately by writing the title, "A Mountain Lodge." The name apparently appealed to the younger children as they decided to draw additional features onto the lodge.

Suddenly Jimmy remembered his mother's remark about *blowing up the bank*. He decided to create several bombs on the mural. Getting carried away, he said he needed more bombs to "knock out Sissie." It was Hugh who intervened to stop Jimmy from annihilating his sister on paper.

Family's Perception Regarding Roles

The family was asked, "While drawing this picture, was there a leader? If so, who was it?" Hugh claimed, "There is no leader." Mother, to prove she held this important role, declared, "I went first when I made a scribble." Jimmy, jockeying for the authority position, chimed in, "Yeah, but I helped with the mountain and made those big bombs!"

When Sissie was asked her thoughts, she replied in a whisper, saying that although both her brothers created the mountain, Jimmy had almost destroyed it with bombs. The therapist said the statement implied a combined leadership, shared by the boys.

In a most gentle way this author related her own observations:

1. Hugh was the leader since he instituted changes in the picture and stopped the extra bombings which would have wiped Sissie out.
2. It seemed Mother had trouble communicating clear messages and was unable to explain her actions.
3. Although Mother asked for suggestions, Hugh's input was ignored.

Mrs. Akima admitted she was unaware of these factors and appeared genuinely interested in gaining this insight. Hugh, relieved when he heard the therapist validate his own feelings of being discounted, gave the therapist a look of appreciation for understanding him.

Since Mother had revealed a lack of control in her drawing, the clinician utilized this fact to tell the children, "Your Mother's feelings of rejection have left her in a *vulnerable* and *confused* state." Hugh in particular was notified to "lay off your Mom since she is not in any shape right now for additional pressure or confrontation." He was able to take in the suggestion, since he now saw the therapist as an ally and a family therapy expert.

The Akimas were notified their family system was in a crisis, since there had been a major shift in roles with the father/husband gone. Hugh was now acting as "the head of the family" while Mother, overburdened with new responsibilities, was having a very hard time keeping abreast of the many needs that had to be attended to. The family was told it was not unusual for younger siblings to resent a new authority figure, especially when it was an older brother. The author added that it was understandable that their current situation had brought about a great deal of frustration and anger on everyone's part.

Dynamics

Hugh was the force and power behind the newly structured family system. He carried the *authority figure* role. This was witnessed through his ability to confine Mother's immature actions by correcting her symbolic regressive scribble and modifying it into an understandable statement. He also contained his younger brother's out-of-control drawing behavior.

Aside from the characteristics gleaned from the family art task, the author thought it was highly probable that Hugh suffered from unresolved Oedipal conflicts, which were escalated by Father leaving home. "The-man-of-the-house" role played into this dynamic and also placed burdening responsibilities upon his shoulders. In addition, the adolescent's task of individuation was made more difficult due to the family's traumatic situation. Hugh's acting-out behavior was a defense for masking his depression and conflicts.

Jimmy played the role of the *family clarifier* and *exhibitor of feelings*, which other members repressed. His major function was to display the family's anxiety. During the art task he portrayed his *clarifying position* through the following:

1. asking what the mural theme would be;
2. pressing Mother to explain her statement;
3. asking questions in an attempt to seek logic;
4. helping his brother to concretize Mother's vague and abstract scribble; and
5. giving positive reinforcement to his brother for making Mother's confusing symbolism into a reality-oriented object.

As the *exhibitor of family feelings,* Jimmy wanted to include in the picture a bank "with money in it," indicating the family's financial insecurity. He also symbolically carried out Mother's destructive wishes via his drawings of the bombs.

Jimmy's three symptoms were symbolic of the family's anxiety. First, the nail biting was an obvious display of being *nervous* and allowed the regressive oral action of placing his fingers in his mouth. Second, the nightmares exhibited the very state in which the family lived. The third point concerning Jimmy's "crazies" and acting "weird" portrays the family's need to designate such a role to one of its members.

Sissie's role was that of *the passive member;* her participation both verbally and graphically was at the bare minimum. She was also the *recipient of other members feelings;* for example, Jimmy's displaced anger, also Mother's guilt and shame.

Sissie, who had been "Daddy's little girl," suddenly experienced herself without a father to care for her; the loss stirred up a great deal of anger. She kept her mouth shut, out of fear of revealing the rage that might fly out.

Mother's anxiety and faltering ego were revealed by the manner in which she expressed her uncontained, inappropriate responses, both artistically and verbally. Her suggestion that if a bank is drawn it "should be blown up" indicated her unconscious destructive rage. It was the *children's ego strength which bailed this parent out and set her in the direction of reality.* Mother's current role was in a state of flux and not yet defined. The *role reversal* between Mother and her eldest son put her in the pseudo position of authority, while she actually functioned as a dependent person who required structure and parameters.

SESSION THREE/*Conjoint Meeting: Mother and Hugh*

A conjoint meeting was held since Jimmy and Sissie were ill.

Hugh came into the art therapy room obviously furious. Without any instructions he began looking through the photo collage box which was on the table. At the same time Mrs. Akima reported Hugh's constant complaints about attending school. He threatened her with truancy unless she transferred him to another school where his close friends were enrolled.

Rather than allowing mother and son to continue haranguing one another, the author instructed them to *make a collage which depicted the advantages and disadvantages of Hugh attending his currrent school.* This directive was given to provide each person with a chance to present his or her point of view.

When Hugh was asked to share his artwork first, he belligerently held up his collage, obviously expecting a big argument. Hugh represented the *advantages* of his school through pictures of *ball players.* For the *disadvantages* he picked out a *classroom* scene adding the words, "The kids are smart; it's hard to be tops." Under a photo of a group of adolescents he wrote, "The kids are stuck up."

Surprisingly, Mrs. Akima listened to her son. Rather than hassle Hugh, she simply resorted to showing her own collage. For the *disadvantages* of going to the school of his choice, she portrayed a *boy waiting for a bus,* a photo of a *woman and a teenager yelling at one another,* and a picture of *pills* indicating the drug abuse problem in the school of his choice. For the *advantages* she drew a *book* that represented "getting a fine education." Hugh's reaction to his mother's artwork was disgust, since he was not open to her point of view.

When Mrs. Akima examined her son's collage more closely she looked surprised, claiming she did not know her son was having difficulty in being an outstanding student. In the past Hugh always had very fine grades. It was only when the principal called that she discovered her boy was no longer a top student in his class. Nevertheless, she perceived this as her son's unwillingness to work hard rather than with difficulty in competing with his exceptionally intelligent peers. She addressed this issue in a kindly way, engaging her son in a meaningful discussion. When Hugh recognized the quality of his mother's involvement, he confided in her, relating the academic and social struggles that he was having in school.

Fortunately Mrs. Akima did not push her point of view about the excellent educational opportunities nor about the drug situation in the school of Hugh's choice. The essential dynamic was Mrs. Akima's response to her son's feelings and thoughts. Hugh later expressed, "It was the first time since Dad left that my mother really listened to me."

SESSION FOUR/*Family Meeting: Mother, Hugh, Jimmy, and Sissie*

During the following week when the family came to the art therapy session, both Mother and Hugh reported they were surprised by the improvement in their relationship. Mrs. Akima related her son had not complained about school during the entire week.

With a change of emphasis, she now complained about the constant fighting between *Jimmy and Sissie*. For this reason the therapist selected *Jimmy and Sissie* to become a *team*; they were told to *work together while your mother and Hugh act as observers*.

The observation technique was purposely chosen to give Mrs. Akima a chance to watch the therapist as a role model while working with the quarreling siblings. Jimmy and Sissie were then instructed *to create a scene together utilizing construction paper and plasticene and to work cooperatively*.

As the project began, Jimmy asked his sister what she wanted to do. Sissie merely responded with a shrug, but after a few seconds she decided to use the plasticene. Jimmy asked his sister, "What are you doing?" Although she failed to answer, Sissie formed a *little girl*. Jimmy, aggravated by her lack of communication, picked up a piece of plasticene and purposely dropped it on the figure. Sissie was furious.

The author told the children to *back up their actions* to where Jimmy would again ask his sister what she wanted to do. After he complied with the instructions, Sissie was instructed to please *reply to your brother's question since clarification would keep him from getting aggravated and would help him be cooperative*. In the replay, when Jimmy asked his sister, "What are you doing?" Sissie looked at him and said, "I want to make Jacqueline out of plasticene." (This was a neighbor friend of Sissie's who had moved away.) "Maybe you can make a doll for her," she told her brother. Jimmy was very pleased to be invited to participate and set himself to work. The author withdrew from making any further interventions as the two children manipulated the media and talked about Jacqueline, wishing she still lived on their block (Figure 66).

After the plasticene *figures* were finished, Sissie and Jimmy decided to use construction paper to duplicate the *house* their friend had lived in. They placed the models of Jacqueline and the doll into it.

The therapist's intervention gave mother insight on how important it was to intervene when her children needed an adult to assist their interaction. It was pointed out that Jimmy needed help getting answers to prevent his destructive behavior, and Sissie needed someone to facilitate her communication. The children were given positive reinforcement with Sissie reaping rewards for voicing her thoughts, and Jimmy for his cooperative response. The art therapy directive had also offered the siblings an opportunity to enjoy a mutually creative venture.

When asked about further information regarding Jacqueline, the Akimas explained how her family had suddenly moved away when Sissie

Figure 66. Misses a friend

was away at camp. No one had written Sissie about the situation and she was hurt when, returning home, Jackie was gone forever! The family admitted they had not talked about the loss with Sissie. Mother believed it was better ignored since she thought her daughter would get terribly upset, especially since the two girls had been inseparable. The therapist informed the family about the significance of dealing with "losses," stating, "Perhaps you are remembering Jacqueline because she, like your father, did not give you an opportunity to say 'good-bye.'"

After thinking about the therapist's statement, Jimmy skipped over the reference to father as he declared, "Yea, Sissie has been sad for a long time. Whenever I wanta talk about Jackie she runs to her room or hits me." Placing the focus upon Sissie, the author told her to "draw a picture of how you are feeling right now."

Sissie willingly drew a *sad girl with tears falling down her face.* When questioned about its meaning, the child identified the picture as a self-portrait, relating how she still dreamt of her friend and missed her dreadfully (Figure 67). Again, when the author connected Sissie's dreams to Father's abandonment, the rest of the family joined in to avoid dealing with this issue and instead discussed Jacqueline as a cheerful and pleasant little girl. They admitted she had lent a bit of excitement to their household and spoke about their fond feelings towards the child.

Since the family was in touch with their emotions around the neighbor child's separation, they were instructed *to express your feelings about Dad leaving home*.

Hugh's denial was exhibited through his big *zero*, stating he had "no feelings." He said his father at home or gone was all the same to him. Similarly, Sissie's avoidance was seen in the drawing of *herself* with "a regular face," also negating any feelings of insecurity or anger. Mother's *hearts* represented her continual positive wishes that her husband would return. It was only Jimmy who expressed his true emotions when he decided to use a *photo* of a *man with his hair standing up on end*, then drew on the *body*, as he declared, "It's scary since Daddy left. It makes me worry" (Figure 68). The author wondered aloud if other family members sometimes felt the way Jimmy did? Without hesitation Hugh and Sissie answered with an emphatic "No," while their mother, obviously hanging on to her thinly veiled defenses, abstained from answering.

With the exception of Jimmy the family formed a bonded defense, which circumvented dealing with the issue of abandonment. Each member's resistance manifested itself in a different way. Mother used wishes and fantasies that her husband would return; adolescent Hugh used acting-out behavior and Sissie used her selective mutism. The collusion prevented the

Figure 67. Sissie feels sad

Figure 68. Jimmy is scared

feelings of rage and guilt to be expressed and worked upon. Nevertheless, as this matter was paramount to the goals of this family's treatment, the clinical decision was to go along with the resistance for the present and to make other attempts to deal with the suppressed emotions in the future.

SESSION FIVE/*Family Meeting: Mother, Hugh, Jimmy, and Sissie*

When the family walked into the therapy room and took their places around the table, Hugh sat as far from his mother as possible, giving her angry glances. To deal with these emotions, *Hugh and his mother were selected* by the therapist *to become a team.* They were instructed to *do something together while Jimmy and Sissie act as observers this week.*

Hugh looked to Mother for some instruction or comment. Ignoring him she picked up her own piece of construction paper and cut out a *female figure.* Hugh shoved his chair away from the table indicating feelings of rejection. Oblivious to her son's actions, Mrs. Akima continued to be immersed in her project. Her son sat disgusted with his mother's lack of interest in him. He grumbled aloud about her failure to follow the therapist's instructions.

About 10 minutes later, Hugh picked up his own piece of paper and began to cut it out. However, he made another attempt to communicate with his parent by asking her what their theme would be. Appearing to be deaf, she did not reply. In an attempt to get his mother to answer, Hugh bombarded her with a number of questions. Mrs. Akima was jolted by her son's demands, having difficulty in thinking of quick responses. She looked frightened by the pressure that was exerted upon her. Blocked from offering any replies she sat passively and refrained from answering. Feeling that his attempt to communicate was useless, Hugh gave up on his mother altogether and turned his attention totally to cutting out a *male* figure.

When Jimmy and Sissie's team was asked to report what they saw happen between their brother and mother, Sissie commented, "Mom didn't answer Hugh but I think she should." Jimmy added, "Hugh asked Mom lotsa questions fast. He didn't even give her a chance to answer."

Agreeing with these observations, the therapist added, "It must be hard on Mom and Hugh since they don't have a give-and-take conversation. It seems when Hugh's questions go unanswered he feels Mom is ignoring him, and it's understandable why he becomes frustrated, upset, and angry. On the other hand, Mother's thinking pace is probably slower than Hugh's. I think that's why she gets overwhelmed by the way he grills her with questions and is demanding of instant answers." Mrs. Akima and Hugh both understood these dynamics since the explanation made sense to them.

The next art therapy directive for Hugh and his mother was to *use the two figures which you made and create an environment for them, then give each figure a voice.* The therapist added, *This time, Hugh, you are to ask only one question and your mother will answer you. For the rest of the exercise both of you are to continue to take turns with your questions and answers.*

It surprised this author when Hugh did not resent her directions. He asked his mother one question, "What kind of environment should we make?" Mrs. Akima suggested, "A trip scene," adding, "Where should this scene take place?" Hugh wondered, "Up in the mountains for skiing—is that ok?" Mother replied with a "yes." When the project was completed, it showed a *male and female figure ''going down the slopes enjoying themselves''* (Figure 69).

The observation team was asked about what they had seen. Jimmy said, "That was real good. Hugh and Mommy talked to each other. They

Figure 69. Mother and Hugh remediate

didn't get mad or holler." Sissie nodded her affirmation. However, wishing to encourage her speech, she was asked to report the way in which the scene was created. Sissie complied, hardly noticing the length of time everyone listened to *what she had to say*. She gave a very accurate and vivid account of the interaction.

The therapist suggested that Hugh and his mother *try to carry out the same give-and-take style of communication at home.*

SESSION SIX/*Family Meeting: Mother, Hugh, Jimmy, and Sissie*

After the preliminary greetings the family was instructed to *find magazine pictures which portray nice people and not-nice people*. This directive was designed to deal with Mother's desire to keep Father's abandonment a secret. Although it was assumed to be due to her feelings of shame and guilt, it was necessary to examine the family's value system on this subject.

Of major significance were the collages made by mother and daughter. For the *nice* people, each selected pictures showing *females with their mouths closed*. Mother's photo was of a *boss yelling, overloading his secretary with work*. The secretary responded by *squeezing her mouth shut tight*. Sissie's picture, which was similar in concept, also showed the female in a subservient position. It portrayed a *man who was giving his wife a pile of clothes to wash while his wife, with a big smile, accepted the instructions*. For the images of the *not-nice* people, Mother picked an *older woman who was flirting with a young man* (she did not realize the photo resembled Hugh), and Sissie chose a picture of a *child laughing with a mouth full of food*.

For the male responses to the *nice* people photos, Hugh pasted a *group of people in a discussion as they sat around a conference table*, while Jimmy had chosen a *man handing his children ice cream cones*. Hugh's *not-nice* picture contained a *seductive female trying to hitch a ride* and Jimmy selected the image of a *boy kicking another child*.

The collages stimulated a lively discussion among the family members. Attention was given to Mrs. Akima's and Sissie's understanding of nice people, who, if they were females, kept their mouths shut and acted as recipients not initiators. Both Sissie and her mother, influenced by their Asian culture, believed women were to be quiet, polite individuals who needed other people to take care of them.

The therapist tied in these beliefs with Sissie's selective mutism as an extreme function of the "being nice" notion. However, the greatest stress was placed on Sissie's verbal withdrawal due to the fear of *giving away the secret of Father's abandonment*. The clinician explained that one of the reasons Sissie had resorted to a note-writing communication was due to its being a safer way and prevented her from telling what was going on in the family.

While these interpretations were being made, Sissie gave the therapist furtive glances. She was unsure about her feelings towards this therapist who guessed so correctly. Could such a person be trusted? The child was in a state of conflict, since she had always been cued to keep things inside. She was not certain if it was all right to go against a pattern that Mother had set up, especially since she was solely dependent upon this one parent. Sissie neither acknowledged nor disagreed with the therapist. She merely stared at the author and kept her lips pressed close together.

SESSION SEVEN/*Family Meeting: Mother, Hugh, Jimmy, and Sissie*

During this session, Sissie appeared less tense and fearful. Although she was not friendly towards the therapist, she appeared to be more relaxed.

To observe the interaction between the males and also the females, the family was divided up into a mother-daughter and a brothers team. Each team was directed to *create your own construction paper sculpture*.

Hugh was leader while the boys built a *house*. He incorporated Jimmy's ideas as they worked together cooperatively. Hugh accepted the responsibility to be sure the *construction* was solidly built. The brothers obviously enjoyed themselves during the project and were pleased with the finished product.

In contrast to the boys' team, Sissie and her mother had trouble working together as a unit. Each person used her own art materials and worked individually without consulting one another. At one point when Mrs. Akima was in the process of making a *rainbow* and Sissie was creating a *bull*, Mother commented to her daughter, "A cow or a calf would be better than a bull with horns." When Sissie heard her mother's dissatisfaction, she pursed her lips together and ignored her. After a while, Sissie asked her mother to "make some grass for the bull to eat." Mrs. Akima appeared not to hear her child as she concentrated on her own rainbow. Although several additional suggestions were made by Sissie, they were never acknowledged. Finally, Sissie wrote on a piece of paper, "This bull is angry" (Figure 70). Mother, looking at the paper, retorted, "I don't know why your animal has to be angry!"

When both teams finished their artwork, the author suggested *all the constructions be combined into one total sculpture*. Everyone agreed the bull would look fine next to the house. However, it was the rainbow's placement that gained the most attention and friction. When Mother wanted to put it over the house, the boys objected. Then she placed it over the bull, but Sissie, who was still angry with her Mom for her lack of communication, resisted the idea. What to do with the rainbow presented a minor dilemma. Finally Jimmy offered to make some white clouds so his

This bul is angree

Figure 70. An angry bull

Mom could place her rainbow over it. This suggestion seemed to appease everyone, and the project was completed.

The family discussed the interactions involved in the team's work and the unified effort. The mother and daughter interplay provided the therapist with yet another opportunity to interpret one of the reasons for Sissie's mutism. It was apparent that when Mother ignored Sissie's verbal attempts to communicate Sissie resorted to writing out a message. The therapist noted the verbal message was not acknowledged, whereas the written one gained attention and thereby received reinforcement. At that point, Sissie spoke up loud and clear to declare, "That's right, my mother doesn't pay any attention to me. I know when I write her a note she has to read it."

The concreteness of this example forced Mrs. Akima to realize the role she played in Sissie's mute behavior. This particular incident had an impact on the family and was referred to during other sessions. It had a major effect on the future dynamics between the mother and daughter.

SESSION EIGHT/*Family Meeting: Mother, Hugh, Jimmy, and Sissie*

The family reported the improvement of their home life. They were told to *use the plasticene to create whatever you choose* (as a way of continuing work on family communication).

The report on this art psychotherapy session will focus on Sissie only, as it was of prime significance. The child's free-choice sculpture revealed a "stone snow-lady who was scared but was acting brave." The frozen-woman seemed to express the child's perception of her mother's inability to be emotionally comforting. When Sissie sensed what she had revealed, she ended the story by claiming it was "just a dumb story."

Nevertheless, the therapist utilized this tale to interpret how Mrs. Akima needed to be a *stone snow-lady* in order to survive the family's traumatic crisis. Sissie was given credit for understanding that her mother was "scared but still managed a brave front." The three children confessed they felt better when Mother acted strong because they themselves were so fearful. Yet, they admitted feeling uneasy when "mother acts funny" or "when she cries a lot or doesn't pay any attention to us."

Realizing how her lack of communication was frightening and frustrating to her sons and daughter, Mrs. Akima requested treatment for herself in addition to the family sessions. The therapist agreed to see Mrs. Akima individually and defined her immediate treatment goals: 1) facilitating availability to the family; 2) providing the children with more structure and parameters; and 3) improving communication skills. The therapist's unspoken agenda included ego strengthening, self-expression, and an insight orientation.

SESSION NINE/*Family Meeting: Mother, Hugh, Jimmy, and Sissie*

Early in the session, the family members referred to the times when Jimmy was "a weirdo and got the crazies in him." To deal with this problem the family was asked to *draw Jimmy in this state.*

Mother's picture showed Jimmy *flipping up and down on the bed*, "like a fish out of water." Hugh drew his *brother running around the living room* "as though he were in a marathon race"; Sissie portrayed him *racing throughout the entire house*, while Jimmy made himself scooting around "like crazy." Hands were unconsciously omitted in his pictures, demonstrating a sense of helplessness (Figure 71).

When Jimmy spoke about his artwork he said, "I can't help myself," admitting his own actions scared him terribly and voicing a strong desire to stop this behavior.

The author notified the family, and Jimmy in particular, about the success she had in helping children with this problem, informing them it required the united effort of the entire family. They could help Jimmy stop his out-of-control behavior. In response to this news, everyone

Figure 71. Lack of self-control

looked amazed. It was difficult for them to believe they could play a part in changing the actions of a family member, yet they were eager to hear about the way in which they could make a contribution.

The Akimas were told they were not to refer to Jimmy as a "weirdo" or "getting the crazies in him." It was explained that people who are given a label oftentimes manage to live up to it as a self-fulfilling prophecy. The family found the request simple enough and agreed to stop labeling Jimmy inappropriately.

The second instruction was particularly emphasized. Mother and Hugh were informed when Jimmy began to run around they were to help him stop by grabbing and holding the child firmly. As they did so, they were instructed to say "*I am going to protect you and help you hold on to yourself.*" Jimmy was notified this would not be a punitive gesture; it would be an act which would aid him in containing himself. Stress was placed on the importance of it being an experience where the total family lent a hand to dissolve behavior which was undesirable.

SESSIONS TEN AND ELEVEN/*Family Meetings: Mother, Hugh, Jimmy, and Sissie*

In the next session, Jimmy reported that no one had called him "weirdo" or referred to his "crazies." He proudly announced he had run around the house only two times during the entire week. Mother related that the first time she grabbed Jimmy and talked to him, he informed her, "You're not saying the words *exactly like Mrs. Landgarten.*" He told Mother she had to "say it *right* . . . '*I'm going to protect you and help you hold onto yourself.*'"

During the following session, Jimmy pleased with himself, smilingly boasted, "I acted like a weirdo only one time last week." Mrs. Akima agreed with this report and related other improvements as well; Jimmy had slept without being awakened by nightmares and was managing to control his nail biting. The entire family gleamed with pride over Jimmy and themselves for the roles they played in helping him master his problems.

SESSIONS TWELVE THROUGH FOURTEEN/*Conjoint Meetings: Mother and Jimmy*

There were several sessions when Mrs. Akima showed up with Jimmy alone for the family appointments. She apologized for Hugh and Sissie's failure to attend the art psychotherapy meetings, reporting that her older son and her daughter no longer saw any reason for treatment. The household was in a better frame of mind and their relationships had greatly improved. The clinician interpreted their resistance as a way of refusing to deal with the issue of separation.

The mother and son conjoint meetings revolved around the feelings evoked by the missing members. Jimmy was resentful and in the art he portrayed himself as being dumped with the title of the child with the *most problems* since he was still in treatment. Mother's art expressed her anger, frustration, and self-deprecation for being unable to control Hugh and Sissie, that is, to be strong enough to convince them to continue therapy. Another issue that was explored was the management of Jimmy's behavior. The child continued to maintain self-control. His drawings revealed an increase in self-esteem and an ability to separate himself out from the family and to experience himself as an individual.

While exploring the shift in family roles and how it affected each family member, Mother presented herself with greater authority and more availability to the children. Although life was still difficult, her self-awareness helped her to function at a higher parental level. Jimmy could view his role change since he realized he was receiving attention for positive behavior rather than negative, claiming he was no longer being "picked on." In actuality, his work towards individuation made him less available to act out the unconscious conflicts and confusions of other family members.

It was unfortunate that Hugh and Sissie did not avail themselves of the opportunity to examine their own shift in roles. It would have clarified their changing status within the context of the family system and the way in which it affected everyone.

SESSION FIFTEEN/*Conjoint Meeting: Mother and Jimmy*

By the fifteenth session it was obvious that only Jimmy's positive transference kept him returning to the art therapy meetings. The clinician realized he would probably stop coming to treatment in the near future. This suspicion was confirmed when Mother supported her younger son to join an athletic school team which would prevent his art therapy attendance. In defense of their actions, Mrs. Akima and her son gave glowing reports of their family life (which appeared to be authentic) and of Jimmy's continued improvement.

Although Mother, on a conscious level, wished the entire family would come for treatment, she claimed she was unable to gather everyone together since they had many after-school involvements such as athletic, academic, and social commitments.

The author insisted the entire family return to the office, stating it was very important to give Hugh and Sissie a chance to say good-bye to the therapist. This was particularly stressed since it was believed to be an essential step in the direction of a corrective experience. The necessity for the family to deal with termination was especially significant since they were now using their father's model of avoidance.

SESSION SIXTEEN/*Conjoint Meeting: Mother and Jimmy*

Mrs. Akima insisted that she tried to get the whole family to attend a terminating session. In spite of her efforts, she managed to bring Jimmy only. She informed the therapist the child would start his team practice the following week. The author believed this was a way of having the clinician to herself. Although this interpretation was made, Mrs. Akima denied it.

To facilitate Jimmy's final session, Mother and the child were invited to create artwork utilizing the theme of "saying good-bye." Mrs. Akima was directed to *think about the good-bye in terms of ending the family art therapy* and Jimmy was told to *get in touch with your feelings about discontinuing coming to the office.*

When Jimmy asked the author to join them, she agreed.

The child used the photograph of a *sad boy* to which he added the *body* and a *soccer ball.* He said he was glad to be stopping therapy because he was a "good soccer player" and loved the game. If he continued treatment he would have to get off the team since they practiced after school (Figure 72). The child concluded that since he had stopped his "bad things" and the "nightmares had disappeared," he did not understand why he should continue coming to therapy with his mother, when the rest of the family no longer attended the meetings.

On the other hand, Jimmy expressed his ambivalence by relating his sadness about giving up seeing the therapist. He asked her if she could come to their home to visit them. In a gentle manner, the author responded to Jimmy by explaining the therapist's role. The author's *self-portrait* was then shared. It represented her pleasure in his positive gains and showed her pride in him for changing his unwanted behavior. The clinician included her sadness over saying good-bye, yet wished him well.

Mrs. Akima allowed herself to experience her dejection while the good-byes between Jimmy and the author were being affirmed. Although Mother shared her feelings of depression, she could not understand why they went so deep. The therapist interpreted them as the emotions that get stirred up around the issue of separation and loss and claimed they were due to the unfinished feelings around her husband's

Figure 72. Ambivalence about termination

abandonment. When Jimmy heard this statement, he accidently knocked down the "sad feelings" artwork. The clinician announced it was not unusual to have angry feelings connected to sad ones. It was all right to feel furious with his Dad since the latter was no longer available to give them love and security. *With the absence of Hugh and Sissie, the mutual bond of resistance towards dealing with the abandonment was dissolved.* Both Jimmy and Mrs. Akima began to cry as they admitted their anger towards their father/husband.

The therapist found it frustrating to end the session when the core of the work had just begun.

When closure was brought to the session, Jimmy asked if he could take home some sheets of paper and crayons. As a farewell gift and a transitional object, he was permitted to select 10 sheets of paper and a small box of crayons.

On his way out of the office, the therapist overheard Jimmy telling his mother, "Hugh and Sissie will be sorry they didn't come this time." It was assumed, this remark was probably due to the gift; however, on a psychological level the child realized he had been given a therapeutic environment where angry feelings were expressed and accepted.

SESSIONS SEVENTEEN TO TWENTY/*Individual Meetings: Mother*

Mother was seen individually for several sessions to continue work on parenting skills and in hopes of continuing family treatment in the near future. However, the family made a sudden departure from Los Angeles, moving to the east to be near relatives. Follow-up information on the Akima family has not been available to the author.

COMMENTS

In spite of the remarkable gains that the Akimas accomplished in the short period of a few months, this case is viewed by the author as a "failure." Although the family members were helped to gain control over their actions and to obtain insight to the family system, the implicit source of their manifest behavior was blocked by the *children's flight into health.* Their premature termination was viewed as an escape mechanism. It prevented them from dealing with the traumatic effects that Father's abandonment left on their psyche. Without work on separation and loss, the author believed future relationships could be impaired.

SUMMARY

The father's abandonment was a psychological traumatic event which Mother refused to accept. Due to her denial, the feelings which the unexpected separation caused were repressed by herself and the children. The unexpressed fears, rage, and depression were manifested in various ways. Mother became an immobilized, ineffectual parent. Her eldest child, an adolescent, established himself as the authority figure. He argued with his mother incessantly and began to perform poorly in school. The 10-year old boy served as the mirror-image of the family members' anxiety, through nail-biting, repeated nightmares, and a strange, frenetic way of running around the house in circles. The eight-year-old girl, resorted to selective mutism, seldom speaking at home and communicating through written notes to her mother.

The family system was unbalanced and in a state of flux. Role confusion and double messages added to the psychic chaos.

In spite of the brief treatment, the children's symptoms disappeared. The author believed these miraculous positive changes to be a *flight into health, as a family defense against dealing with the abandonment trauma.*

Without continued therapy, the author believed the gains to be of a superficial nature and that their relationships in the future would be impaired.

RECOMMENDED READING

Anderson, R. Where's Dad? Paternal deprivation and delinquency. *Archives of General Psychiatry, 18,* 641–649, 1968.

Baittle, B., & Offer, D. On the nature of male adolescent rebellion. In S. C. Feinstein, P. L. Giovacchini, & G. A. Miller (Eds.), *Adolescent Psychiatry, Volume I: Developmental and Clinical Studies.* New York: Basic Books, 1971.

Bank, S. P., & Kahn, M. D. *The Sibling Bond.* New York: Basic Books, 1982.

Biller, H. B. Father absence and the personality development of the male child. *Developmental Psychology, 2,* 181–201, 1970.

Billig, A. L. Fingernail biting: The incipiency, incidence and amelioration. *Genetic Psychology Monographs, 24,* 123–218, 1941.

Bowlby, J. *Attachment and Loss: Volume 2, Separation.* London: Hogarth Press, 1973.

Brown, S. Family therapy. In B. Wolman (Ed.), *Manual of Child Psychopathology.* New York: McGraw-Hill, 1972.

Browne, E., Laybourne, P. C., & Wilson, V. Diagnosis and treatment of elective mutism in children. *Journal of the American Academy of Child Psychiatry, 2,* 605–617, 1963.

Davis, D. A Management program for elective mutism. *Journal of Child Psychotherapy, 4(3),* 246–253, 1977.

DiLeo, J. H. *Children's Drawings as Diagnostic Aids.* New York: Brunner/Mazel, 1973.

Douglas, J. Broken families and child behavior. *Journal of the Royal College of Physicians (London), 4,* 203–210, 1970.

Ferri, E. *Growing Up in a One-Parent Family: A Long-Term Study of Child Development.* National Foundation for Education Research. Atlantic Highlands, NJ: Humanities Press, 1976.

Glasser, P. H., & Glasser, L. N. (Eds.). *Families in Crisis.* New York: Harper and Row, 1970.

Hadley, T., Jacob, T., Milliones, J., Caplan, J., & Spitz, D. The relationship between family development crises and the appearance of symptoms in a family member. *Family Process, 13(2),* 207–214, 1974.

Halpern, W. I., Hammond, J., & Cohen, R. A therapeutic approach to speech phobia: Elective mutism re-examined. *Journal of the American Academy of Child Psychiatry, 10(1),* 94–107, 1971.

Harrison, S. I., & McDermott, J. F. (Eds.). *Childhood Psychopathology.* New York: International Universities Press, 1972.

Hayden, I. L. Classification of elective mutism. *Journal of the American Academy of Child Psychiatry, 19(1),* 118–133, 1980.

Hertz, M. R. Projective techniques in crisis. *Journal of Projective Techniques and Personality Assessment, 34,* 449–467, December 1970.

Hesselman, S. Elective mutism in children 1877–1981. *Acta Paedor Psychiatry, 49,* 297–310, 1983.

Hetherington, E. M., & Deur, J. The effects of father absence on child development. *Young Children, 26,* 233–248, 1971.

Kagel, S. A., White, R. M., & Coyne, J. C. Father-absent and father-present families of disturbed and nondisturbed adolescents. *American Journal of Orthopsychiatry, 48(2),* 342–352, April 1978.

Kolvin, I., & Fundudis, T. Elective mute children: Psychological development and background factors. In S. Chess & A. Thomas (Eds.), *Annual Progress in Child Psychiatry and Child Development.* New York: Brunner/Mazel, 1982.

Lamb, M. The effects of divorce on children's personality development. *Journal of Divorce, 1,* 163–174, 1977.

Landgarten, H. B. Art therapy as a primary mode of treatment for an elective mute. *American Journal of Art Therapy, 14,* 121–125, July 1975.

Landgarten, H. B. Individual treatment: Case history of an elective mute. In *Clinical Art Therapy: A Comprehensive Guide.* New York: Brunner/Mazel, 1981, pp. 91–105.

Morawetz, A., & Walker, G. *Brief Therapy with Single-Parent Families.* New York: Brunner/Mazel, 1984.

Marris, P. *Loss and Change.* London: Routledge and Keegan Paul, 1974.

Miller, A. Identification and adolescent development. In S. Feinstein & P. Grovacchini (Eds.), *Adolescent Psychiatry.* 2, New York: Basic Books, 1973.

Morin, C., Ladouceur, R., & Cloutier, R. Reinforcement procedure in the treatment of reluctant speech. *Journal of Behavioral Therapy and Experimental Psychiatry, 13*(2), 145–214, 1982.

Morris, J. V. Cases of elective mutism. *American Journal of Mental Deficiency, 57*(4), 661–668, 1953.

Naumburg, M. *Studies of the "Free" Art Expression of Behavior Problem Children and Adolescents as a Means of Diagnosis and Therapy.* New York: Coolidge Foundation, 1947.

Nolan, J. D., & C. Pence. Operant conditioning principles in the treatment of a selectively mute child. *Journal of Consulting and Clinical Psychology, 35*(2), 256–268, 1970.

Nye, F. Child adjustment in broken homes and unhappy unbroken homes. *Marriage and Family Living, 19,* 356–361, 1957.

Offer, D., & Offer, J. B. *From Teenage to Young Manhood.* New York: Basic Books, 1975.

Putstrom, E., & Speers, R. W. Elective mutism in children. *Journal of the American Academy of Child Psychiatry, 3,* 287–297, 1964.

Reed, G. F. Elective mutism in children: A reappraisal. *Journal of Child Psychiatry, 4,* 99–107, 1963.

Robson, B. *My Parents Are Divorced Too. What Teenagers Experience and How They Cope.* Toronto: Dorset, 1979.

Roman, M., & Blackburn, S. *Family Secrets.* New York: Times Books, 1979.

Roman, M., & William, H. *The Disposable Parent.* New York: Holt, Rinehart and Winston, 1978.

Sprenkle, D. H., & Cyrus, C. L. Abandonment: The stress of sudden divorce. In C. R. Figley & H. J. McCubbin (Eds.), *Stress and the Family: Vol. II, Coping with Catastrophe.* New York: Brunner/Mazel, 1983, pp. 53–76.

Stierlin, H. *Separating Parents and Adolescents.* New York: Quadrangle, 1974.

Vogel, E. F., & Bell, N. W. The emotionally disturbed child as a family scapegoat. *Psychoanalytic Review, 47*(2), 21–42, 1960.

Wakerman, E. *Father-Loss.* Garden City: Doubleday, 1984.

Wallerstein, J., & Kelly, J. The effects of parental divorce: The adolescent experience. In S. I. Harrison & J. F. McDermott (Eds.), *Childhood Psychopathology.* New York: International Universities Press, 1978.

Wechsler, D. The incidence and significance of fingernail biting in children. *Psychoanalytic Review, 18,* 201–209, 1981.

Wolff, S. *Children Under Stress.* London: Allen Lane, 1969.

Zuk, G. The side-taking function in family therapy. *American Journal of Orthopsychiatry, 38,* 553–559, 1968.

CHAPTER 7

Intact Family with an Acting-out Adolescent

INTRODUCTION

The achievement of autonomy and a new self-concept is the major task of adolescence. During this stage of the family life cycle, a similar goal must be met by the parents who are facing an "empty nest" future. Thus, the two generations are simultaneously grappling with the conflict of dependence versus independence. The ambivalence that accompanies this struggle exacerbates the push-pull phenomenon, mixed messages, and confusion on the part of both parties.

It is essential for individuals in the adolescent stage of development to increase their self-responsibility. Therefore, it is important to view and reapportion the power within the family system. This dynamic requires a diminishment of control on the part of the parents, with a simultaneous escalation of the teenager's position.

In the efforts to "grow-up" and be their "own person," adolescents may resort to defensive strategies, with rebellion being a frequent manifestation. In the attempt to detach themselves, youngsters resort to challenging behavior, with a tendency to press upon the vulnerabilities of others. These actions bring the negative aspects of the family's life to the forefront.

As the teenagers strain to loosen their ties, the parents must be able to comply with their children's needs. Milton Erickson described this process as a necessity to "wean" parents away from children (in Haley, 1973). For those mothers and fathers who never completed their own "second individuation," during adolescence, decathexis is especially arduous or impossible. This author believes that when *parents* have adolescent children they must undergo their *third individuation* before growth can continue and genuine maturity can be attained.

The path towards autonomy is a difficult one, particularly when the entire family is dealing with *separation and loss*. For the adolescent, the loss is his or her childhood; for the parent it is a loss of the offspring's continued presence; and for all the members, it is the loss of the family's former structure.

CASE ILLUSTRATION

The major focus of this family art psychotherapy case history is the adolescent struggle of separation and individuation. Twenty-four weekly sessions were held for the family. The young adult male member who was attending an out-of-state school was unable to participate in the therapy. Treatment also included three individual appointments with the designated patient and a single conjoint meeting for the parents.

PRECIPITATING EVENT

When 17-year-old, Ellen Sullivan received two traffic tickets within one month, a judge required that she attend a traffic class and counseling.

Ellen's mother, Mrs. Sullivan, phoned the therapist for the appointment. Besides relating the court demands, she added her own concerns. Her daughter had recently undergone a negative change in attitude as well as a drop in school grades.

Before the appointment time was set, the clinician related the requirement for a family session during the evaluation period. Mrs. Sullivan responded with reluctance, stating such an arrangement was questionable as her husband was adamantly "against therapy of any sort." The author insisted the family session was a necessary part of the assessment phase. The importance for *all* members to attend was stressed; this meant the inclusion of Mr. and Mrs. Sullivan, Ellen, as well as Judy, the 15-year-old sister. Junior, a brother, 19 years of age, was attending an out-of-state university.

The next week, Mrs. Sullivan telephoned to relate her husband's consent to "get it over with." He believed there was little choice in view of the court's orders. Apparently, the message he gave his wife was that the therapist would not want to have him back again once he made his position clear.

SESSION ONE/*Family Meeting: Father, Mother, Ellen, and Judy*

Mrs. Sullivan, who was pleasant during the introductions, appeared older than her 51 years. She was very plain, with pale skin, straight salt-and-pepper hair, and no makeup.

Mr. Sullivan was obviously annoyed when he greeted the therapist. He seemed younger than his 55 years. His pitch black hair brought attention to his large dark eyes and strong chin. He looked like someone who worked out in a gym and took care of himself. He was meticulously dressed, in fine taste, with matching slacks and tie, shoes and socks. His jacket and shirt were subtly contrasting.

Neither daughter resembled her parents. Ellen's face was heavily made up and her casual clothes were carefully selected. She projected the image of someone who was sophisticated yet "tough." Like her father, she was angry about the appointment. In contrast, Judy looked pleasant and was quietly polite, offering her hand as she greeted the author. She wore only a little makeup, being naturally attractive and with a sense of vitality and warmth about her.

Before Mr. Sullivan seated himself, he informed the author of his irritation about being at the meeting. Ellen, too, complained and questioned the "family" format. Mrs. Sullivan looked embarrassed by the conversation but said nothing, while Judy attempted to bring about a discussion on the clinician's theoretical framework.

The Sullivan family, who had not been aware that they were to be seen by an "art psychotherapist," questioned the degrees and licensure of the author. Although the answers fulfilled their expectations, the *art* part elicited scrutiny. The author, did not see a need to defend the unusual modality and merely notified the Sullivans, "This is my approach and it will be utilized for the evaluation. After that time, a recommendation for type of treatment will be made, such as individual or group for Ellen, or possibly family therapy. The modality that would be most therapeutic will also be stated at that time. All of you will have an opportunity to discuss your responses to the proposals."

Although Ellen and her father continued to talk about their dissatisfaction, the author declared the need to begin the diagnostic interview. The family was told they would be participating in an *art task experience* as part of the assessment process. Although Mr. Sullivan grumbled about it "being a funny way to help Ellen with the judge's recommendation," the therapist, ignoring the comments, simply placed two sheets of paper down on the table along with four different colored markers. Ellen colluded with her father's resistance, claiming the idea of any type of therapy was "stupid, especially one that included art." The author, disregarding the comments, proceeded to give the instructions for the family to *divide up into two teams*.

In spite of Father's and Ellen's declarations that they would be better off without each other as partners, they decided *not* to move their side-by-side seating positions, thus forming one team. This gesture automatically left Mother and the younger daughter as the other dyad, who willingly accepted the situation without comment.

Nonverbal Dyad Art Task

All the members were instructed to *select a color marker, then each team is to create a single drawing without anyone speaking during the process.* Assurance was offered: *Any type of picture or design will satisfy the purpose of the task.*

Dynamics of Ellen and Father team. In spite of Father's and Ellen's resistance to the idea of art, they began drawing immediately. Each started on their own side of the page, making a *figure that represented their own sex*. As soon as these were completed, the partners appeared to be mind-reading as they got up, and without speaking switched seats. It was undoubtedly a learned response portraying the entangled relationship. Father proceeded to draw a *bedroom around the girl's figure*. This may have indicated his intrusion upon his daughter's privacy or possibly clues to his unconscious or conscious sexual feelings towards his child. Ellen drew *a little kitten onto the male figure*. Since it was placed over the genital area, it may have had sexual implications. Another alternative could be Ellen's identification with the kitten, perhaps wishing to be cuddled and nurtured.

In the beginning, the pair appeared to be enjoying their creative involvement with one another. However, this was short-lived for Father became irritated with his daughter when she did a sloppy job on coloring in the picture. Although it appeared to be an unconscious act, Mr. Sullivan made a *dog barking at the cat*. His animal was a metaphor for his anger evoked by Ellen's refusal to conform to his expectations.

When the therapist notified the dyad to stop, they resisted the rules, continuing to draw. Although told to speak while titling the picture, the couple brushed the authority's instructions aside to complain about their partner's participation. The pair never titled their artwork because they ran out of time (Figure 73).

Dynamics of Judy and Mother team. Judy and her mother worked autonomously. Each stayed on opposite sides of the page, totally involved in her own configurations. Mother drew a *landscape* while Judy

Figure 73. Father and Ellen team

portrayed a *family group*. The pair stopped as soon as they were told to do so. Embarrassed by the other team, they tried to ignore them. The title, "A Family and a House," was conceived by combining their subject matter, yet each person wrote her own contribution onto her part of the picture.

Team Reversal and Verbal Dyadic Art Task

To understand the interaction with each parent, the girls were told to *switch parental partners*. When Judy asked if talking was permitted this time, they were given their own choice. Everyone decided to speak.

Dynamics of Father and Judy team. Father told Judy to draw a home computer and he would add something onto the screen. Judy complied by carefully delineating a *word processor*. Father, pleased with his daughter's efforts, added a *graph onto the monitor*. The partners paused to admire their picture before proceeding to add the details. When their artwork was completed, Judy did not seem to mind the way her parent had failed to consult her, as he automatically titled the picture, "Our Computer" (Figure 74).

Each person responded to one another very differently than they did with their former partner. The interaction portrayed Father as the undisputed leader. He offered the direction and Judy carried it out in a careful, neat fashion. Mr. Sullivan gave his daughter positive reinforcement and the pair derived satisfaction from their results. Both the content and the process indicated compulsive features on Father's part.

Dynamics of Mother and Ellen team. Ellen instructed her mother to draw a mountain range. Without any discussion her mother obeyed, placing *mountains* where her daughter had designated the placement. After Ellen included *clouds*, she told her mother to put in some *rain* "to water the landscape." Mother complied with the instructions and the team admired their results. Ellen, similar to Father, automatically titled the picture. She named it "Escape." Although Mother looked puzzled about the meaning, she failed to question her daughter (Figure 75).

In this team, Ellen did not have to compete with her mother for leadership, as Mrs. Sullivan was very willing to let her daughter take charge. This dyadic interaction was similar to the dynamics of the Father-Judy team, where there were clear-cut roles of leader and follower.

When Ellen informed her mother to make rain for the mountains, she

Figure 74. Father and Judy team

Figure 75. Mother and Ellen team

might have been asking for her own nurturing needs to be met. The title "Escape" could have indicated a wish to get away from home. Nevertheless, it appeared as if Ellen found relief in her relationship with Mother, since Father had difficulty in allowing autonomy.

Nonverbal Family Art Task

Without any discussion, the next nonverbal family art task followed immediately. The Sullivans were told to use *your same colored markers while the entire family makes a mural together, obeying the nonverbal rule.*

With the mural paper tacked onto the wall, Mr. Sullivan approached it, mumbling about the "cost" of the session. Ellen, directly behind him, chimed in with, "It's a waste of time." She wondered what the judge would say if he could watch them "doing this stuff."

Both Father and Ellen placed themselves in the center of the page. For this reason, Mother and Judy flanked themselves on both ends. Judy quickly moved to be next to Father, leaving Mother to place herself beside Ellen.

Father began the mural by drawing a *baseline* at the bottom of the page, immediately followed by Ellen who set a *tree* upon it. Mother went next, adding some *flowers*; but before she finished, Father interrupted to put in a *building*, then he added a *pathway* which led from his building to Ellen's tree. Judy, after assessing what had already taken place, participated by putting a *fence* around Father's structure. Mr. Sullivan became involved as he meticulously added *windows* to his building, while the others implemented *details* onto their own part of the picture. At one point, when Ellen colored in Father's path, he stopped to watch her, apparently to see if she did it neatly.

The therapist asked the family to stop and to give the mural a title. Again, Ellen and her father continued to draw as Mother and Judy stepped back in obedience. Without consultation, Mr. Sullivan decided to name the mural, "The Business Office." His eldest daughter flared up accusing him of being a dictator. She declared, "The least you could do is find out everyone else's opinion." Ignoring her, Father turned to his younger daughter instead and asked her for a suggestion. Judy ventured to offer, "The Building in the Park," since she thought it encompassed everyone's graphic efforts. The family agreed with this idea and once again Father took over to print the title across the top of the page (Figure 76).

Family dynamics. The family lined up before the drawing wall in a significant way, with Father and Ellen seizing the central position and Judy seeking to be near Father, and Mother near Ellen.

Father's dynamics illustrated the foundation he provides for his family as seen by his "baseline" contribution. In keeping with his former pictures, his "building" exhibited his tendency to be concrete. Once again he made a direct connection with Ellen by placing a path from her tree to his structure. Father's meticulous drawing again portrayed him to be obsessive. As Mr. Sullivan repeatedly ignored the author's "stop" signal, his power struggle for authority was exposed. His wish to be "boss" in all situations was further evidenced by titling the mural without consultation. Mr. Sullivan, who resented Ellen's confrontation, chose to reject her by asking Judy for ideas.

Mother's dynamics proved her to be mild mannered. Her pictures of flowers revealed a tendency to use her denial as a defense. She avoided her husband by physically placing herself away from him. Even her flowers were distanced from his graphics.

Ellen's dynamics portrayed a struggle with the authority figures. This was displayed in her competition with Father as well as her unwillingness to stop or to title the project as directed by the author. Ellen's

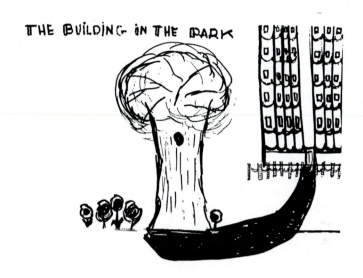

Figure 76. Family mural

gesture of filling in Father's path indicated her involvement with this parent.

Judy's dynamics showed her to be a reactive family member. She viewed contributions of others before becoming involved herself. She symbolically attempted to contain her father by placing parameters (the fence) around his building and took advantage of his attention when he chose to ignore Ellen.

Verbal Family Art Task

The family was introduced to the third technique. They were instructed to *draw yet another picture together. This time you are permitted to talk.*

Mr. Sullivan was agreeable to the directive, stating, "drawing together wasn't too bad." However, he was unable to resist making another sarcastic remark about the financial consideration. This time Judy made an effort to quiet him with, "Oh, Daddy," while Mother hurriedly followed with the proposal to begin the project.

To start off the art task, Mr. Sullivan advised his family to "get going and make a plan." It was Judy who thought of utilizing the theme of "going on a journey." Ellen, who supported the idea, suggested they begin by drawing "a ship on the ocean." Before any further conversation took place, Mr. Sullivan eagerly placed a *horizon and waves* onto the page, but when he began to make the ship, Ellen interfered. She objected to Father "taking over again!" Obviously embarrassed, Mr. Sullivan backed off to let the women participate. They drew a *large ship, billowy clouds,* and a *bright sun* and were delighted with the outcome. However, Father, believing the picture was unfinished, stated, "Important parts are missing." He wanted to add *lifeboats, life preservers,* and *a flag,* to make the mural complete. Since no one objected, he included those items. Nevertheless, Ellen's feelings were symbolically displayed when she added a *shark* at the last moment.

While everyone was admiring their product, Mr. Sullivan took the initiative to fill in the title, "Going on a Journey" (Figure 77).

Figure 77. Family mural

Family dynamics. The family verbal task was purposely given after the nonverbal art to see whether the members would use the opportunity to communicate.

Father began by asking the family for suggestions. Nevertheless, he aborted anyone else's efforts to begin when he decided to go first. Father's horizon and waves provided a base for the family to build upon. He backed off to make room for his family after he was admonished by Ellen. Mr. Sullivan's protective symbols of life savers and lifeboats portrayed his fear of separation and loss. He reestablished his authority role when he took the liberty of writing down the title without consulting the others.

Mother, embarrassed by her husband's financial complaints about the art therapy, tried to squelch his behavior by suggesting that the family begin the art task. After that, she did not make any further attempts to implement any authority; instead she functioned as a responder to the suggestions of others.

Ellen, the designated patient, displayed an openness to her sister's suggestion of the mural's theme, "Going on a Journey." She injected her own ideas by proceeding to make a ship on the ocean. Ellen, enraged with her father, freely complained about his tendency "to take over." Her confrontation caused Mr. Sullivan to back off and allow other members to make contributions. Ellen, who viewed Father's life supports as a metaphor for overprotectiveness, silently, yet graphically aggressive, responded with the picture of a shark. The hostile image was evidence of her rebelliousness towards Father.

Judy made a vague attempt to prevent Father from embarrassing the family by his demeaning attitude towards the art psychotherapy modality. She took advantage of the opportunity to communicate by furnishing the family with a theme. Judy made graphic contact with her mother and sister.

Role Perceptions

When the four art tasks were completed, the author led the family into a discussion about their perceptions of the family roles of each person. Focusing on the group mural, the members were asked, "Who was the leader?" and "Who was the least active person?"

Without hesitation, Ellen volunteered that her father had definitely been "in charge." Mother had the same impression. Even though Judy also agreed, she defended her father by adding that he "had kept the project going."

Mother felt compelled to admit her own passivity while Judy confessed a similar role; however, she gave herself credit for deciding on the mural's subject.

Although Father started out by agreeing with the perceptions of others, he could not resist fingering the lines of each color on the artwork. He practically measured out each member's contribution to prove the validity of everyone's activity. Mr. Sullivan spoke at length about the active persons versus those who were passive. Ellen, frustrated with Father's compulsiveness and verbosity, reacted to him with disgust.

The Sullivans were asked if they discovered anything about their interactions during the last exercise. Father addressed the cooperative spirit once "a plan" had been laid out. Ellen mumbled "a plan" was possible only because he backed off from taking over entirely. In a stronger voice she added, "You should try that more often!" Upset by the remarks, Mr. Sullivan flashed Ellen an angry look. Wishing to deflect attention from the Father and Ellen interaction, Mother began to talk about the mural. She said it was "nice to do it because we didn't argue."

However, Ellen was still dissatisfied and continued to examine the mural. She noted, "The females played *inferior roles*." They "merely *added* things to the picture since the baseline had already been made by Daddy". She pointed to Father's authority role as evidenced by his making the first and final marks on the art. Ellen also found significance in Father aggressively writing in the title. She adamantly claimed it was symbolic of how he took over and infantilized his children because he failed to recognize their capabilities. She glanced at Judy to cue her in for support. Even though Judy's facial expression portrayed agreement, she was reluctant to be harsh with her father and gave him "credit" for the mural's success instead of dealing with this issue.

The family discussion ceased for a few minutes as the members considered the meaning behind their mural. Ellen initiated the conversation as she commented, "Father's waves were choppy and didn't make the journey very easy." Feeling picked upon, Mr. Sullivan defended himself by calling attention to the safety guards, which he included such as the lifeboat and life preservers.

Mrs. Sullivan pronounced that the protective devices were typical of her husband since he was truly a caring person and a good provider. Regardless, Ellen insisted on citing an *overabundance* of life preservers, interpreting them as symbolic of father's overprotectiveness and a lack of motivation "to let go" of his children.

Due to the lateness in time, the therapist had to curtail the discussion and bring an end to the session. Although Mr. Sullivan wanted to go beyond the appointment time, the author was firm in ending the session. The members were told to think about their experience and next week the family art psychotherapy would be continued.

Summary of Roles

Father functions as the person of power in his family. Mrs. Sullivan and Judy are willing to accept his position and possibly benefit from his clear-cut, strong role. His anxiety over separation and loss keep him from allowing the family to function autonomously.

Ellen, who is struggling with her own adolescent individuation task, resents the bond that has existed between Father and herself. Her confrontations with this parent are attempts to free herself from the dependency role in this relationship. Rebellious acting-out behavior at home, in school, and by breaking traffic laws may serve to mask an underlying depression.

In *Mother's* dependent role, her own needs are met by having a protective and controlling husband. Her weak parental position encourages a role reversal between Ellen and herself.

Judy acts as the family "accommodator" and is a subtle influence in controlling Father. Her passivity is modeled after Mother.

SESSION TWO/*Family Meeting: Father, Mother, Ellen, and Judy*

The Sullivans entered the art therapy room and after greeting the therapist took the identical seats they had before.

As Mr. Sullivan glanced at the drawing wall he noticed the family mural was still in place. After seeing a new art media on the table, he tried to second guess the clinician, "Are we going to examine ourselves today with different art materials?" Instead of giving an answer, the therapist wondered about Mr. Sullivan's fantasies. In a sarcastic tone of voice he said, "Maybe the magazine pictures will tell us why Ellen is getting those traffic tickets." Ignoring his snide remarks, the therapist questioned if that was possible. Mr. Sullivan became serious when he mumbled, "I suppose it could." Nevertheless, he managed to add in a louder voice, "It should, for the cost of this art therapy." In spite of the women reacting with annoyance over the negative innuendos about the art therapy treatment, they said nothing.

Without the establishment of a therapeutic alliance, it was premature to deal with Mr. Sullivan's chiding remarks. Therefore, the therapist went on to gather further information about the participants. In an effort to understand the family's value system, magazine collage material was set forth. The four-part instructions required each person to do the following:

1. *Choose photos that remind you of something from your family's past.*
2. *Choose an image of the present.*

3. *Choose an additional picture that represents your wishes for the future.*

4. *When choices have been made, paste the images of each tense onto a separate page and include the meanings under each photo.*

When the family finished their project, the clinician collected the collages and divided all of them up according to tense. All of the *past* pictures were then tacked on the wall in one cluster, the *present* in another place, and *wishes for the future* in its own space.

The arrangement made it possible for the members to get a conglomerate view of their memories and wishes.

Past Photographs

Mother's photo displayed a *group of younger children raiding the refrigerator.* The statement underneath the picture was "happier times when the kids were young." Although the woman in the photo did not look pleased, no one seemed to notice or comment on this fact (Figure 78).

Father's picture was a *silhouette of a man, woman, and three children. They appeared to be superimposed upon a graph. The man was lifting the graph line over everyone's head.* Mr. Sullivan used the photo as a metaphor for "the

Figure 78. When the kids were young

energy I put into protecting my family," adding, "I've always been a good provider and tried to keep them safe" (Figure 79). Although the women agreed with his statements, Ellen believed that this very fact was part of their problem, for her father did not seem to realize she had grown up and could take care of herself.

The therapist was struck by the similarity in Ellen's and Judy's examples. Both of them had chosen pictures of a father with his youngster. *Ellen's* photo showed a *man carrying a child on his shoulders*; it represented "Daddy carrying me around at Disneyland. He always did that when I got tired. I remember how good it made me feel, being so high up in the air" (Figure 80).

Smiling as she listened to her sister, *Judy's* memories also revolved around pleasurable moments with "Daddy." She pointed to her example of a *child sitting on a piano bench clapping her hands as the man played the piano*. She remembered how much "fun it was when Daddy played the piano and we use to sing and dance to his music. We had some good times together" (Figure 81).

Although the girls' pictures brought back other memories of their childhood, Mrs. Sullivan looked dejected. When the therapist reflected upon this and wondered if she felt "left out" because the girls' pictures included only their father, Mrs. Sullivan denied any feelings of neglect. The rest of the family also chose to evade this issue.

Photographs of the Present

When *Father* declared his *present* picture of *robots boxing in a ring* represented "Ellen and myself always fighting with each other," the other participants remained quiet (Figure 82). The therapist interpreted this photo as an acknowledgment on Father's part to work on his negative relationship with Ellen rather than focusing on his daughter's traffic violations. Mr. Sullivan seemed pleased with the way the clinician had explained his priority.

Judy's collage demonstrated a *man on the phone dialing for help* as an indication of the "family's need for counseling" (Figure 83). Again, comments from the other participants were not forthcoming.

Mother's thoughts of the *present* were expressed through the picture of a *man being overworked in his office* (Figure 84). She claimed the image was "typical" of her husband. When Mrs. Sullivan was questioned about the underlying message of the photo, she had difficulty in comprehending the therapist's meaning. The clinician asked if it was basically a complaint that Mr. Sullivan spent too much time away from home, or did it stand for some other concern? She was insulted by the thought of her

Figure 79. Protects the family

Figure 80. On Daddy's shoulders

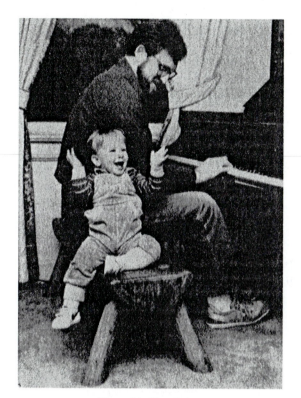

Figure 81. Good times

Figure 82. Fighting

Figure 83. Need for counseling

offering "a complaint" and was quick to explain that she was concerned about her husband's health because he "was so overworked." Mrs. Sullivan reported her husband's terrible headaches and his being a candidate for a heart attack since his father and siblings were all prone to heart disease. The girls looked as though they, too, feared their father's future. However, instead of expressing their dismay, they turned the conversation around to Father's unwillingness to care for himself.

Ellen's picture contained walking feet. She related, "I'm moving on. I'm going away on vacation in a few months, then I'm off to school" (Figure 85). Father brought attention to Ellen's picture as the only one that was self-oriented. When he mentioned her narcissistic involvement, Ellen was offended and responded defensively. The author informed Mr. Sullivan that self-interest was indigenous to the adolescent stage of development; he might consider viewing some of his daughter's reactions in that light.

Photographs of the Wish for the Future

Both Judy's and her mother's photos referred to hope for improved family relations. *Judy's* message was revealed through a magazine cutout of *plugs being connected to a circuit board*. She called the picture, "Better Communication for Our Entire Family" (Figure 86). A *crowd of people laughing and enjoying* themselves was selected by *Mother*. She had hoped her family would be like that once again (Figure 87).

Ellen dealt with herself only. Her wish for the future demonstrated several *young affectionate couples*. It alluded to her desire to have a boy-friend in the near future (Figure 88). When Father again commented on Ellen's self-involvement, the therapist reminded him about this being an adolescent's paramount need. She added that the task of this stage of development dealt with the issues of separation, individuation, and finding a significant other.

The clinician affirmed Ellen's male interest as a natural process for her age. Even though the family validated this information, Mr. Sullivan's acknowledgment was without enthusiasm. He could not resist kidding his daughter by saying, "You'd better find a boyfriend who is educated

Figure 84. Overworks

Figure 85. Moving on

and could afford to provide you with all of the things you are used to."
As expected, his comments drew a nasty look from Ellen.

Father was the last person to explain his picture of a *man who was walking in the rain holding up an umbrella.* Mr. Sullivan announced he was not as self-destructive as the family believed. He had selected this photo as a wish for the future because he planned on learning to "protect" himself (Figure 89). The very fact that Mr. Sullivan was considering this matter appeased the women. He responded to the positive reinforcement from his wife and daughters by making a declaration to *change.* He wanted to be less involved and less dependent upon his family for his well-being.

Although it appeared Mr. Sullivan was aware of his counterproductive enmeshment and a need to distance himself, he went on to talk about his worries over Ellen. He reported poor grades, staying out late at night, and possibilities of drug or alcohol abuse. He was not sure if her traffic tickets were a result of "being stoned" or a general reckless attitude. When Mr. Sullivan began to blame Ellen for his headaches and chest pains, the therapist intervened and did not permit him to overload his daughter with guilt. For this reason he was *handed plasticene* with a request to *create a symbol which stands for your feelings about the situation*. Although Mr. Sullivan may have felt uncomfortable with the clinician's intervention, he took the plasticene in hand and began to mold it into a shape.

In the meantime Mrs. Sullivan appeared nervous about the way the author had handled the situation with her husband. Judy, who also appeared anxious, quickly offered to soften the plasticene for her father.

Only Ellen sat by, curious about the way her father would respond to this female authority who gently but firmly ruled this therapy session.

Although Mr. Sullivan was carrying out the art task, he could not resist saying, "As long as I'm paying for this plasticene, I might as well come up with something." The therapist chose not to give her interpretation of his need to minimize his participation because he had decided to get something for himself in this session.

Mr. Sullivan carefully squeezed out a number of *bricks*, setting one on

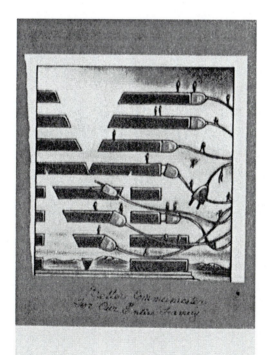

Figure 86. Improved communication

Figure 87. Happy again

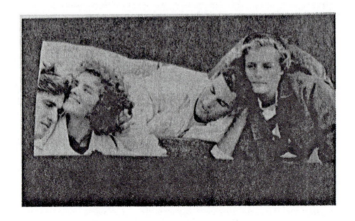

Figure 88. Wish for a boyfriend

Figure 89. Self-protective

top of another until he had built a *wall*. When asked what feeling it represented, Mr. Sullivan admitted, "I'm not sure, but my head and chest feel like a ton of bricks." The author interpreted the sculpture as the way in which he *blocks* off his feelings and somatizes instead. Mr. Sullivan argued with the interpretation as he pointed to another brick wall which was on display in the office. He claimed he had merely chosen to copy what he happened to be looking at. The author called attention to the other objects that were in his line of vision and questioned the reason for selecting the brick wall in particular. When it was apparent a reply was not forthcoming, the clinician reminded Mr. Sullivan he had failed to follow the instructions to "portray your feelings about the Ellen situation." This time he acquiesced, as he replied, "You've got something there." The rest of the family looked relieved as this admission was a way of expressing his respect for the therapist and her techniques.

As the session was ending, the clinician notified the family there would be six or seven art psychotherapy sessions altogether, which would be considered the assessment period. At the end of that time, recommendations would be forthcoming regarding treatment plans and the therapeutic modality.

COMMENTS

The developmental history of the designated patient which is usually taken during the first or second appointment was delayed. In this case, since family work was effective and beneficial to Ellen, the author believed that breaking the rhythm of the family meetings was inadvisable.

SESSION THREE/*Family Meeting: Father, Mother, Ellen, and Judy*

The family greeted the author and seated themselves in the same seats once again. Father immediately got "down to business" as he began to give an account of Ellen's misbehavior since the last meeting. Rather than allow Mr. Sullivan the opportunity to make a weekly report, the therapist used the art task to redirect the family's focus. To tie in the last week's session with this one, the participants were instructed to *cut out a construction paper symbol that represents your thoughts or feelings about the last family meeting.*

Before beginning the project, *Father* remarked, "Here we go again." Nevertheless, he went along with the directive and *tore out a configuration which he ripped and crinkled.* During the group discussion he explained the crumbled product: "Part of the session has been 'fine,'" adding, "but part of it left me with a messed-up feeling." The therapist related his figure of speech as significant to his problem of somatizing.

It was interesting to see the visual similarity in the artwork of Mother and Judy once again. They both created *round shapes. Mother* claimed her art stood for the family's positive attitude when they left the office last week, whereas Judy talked about her art as relevant to the family's meaningful participation in the last session.

In contrast to the former meeting, Ellen's attitude had softened. Her *paper sculpture* was three-dimensional. It was pleated in accordian fashion as a metaphor of the way each person tended to "open up, then backed off." She elaborated on the way Father often closed himself from his feelings and how Mom and Judy usually "managed to stay out of trouble." Judy was quick to inject the fact that Ellen had not taken any "risks" either. Father, agreeing with the remark, declared, "Yeah, I was on the *hot seat* last week." He then switched away from being reflective and, turning to Ellen, began to tease her as he said, "I bet your paper sculpture couldn't even fly in the air." Ellen, who took the remark at face value, angrily retorted, "It wasn't a toy! It was a reply to Mrs. Landgarten." The two of them bantered back and forth, with Father teasing and Ellen hostile and serious, continuing to reply to his remarks.

Because of Mr. Sullivan's and Ellen's verbosity, the author decided to deal with the situation through the art. Therefore, Father was told to *draw a symbol of what you were feeling when you made your remark about "the paper structure not being able to fly"* and, also, *a symbol for the response you expected from Ellen.* Ellen, in turn, was to portray *how you perceived your Father's remark.* Mother and Judy were directed to *relate your own observations.*

Father, instead of making an emotional symbol about how he felt, printed *Okay* on the page. However, for his expected response from Ellen, he made *a bolt of lightning.* The therapist failed to accept the "Okay" symbol and pressed him to search for his feelings, reminding him of his words about being on the *hot seat.* After a few thoughtful moments, Mr. Sullivan stated, "I was probably provoked." The therapist added, "And?" "And," he said, "I suppose I was kinda angry, too." When the author then questioned the meaning of his lightning metaphor, he replied, "I got just the kinda response I expected. I knew I'd get a rise out of her." Rather than comment on the dynamic formulation, the clinician chose to delay it by turning the attention to *Ellen's* pictorial statements of a *wavy arrow,* which *pointed downward.* Its meaning was one of "being put down all the time and," she said, "I'm sick and tired of it!"

The author, desiring to give everyone a chance to deal with the material, went on to ask Mrs. Sullivan and Judy to talk about their artwork. *Mrs. Sullivan* shared her drawing of *pennies.* She said her husband's teasing "made no sense," since he knew it would only cause friction between Ellen and himself. In contrast, *Judy* made a *joker's playing card,* as she explained "Daddy was only kidding. I wish Ellen wouldn't answer him or she should catch on when he kids her."

The therapist collected all of the artwork and arranged them accordingly: Judy's *Joker,* Ellen's *downward arrow,* Father's *lightning bolt,* and Mother's *no sense pennies.*

The family was told their visual statements were indicative of their family dynamics which were probably played out at home in one way or another. *Father* acting as *the joker* towards Ellen does this to defend himself from his own uncomfortable emotions. *Ellen,* who is feeling "put down" as represented in her *downward arrow,* gives a *lightning bolt* response. Even though it made *no sense* to *Mother,* Ellen and her father continued to engage each other through arguments (Figure 90).

The clinician's statements caused the family to contemplate their interactions. After a few minutes the silence was broken by Mr. Sullivan who admitted, "It all seems to make sense but I've gotta give what you said more thought."

Figure 90. Family dynamics

The therapist continued to pursue the family's style of dealing with each other. Mr. Sullivan was asked if he sometimes displaced his rageful feelings onto Ellen? Perhaps there were times when this daughter was the recipient of his anger, even though it did not rightfully belong to her? Before Mr. Sullivan had a chance to answer, Ellen heatedly remarked about the frequency with which she was "dumped on." Father pensively agreed to examine this phenomenon.

Mrs. Sullivan and Judy were brought into the discussion as they were asked their opinion. Judy reiterated her belief that "Ellen needed to avoid Dad's bait." Nevertheless, Mother clung to the hope that the household tension would be relieved when Ellen paid more attention to her father's moods. The therapist wondered aloud about the family's responsibility to evaluate their father's feelings before interacting with him. Did that mean Father had no responsibility in the situation? Mother, thrown by those questions, withdrew from a dialogue. The author suggested that the entire family consider their own reactions to Mr. Sullivan and the way in which he managed to involve them.

To bring closure to the session, the female participants were told to *create a symbolic gift for your husband or father.* Mr. Sullivan was instructed *to make something you would like to give to yourself.*

When the task was finished, everyone handed their gift to Mr. Sullivan. Mrs. Sullivan gave her husband a picture of a *forehead with a peace symbol on it*, stating she wished to give him "some peace of mind." Judy gave her Dad a *heart*, declaring it stood for her "love," while Ellen, who was still feeling victimized by Father, made *two parallel lines*, which portrayed Father and herself not engaged in a fight.

Mr. Sullivan's gift to himself was an *"x-ed" out bottle of pills*. He explained it represented his feeling good without a dependency on prescriptions (Figure 91).

The gift technique took the edge off of Father's hurt feelings. It was premature in the family's treatment to let Father leave the session without some closure to his vulnerability. Early in family therapy it is important to offer relief after difficult moments with the parents. Aside from its therapeutic value, it is also realistic to recognize that the authority figure may withdraw from treatment, or possibly sabotage the family's therapy altogether.

When the family left the office, Mother and Judy flanked themselves on either side of Mr. Sullivan, with Ellen trailing behind. The therapist

Figure 91. No pills

wondered if it was easier for Ellen to handle her Father's proximity when she was angry with him. Perhaps positive feelings evoked unresolved Oedipal conflicts and threatened her struggle for individuation.

SESSION FOUR/*Family Meeting: Father, Mother, Ellen, and Judy*

When the family entered the office, Mr. Sullivan sat himself down to question the clinician about the continuance of the family art therapy mode. The therapist notified him this approach would be continued for three more sessions until the evaluation was completed, then recommendations for treatment would be made. At that time the suggestions for the type of therapy would be offered, i.e., individual, family, or group, as well as the modality that would appear to be most productive.

Mrs. Sullivan and her daughters spoke up to voice their desire to continue working within the art psychotherapy model. They believed it delineated the family interactions and helped them to better understand each other. Although Mr. Sullivan listened to his wife and girls, he failed to make any comments.

The therapist informed Ellen that next week she would be seen alone to take her developmental history.

SESSION FIVE/*Individual Meeting: Ellen*

The developmental history portrayed a normal childhood. Ellen met all the milestones with no reported traumas. When she was questioned about her menses, she admitted feeling depressed during that time with a tendency to suffer severe headaches and frequently "flew off the handle." As further sexual issues were discussed, Ellen admitted she had been secretly pregnant the previous year. She reported having a long-term steady relationship with the young man who had impregnated her. Ellen became very upset as she spilled out the facts of an abortion, claiming her boyfriend was very supportive and suffered a great deal of guilt and pain. They disengaged completely last fall, when he went away to college. Ellen asked the therapist to maintain confidentiality, since no one except a best friend knew about the incident.

The clinician, thinking over Ellen's past, noted her drop in grades and acting-out behavior coincided with the time of the abortion. Although the adolescent agreed about the effect that this event had upon her, she began to change the subject.

To keep Ellen focused on this important issue, she was told to *draw the circumstances around the abortion*. Ellen, requesting the collage media, sadly selected a small-sized picture of *two panic-stricken dogs*. They were pasted onto a large surface to indicate the frightened feelings that she and her boyfriend had experienced. Then she turned the page and filled it with a drawing of *red tears*. Before the graphics were completed, Ellen began to cry, her wet tears mingling with the ones she drew.

The clinician encouraged her to mourn the fetus and a period in her life when she and John were in love. As the past could not be retrieved it was essential not to repress but to attend to the grieving process. The therapist helped Ellen to talk about the pain, which she had worked so hard to keep as a secret.

As the session came to an end Ellen was asked to return for another individual session before the family meetings were resumed.

SESSION SIX/*Individual Meeting: Ellen*

To continue with the issue of loss, Ellen was asked to *create art that expresses why you feel lonely*.

Ellen folded the page in half and on one side drew a *heart-shaped locket*. On the other half she made a letterman's jacket, a record, and a *banner*. When asked to explain her symbols, Ellen said the locket represented the loss of her boyfriend and the other three items represented her brother, Junior. When the therapist requested more information about her brother, Ellen explained he was a "very special person who got along with the entire family." Junior was kind, loving, caring, fun to be with, and had an interest in a great many things. She believed he was the one member to whom everyone confided. As Ellen stressed her brother's importance, she realized there had been a general sadness in the house ever since he left last fall for an out-of-state university.

The author empathized with Ellen's loss and questioned her further about feelings of abandonment. Refusing to examine these emotions, Ellen tried to avoid the subject by bringing attention to her *doodle drawings*. Unwilling to be diverted, the therapist noted Ellen had lost the presence of two significant people in her life at the same time, both her boyfriend and her brother. Since this statement struck at the core of her sadness, Ellen began to weep. She sobbed as she concluded the two men she loved the most "deserted" her last fall. The author encouraged Ellen to allow herself to stay in touch with her feelings. She was asked if she wished to *use the art materials to express yourself*. Although she did not answer verbally, Ellen indicated her consent by reaching for the plasticene. As she pressed and squeezed the media, she allowed herself to experience sadness and anger in spite of the rationalization about the reasons for the boys leaving.

When Ellen paused to view her *abstract sculpture*, the author asked her to *describe the form, the positive and negative spaces, and so forth.* She began by relating, "It has a lot of substance. It's round and smooth and nice to feel, and is empty in the center." As she turned the object around, she reported, "The empty part can't be seen on all sides. It's only after you turn it around slowly that you notice it's not a solid piece" (Figure 92). Ellen was told to *stop and write down what you just said.* She did so willingly, then read and reread her words searching for a significant meaning. Just as she was about to give up, Ellen asked the author if the piece validated her feeling of emptiness in spite of her ego strength and positive self-esteem. However, before the therapist could concur with these thoughts, Ellen declared, "It all fits," and dismissed the therapist from answering.

The session ended as the clinician noted that Ellen's acknowledgment of separation and feelings of abandonment would help her to deal with the emotions around those issues. She was told, "The acting-out behavior was a way of avoiding what was going on inside of you. Sometimes it is a defense and a way of masking one's deeper feelings." As Ellen stood up to leave the office, it was obvious a chord had been struck which would need exploration.

SESSION SEVEN/*Family Meeting: Father, Mother, Ellen, and Judy*

The Sullivans began the therapy session by addressing their attempts to "get along better."

As the clinician wished to gather more information on the participants

Figure 92. Empty in the center

and their perceptions of their family, they were each assigned to *draw a house, a tree, and a person, plus a picture of your family*.

Several persons mumbled about their artistic ability being less than adequate. The therapist encouraged them to complete the artwork since their adeptness as illustrators was unimportant.

When the tasks were completed, the products were tacked on to the wall. After a brief glance, it became obvious everyone had placed Junior in the center, even though there were variations on the positions of the rest of the family. Pictures of *Junior* were most outstanding in every way; his figure was the largest, contained the most color, had the greatest amount of details, and so forth (Figures 93A and 93B).

When the author questioned the family about these facts, the Sullivans became deeply involved in a discussion about the missing member. In the main, the conversation was informative as everyone chose to describe Junior's looks, intelligence, kindness, and so on. When the therapist told the family, "It sounds like all of you miss him terribly," Ellen said, "Yes." However, Mr. and Mrs. Sullivan and Judy all diverted the conversation away from this statement. Ellen removed herself from the family to sit back and observe her sister's and parents' reactions. It occurred to the therapist that were it not for her individual art therapy session, she, too, would have avoided dealing with the feelings behind the separation.

To help the family face their inner loneliness, they were instructed to *create a collage about the feelings behind Junior's absence*.

When *Mother* began to look through the collage box she was attracted to a picture of a person reading a book entitled, "The Art of Avoiding Decisions." Although she started to paste it down on the paper, it was discarded and replaced by the image of a *person on a telephone*, which represented her pride in Junior for being a fine student who was always pleased to hear from his family.

Father was quick to choose the photo of a *boy studying*. He informed the therapist, "I miss my son, but he'll be home for the summer before too long" (Figure 94).

In spite of the fact that there was an abundance of collage pictures of young men, *Judy*, resistant to looking at her feelings decided to pick out a picture of a June day, claiming she could not wait for Junior to come home.

Even though Mr. and Mrs. Sullivan and Judy refused to deal with their emotions with any depth, *Ellen*'s picture of a *cat with a large tear running down its face* was dramatically effective. She declared the cat was a metaphor for her own "lonely and sad feelings." Ellen reported, "Junior was the one person who was available to all of us. He has a gift for being interested in everyone" (Figure 95).

Figure 93A. Father's family picture

Figure 93B. Ellen's family picture

Figure 94. Misses son

The therapist reached for Mrs. Sullivan's *discarded* picture with "The Art of Avoiding Decisions" on it. She cut off the word "decisions" and replaced it with "emotions" (Figure 96). The family looked at the message and a discussion ensued. The participants agreed they tried "not to be down" because they did not want to "bother" anyone else with their own loneliness.

No one was surprised that these mutual feelings existed; but they realized expressing them helped to ease the load of depression. Ellen was the family's voice when she said sharing emotions gave her a sense of comfort since she felt less isolated and detached from the rest of the members.

At that point, Mr. Sullivan switched away from the seriousness of the moment by beginning to tease the author, "Say, Mrs. Landgarten, this art therapy stuff isn't so bad after all. I won't even mind paying the bill if you can get our family straightened out." The therapist pointed out how Mr. Sullivan found it difficult to stay with the emotional aspect of treatment, stating that he often leaned on *teasing* as a diverting mechanism. The meeting was called to a halt, since the therapy time was over.

On the way out, Mr. Sullivan could be heard saying, "Who would think that *art* could *help people*?"

Figure 95. Lonely and sad feelings

SESSION EIGHT/*Family Meeting: Father, Mother, Ellen, and Judy*

After the initial greetings, the author informed the family of the following recommendations:

Since Ellen would be leaving for her vacation in approximately four
months, the treatment had to be on a short-term basis. Under these
conditions the continuance of family therapy would be most productive,
not only for Ellen but also for the rest of the members.

The Sullivans were given the opportunity to either remain in clinical
art therapy or to be referred to another psychotherapist who would treat
them within a classical treatment approach.

Ellen was the first to declare her desire to stay in therapy with the
author, as she announced, "You know all about us. I even like the art."
Without any hesitation, Father agreed. He jokingly added he wanted to
stay with the art therapy because he was now familiar with the author's
approach. Once more he referred to getting his "money's worth." Judy
and her mother also believed they had already been helped. They testi-
fied that Ellen and Father had become less argumentative. For these

reasons the family committed themselves to remain in art psychotherapy.

With the treatment matter settled, work on communication began as
the *entire family* was told to *make a single piece of art. You can select your own
theme and media.*

Father began by asking his family for suggestions. When none were
forthcoming, he wondered if they were open to using a combination of
art materials? The women liked the suggestion and decided to apply it
towards developing an *abstract design.*

In deciding the way to go about making the project, Mr. Sullivan
offered to cut the construction paper into strips, mentioning the women
could follow by weaving them together. He proposed the final piece
could be mounted onto a background or suspended in mid-air. Since
Father's ideas sounded very creative, the females encouraged him to
begin.

Mr. Sullivan took his cutting job very seriously. In his usual compul-

Figure 96. Therapist changes discard

sive style, he picked up a ruler from the therapist's desk and used it to make certain he marked off the edges straight and exactly the same length. In his determination to do his job well and with accuracy, Father took up a great deal of time. Although his wife and both daughters were impatient, it was Ellen who said, "Come on, Dad, finish up already, or we'll never get a chance to do our part." Disregarding his daughter, Mr. Sullivan kept right on measuring the paper, then finally proceeded on to his cutting. As Ellen kept urging her Dad to "finish up already," quite by accident he miscut the size of some of the paper strips. In his frustration Mr. Sullivan turned and yelled at Ellen for her nagging him, claiming his error was due to her interruptions. Ellen, obviously embarrassed and upset for being berated in front of the therapist, defended herself in an outburst of rage. Nevertheless, Mr. Sullivan discounted his daughter as he declared her actions were typical of her usual insensitivity towards him. The two continued to argue as Mrs. Sullivan and Judy sat quietly by, looking helpless.

When it was obvious the family had given up on the project, they were told to "stop and think over what has happened in this session." A reflection upon the dynamics began as the attention was then taken away from Mr. Sullivan and Ellen and directed towards Mother when she was asked to describe her observations. Mrs. Sullivan began by defending her husband: "He was trying to do his best when Ellen hurried him," she said. However, when Mother saw the hurt look on her eldest child's face she added, "Although Ellen didn't mean to place stress on her Dad, it did upset him. I guess it wasn't Ellen's fault that my husband was taking such a long time, and it was getting late."

Judy was the next person to be asked her opinion. Believing Ellen needed support, she said, "My sister was right, Daddy was being so careful, he was using up all our time. The rest of us would have never gotten a turn."

Then Ellen was questioned. In a disgusted tone of voice she said, "Oh, what's the use?" adding, "Dad will never change! He won't listen anyways, he'll just get mad."

Mr. Sullivan was the last to be focused upon. He voiced his sense of hopelessness about being unable to communicate with Ellen.

It was essential for the participants to understand their family dynamics. For this reason the clinician examined the chain of events that led up to the argument.

1. Father, who had in a past therapy session been accused of being unfair and too authoritarian, seemed to make a point of asking for suggestions.

2. In spite of the opportunity to offer their ideas, the women did not do so.
3. Father asked his wife and daughters about the possibility of combining media. They readily agreed, adding their own idea of an "abstract design."
4. Again Father, attempting to organize a plan, related the method to be utilized for the construct.
5. The females encouraged Mr. Sullivan to begin.
6. He may have taken the job too seriously, although it was typical of the way he always functions.
7. No one offered to help him with the cutting job once he started.
8. All the women became frustrated.
9. It was Ellen alone who had the courage to *voice her* opinion.
10. Father did not state his frustration with trying to do a good job while being urged to hurry. Instead, he chose to disregard Ellen and to continue his task.
11. Ellen, feeling ignored, repeated her comments.
12. Father, feeling rushed, began to experience himself under stress.
13. His own error infuriated him further.
14. Father's anger towards himself was displaced upon Ellen.
15. Ellen, hurt by Father's put-down, retaliated by expressing hostility.
16. Father, hurt by Ellen's response, resorted to getting even by demeaning her again.
17. Neither person acknowledged their own feelings aloud. Instead, they verbally injured their opponent.
18. Judy and Mother resorted to a passive stance. They may have felt guilty because Ellen had done their work by expressing their own thoughts to Mr. Sullivan.
19. Everything fell apart and the art task, which the family was asked to do, was never completed.

The family was asked to think about the statements that had just been made. A few minutes later the Sullivans were told to talk about exploring alternatives to their interactions. Judy was the first person to offer her opinion, "All of us could have offered suggestions instead of leaving the ideas up to Daddy." Agreeing with her, Mother added, "And someone else could have done the first step of cutting up the strips of paper so that it didn't have to take so long. We all know that Dad always likes to do everything perfect."

Ellen, who was inattentive to her sister's and mother's thoughts, glanced at her father sideways, claiming the females had been placed into an inferior position by him, since he was to do the cutting and the women had to wait to do the weaving. She declared it was typical of the type of job that women always had to do and admitted that particular "ploy" was unacceptable to her from the beginning. The therapist pointed out that by withholding these thoughts Ellen had set up her Dad to displease her. The author interrupted these actions by saying, "Sometimes adolescents become angry with their parents because they find that an easier way to distance themselves. This is done in service of the adolescent task to individuate. That is, they desire to become more autonomous before they go out on their own."

The author wondered if she should ask the family to rework the cooperative art task, or to let them leave the session without any closure. It seemed best to lead the family into introspection on the parts they played. Therefore, a request was made to *look over the collage photos and find pictures which define your own role in what happened in the session today.*

Everyone fell silent when the instructions were given, obviously giving their roles careful thought. As they inspected the collage photos, a general sense of depression seemed to fill the room. The therapist believed this was a sign that the Sullivans were getting in touch with their feelings, rather than resorting to their usual defenses of denial or avoidance.

When the artwork was shared, the participants expressed their astonishment at the personal revelations that were made.

For example, Mrs. Sullivan and the girls were surprised when *Father* displayed himself as a mime who was *overloaded with paperwork* and as *a man who had a smiling façade while his insides were on fire.* Yet another picture contained a *bottle of Bufferin* to exhibit his proneness to headaches. As an afterthought, he added, "I could use one right now." Looking at the author he asked her if she had some Bufferin or Tylenol handy? Instead of answering directly, the therapist asked if he expected her to *take his pain away*? Realizing the symbol of his message, Mr. Sullivan said, "I guess I'll have to cure myself." Yet, in spite of his statement, he printed "Mrs. Landgarten" on the Bufferin bottle (Figure 97).

After considering her role in the group project, *Mother* was saddened by the part she played. She shared several photographs: one was of a *Japanese doll* whose eyes were closed and the other of *"dummies driving a car."* Mrs. Sullivan did not need to make any verbal comments since the pictures dramatically portrayed the story of her "silence" (Figure 98).

When *Judy* took her turn she had trouble in making eye contact. She especially avoided looking at Ellen. Finding it easier to face the collage,

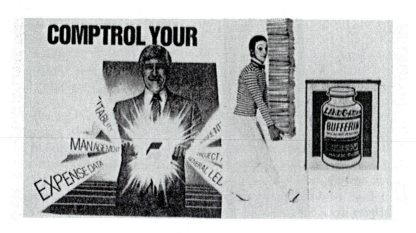

Figure 97. Shares feelings

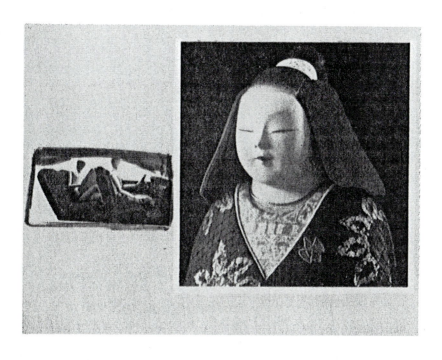

Figure 98. Passivity

she confessed her role to be that "of the helpless child, who just sits by sadly and lets things happen." She utilized another image to reflect the results of that role as she admitted, "It makes me feel guilty." Judy confessed she had never before identified those feelings (Figure 99). Previously, she believed it was Dad's and Ellen's fighting that made her uncomfortable, but she now realized it was due to her own guilt for letting the arguments go on.

The last person to take a turn was *Ellen*. She held up her collage which made three pictorial statements. One was of a *little girl with a defiant stance*. She admitted her identification, stating, "I'm like that little kid in the picture, always looking for a fight." The second picture displayed *two wrestlers in the ring*, which symbolized the verbal wrestling in which she and her father were frequently engaged. The last photo was of *wounded soldiers helping one another to walk*. She described herself as similar to the contents, as "army men who were badly hurt, yet cared enough to try and help each other" (Figure 100).

Everyone was affected by Ellen's presentation, Mr. Sullivan in particular. His eyes were filled with tears and he found it difficult to speak. When he did talk, he preferred to lighten the mood by making a joke, "I

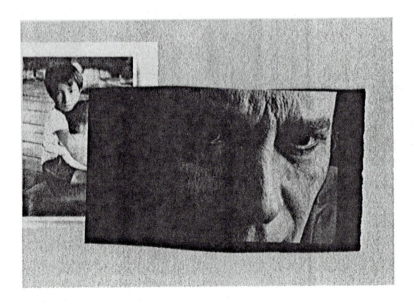

Figure 99. Helpless and guilty

Figure 100. A) Defiant B) Looking for a fight C) The hurt help each other

see one of your soldiers has his head hurt. You know you and I suffer from pains in our heads." Then, holding up his collage, he added, "Hey, maybe I can give your soldiers one of my Bufferin." The family laughed in an attempt to get some comic relief.

The author said, "I guess it's hard to face difficult material." Once again, trying to keep the group from watering down their feelings, the therapist did *not* give a closing technique. Instead, attention was called to the end of the session.

On the way out of the office Mrs. Sullivan and Ellen warmly shook the therapist's hand as an indication of their appreciation for an important session. Mr. Sullivan, who also wished to convey his thanks, gave the author's shoulder a squeeze. Only Judy avoided facing the therapist as she left the room.

SESSION NINE/*Family Meeting: Father, Mother, Ellen, and Judy*

Since the last session had ended with the family in an introspective mood, the therapist decided to see if they would continue an insight orientation or if they needed to back off for a while. Therefore, the Sullivans were instructed to *create a configuration which illustrates something you want to work on in this session.*

Father decided to use the plasticene. In contrast to the bricks which he made in the past (depicting his unwillingness to be in art psychotherapy), he rolled out a series of *green balls*. He said it was the antithesis of the red bricks; their round shapes and green color represented his willingness to "go forth." He professed his motivation to change and to improve his relationship with his eldest daughter.

Similarly, *Ellen's* plasticene *abstract figures* also contained a message to improve her interaction with Dad.

A small *house paper sculpture* was created by *Mother*. She ascribed its meaning as her "hope" to have family differences resolved.

The only person who avoided dealing with any introspection or wishes for a better family life was *Judy*. Her artwork was a simple *doodle* with some spaces colored in. It was typical of what many nine-year-olds learn to do in school. Although the author did not state this, it was believed Judy was maintaining her childlike role in the family. A shift in the family system appeared too threatening for her. Since she had benefited from being the "good" child, while Ellen's title was the "bad" one, she preferred that the family homeostasis were maintained.

After the artwork was discussed, Mr. Sullivan turned to the therapist and questioned, "Well, what do we do next?" Instead of offering a directive, the family was asked, "What do *you think should be done*?" Mr. Sullivan jokingly told the therapist, "Hey, this is what we pay *you* for." However, expecting no reply, he turned to his family for ideas. Ellen, wishing to "do something different," thought it would be interesting if they utilized various types of materials for a three-dimensional piece of art. Father liked the idea and asked his wife and younger daughter what they thought. Mother, who was suddenly thrown by having the spotlight on her, had difficulty in offering any more than "Ellen's suggestion seems fine," with Judy adding, "It's OK with me." However, when questioned about a topic for the artwork, Mrs. Sullivan and Judy again failed to present any ideas.

This situation left Mr. Sullivan and Ellen to make the decisions. Both were undoubtedly determined to have a positive interchange this time. With that in mind, Father encouraged Ellen to produce a subject. She replied with "the theme is not important, but the way we act is." Father seemed to be in agreement, yet he believed a topic would help the family take a step forward towards a united effort. For 10 minutes or so the Sullivans conversed about possible procedures.

The final decision was made by Ellen when she said, "Forget the group experience," and suggested the family *divide up into two teams* instead. *Each dyad would make a paper sculpture and then the two pieces could be combined into one unified form.* Although in agreement, Mother and Judy seemed reluctant to pick a partner; therefore, Ellen chose her sister, leaving the parents to become the other team.

The parents began to make a *houselike* structure. Sighting their artwork, Ellen told Judy, "Let's make paper dolls of our own family." The two girls looked like small children as they engaged themselves in an activity from out of their past. As the sisters worked, they joked and giggled, regressing to their childhood ways.

Mr. and Mrs. Sullivan looked pleased as they glanced at their daughters "playing with cutouts." To the author it appeared that the entire family had stepped back into a time when everyone was happy, when roles were clear-cut, and when power struggles did not take place.

The parents' paper sculpture went along quickly and easily. Basically, Father built the *structure* which stood on a *solid foundation*. Mother added the *details* and *frills* in a complimentary fashion and with no conflict; each person seemed to know exactly what part they would play.

The girls' team functioned in the same way as their parents', with Ellen making the *basic figures* and Judy adding the *details* and *frills*. Again roles were clearly defined. A leader and a follower, each meeting individual needs.

When the teams were finished they were given a plastic tray. Mother and Father placed the house onto the tray while the girls set the dolls in place. Father was pleased when he saw the "Daddy" figure with outstretched hands. He requested that it be placed in front of the door. Mother decided to have "the Mommy cutout next to Daddy" and Judy asked if they could make a swing for the "Baby" to sit on. Father cut out a swing and stood it up next to the house. "Baby Judy" was then pasted onto it. Ellen voiced her wish to have the Ellen doll between Daddy and Mommy. This left the "Junior" cutout for last. The family decided to "put him near the baby" (Figure 101).

The Sullivans admitted the art task had been enjoyable. They were led into a discussion about their past. Each member free-associated to some good times the family had experienced. Junior was brought into the conversation. They were asked where they thought Junior would have chosen as his spot in the scene, as well as what his free-associations might have been. They all believed he would have placed himself "in the middle." At this time the therapist touched on the feelings around the separation of their son/brother. "Perhaps," she said, some of you long for and mourn the bygone days when the entire family was together."

The Sullivans' resistance to this subject was handled by making jokes. Therefore, the therapist decided to go along with it. It also seemed important to allow the family an opportunity to maintain their good feelings, since they had been successful in the joint task.

Figure 101. Teams unite

Comments

Due to the inappropriate timing, the therapist did not point out the similarities in the way Mr. Sullivan and Ellen functioned. Their conflict lay in their power struggle and Ellen's rebellious attitude to experience herself as an individual.

It appeared that Junior's role included keeping the family on an even keel. The removal of his presence had upset the former balance of the family system. The Sullivan's needed to reestablish themselves with a new pattern of functioning since the members' newer roles were still in a state of flux.

The author was mindful of Ellen's leaving in a few months. This act would elicit yet another family structure crisis for the remaining members.

SESSION TEN/*Family Meeting: Father, Mother, Ellen, and Judy*

The family came into the office with the news that they had seen the author on television. She was interviewed on the use of art psychotherapy as a modality for treatment. They voiced their pride in being seen by a "celebrity." The therapist would have preferred that the Sullivans had not witnessed the interview, since this could affect the transference. The clinician asked if the event seemed to alter anything regarding their treatment.

Mr. Sullivan was the first to answer the question. As an accountant, he believed outside confirmation added to "the validity and accountability" of the art therapy approach. He claimed that hearing about the modality on the air gave him added confidence about the type of treatment they were receiving.

On the other hand, Mrs. Sullivan said she felt "good" about the therapy before they saw the show, but it did make her feel "special" to be treated in art therapy. Judy talked about a case that Mrs. Landgarten had discussed on the television program, where a child was helped to make "imperfect art" because he always tried for perfection and was hampered by unrealistic expectations. When asked why this case in particular held her interest, she admitted identifying with this child.

Ellen unabashedly told the author she had been very excited about the T.V. program. She divulged her pleasure at being treated by someone who was so well known in the professional field.

The author found it unfortunate to have a case of galloping transference. In the past, other such examples had been precipitated by similar situations. Since the Sullivans were to receive short-term treatment, the therapist decided to utilize the family's transference fantasies to exacerbate their work towards positive change.

In an attempt to deal with this issue, the family was asked to select *magazine pictures that describe what you think I, the therapist, can do for this family.*

In response to the directive, *Father* very neatly cut out a picture of a *man entangled in tape.* He said he believed the therapist could help straighten him out. He also included a *doctor* image, which represented the therapist, declaring she could possibly cure his headaches and ulcers (Figure 102). Doctor pictures are frequently used by patients during the beginning phase of treatment depicting magical omnipotent expectations from the therapist.

Next to share her collage was *Mother.* It had several photos: one of a *coal miner,* indicating the clinician's ability to "dig into matters," and another of *Lincoln* and *Washington* on dollar bills. She said this demonstrated Mrs. Landgarten as a person who could scrutinize the family's problems and would be honest and truthful about her observations. Her third photo contained a number of different types of *telephones,* which meant Mrs. Landgarten could "offer all sorts of ways to communicate" (Figure 103).

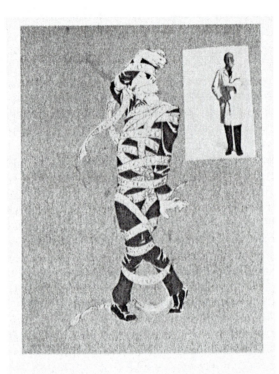

Figure 102. Father believes therapist can cure him

The cutout of a *magazine ad* of "Johnson's No More Tangles Shampoo" was used by *Judy*. It portrayed an unhappy little girl whose tangled hair was being washed with the Johnson's baby shampoo. Judy believed the therapist had access to a special formula which would "smooth out all the family's tangles" (Figure 104).

Ellen was the last person to display her art. She added several *figures to a photo of doors*. She claimed it illustrated her "family reaching for Mrs. Landgarten's office door before they could open up their own inner doors." Another picture showed a *man arising out of a suitcase*. With a great deal of pride Ellen claimed the therapist "had already helped the family come out and unpack their problems" (Figure 105).

When the sharing was finished, the author noted the remarkable powers that everyone had ascribed to her. Despite the protests, she proclaimed a therapist can only help clients to help themselves. However, the family seemed convinced the clinician was merely being modest.

In hopes of reinforcing the Sullivans' working role in treatment, the

Figure 103. Beliefs of therapist's ability

Figure 104. Therapist will untangle problems

Figure 105. Therapist opens inner doors: unpacks problems

therapist asked them to *create a symbol representing your individual contribution to the treatment process.*

In response, Father drew *himself in a hardware store.* He declared art therapy was like the place where he could buy basic building materials that were needed for repair work, yet he realized once he had "the hardware" it was up to him to do the actual work. His wife and daughters were delighted with the analogy and complimented him on his creativity.

A *sponge* had been selected by *Mother.* She said it meant she would soak up everything that was going on and was like a functional object which could "neaten things up." Mrs. Sullivan appeared to accept her position in life.

Judy realistically saw her part as an *interior decorator* "who comes in to make things prettier for the family."

The image of a *bee* was chosen by Ellen. She claimed, "I'm very busy working away on myself." Continuing on, she added her hope for "storing away lots of honey for the future."

All of the pictures contained a great deal of insight. The therapist chose to review them in detail in an attempt to dilute their magical expectations. The family was given credit for their work in therapy and concerted efforts to improve their family life.

Before the Sullivans left the session, Ellen related she had talked with her parents on the way to the office about an individual art therapy session for herself. Although Mr. and Mrs. Sullivan agreed to such an arrangement, Father requested that Ellen's appointments should not interfere with the family meetings. He wanted her sessions to be made in addition to the usual family therapy.

SESSION ELEVEN/*Individual Meeting: Ellen*

While entering the office, Ellen announced she was troubled by a series of dreams, all with similar themes. For this reason she was instructed to *draw some of the events or symbols of feelings contained in the dreams. The graphics can be done in serial fashion or separately, realistically or abstractly.*

Ellen busied herself as she drew a series of pictures: an *automobile*, a *driver's test*, and *traffic lights*. In addition, she symbolized her *father*, her *brother*, and *herself* following with a *gavel* (metaphor for a judge) and a *policeman's hat* (Figure 106). When asked to relate the entire dream, Ellen reported the following:

Figure 106. A dream

I walked out of our home, by myself, leaving the family behind. I got in the car and began to drive it. I was all by myself. I seemed to be glad and frightened at the same time. Then the dream switched to another scene.

Now Dad was driving the car. Our whole family was there. My brother sat in the front seat between my Dad and me. He had a map on his lap and his job seemed to be guiding us in the right direction.

Then the dream changed again. I was driving alone in the car. I parked near a meter. When I came back I was very upset because I got a ticket. I didn't understand why I got the ticket.

Suddenly I was in traffic court. The judge said I had to take a test.

Then I was taking a written driver's test. I knew the answer about the green light for GO and the red light for STOP, but I wasn't sure what the YELLOW light meant. I was upset because I always got an "A" in art.

Suddenly a policeman wearing a hat sat on one side of me. I wasn't sure if it was a lady or a man, since the blond hair seemed unusual. I wondered if it was Cagney or Lacey from television.

In the dream I knew I would get through the traffic class with the police person near me.

I walked out of the class and got into my car. I realized the car was not our family car. I thought maybe I made a mistake but when I looked around I found my notebook there.

Then I woke up.

The author asked Ellen for her free associations to symbols used in her dreams. Although the client tended to divert the meaning by explaining where the images were obtained, she was refocused to examine what the symbols represented. With the help of the therapist, the following metaphors were analyzed by Ellen:

1. Walking out of the house represented *Ellen's attempt to be autonomous.*
2. Going for a ride with Father driving symbolized her *conflict with Father still in control.*
3. Junior using a map guides the car. He has an important position of *helping their lives go in the right direction.*
4. Driving alone is the attempt *to individuate.*
5. The ticket indicates that she *must pay her dues because leaving home places her in a vulnerable* position.
6. The judge stands for the *therapist, the authority figure,* who desires to have Ellen "learn her lesson." (In reality the author is also a professor, who had recently marched in a graduation exercise. The

patient, who had glanced at the author's desk, happened to notice the photo of the therapist in the black cap and gown, although Ellen claimed she did not realize the snapshot was of her clinician.)

7. The green "go" signal and the red stop light represented the *ambivalence towards maturing*.

8. The "yellow" light, which signifies "slow down to stop" or "get ready to go," is the color upon which Ellen is blocked. It portrays her *conflict towards individuation*.

9. The "A's" in art are indicative of *wanting to excel in art psychotherapy* treatment.

10. The police person (authority) with blond hair (like the author) is identified with the Cagney and Lacey, who are fictional police officers on television. Ellen tied this into *the author's appearance on T.V. a few weeks previously*.

11. Ellen feels supported to pass the test (*growing up*) *when she has the police person (therapist) near her*.

12. The stop and go signals indicate that Ellen could put a *stop to her acting out behavior and go ahead in her life*.

13. Ellen gets into a car, other than the family's. At first she believes she is in the wrong car (because it is unfamiliar); however, she realizes *she is taking control of her own life* when she identifies her notebook.

SESSION TWELVE/*Family Meeting: Father, Mother, Ellen, and Judy*

As the family had formed a therapeutic alliance with the author, it was important to help the Sullivans to acknowledge their emotions about Junior's absence.

At first, the therapist asked the family if they wanted to work on anything special. When they did not make any offers, the individual members were instructed to *use any media to portray your feelings about Junior not being at home*.

A *construction paper design* was cut out by *Father*. There was a *clean scissor-cut* edge on one side of it, exhibiting his positive intellectual feelings, and on the other side he tore a *ragged edge* to display it was painful to have someone so dear to him so far away.

Mother expressed her wish to be the next person to review the artwork because she wanted her husband to see they shared the same feelings. Using the picture of a *person crying*, Mrs. Sullivan declared she often felt sad because the house seemed so quiet without Junior there. She explained that her son "brought a lot of sound around the house with his laughter, trumpet, record playing, and his friends who came to the house." As Mrs. Sullivan listed her son's activities, one sensed the vitality that Junior contributed to the household. The rest of the family looked dejected as they thought about the missing member.

Compensatory images were presented by *Ellen*. Using plasticene she modeled symbols of shared activities: *midnight snacks, playing tennis, and listening to records*. The largest piece of art was the model of *a heart*. Ellen said what she missed most of all was Junior's warmth.

Judy, too, believed her brother was available to her; she stressed this through the drawing that depicted *the two of them* "talking about important things."

Although the author acknowledged what the girls missed about their brother, it was pointed out that they had not expressed their feelings about his absence. Therefore, Ellen and Judy were told to *create graphics which specifically illustrate what you feel about Junior's being gone*.

This time *Ellen* drew a big *zero*, clarifying that she often felt empty and depressed but tended to keep busy and not to mope. *Judy* illustrated an *empty room*, which revealed her sadness and the void she experienced.

The entire family was encouraged to continue to talk about how they felt, as well as their reactions to the visual statements of the others.

After their discussion the Sullivans were told to *relate through the art what you DO with your sad or lonely feelings*.

Father knew exactly what he wanted to make. He quickly drew some *Tylenol capsules* and a bottle of *Mylanta*. He notified his family that he was aware his psychosomatic ailments sometimes came from his feelings of loss and unexpressed emotions.

While agreeing with her father, Ellen also could not resist adding, "You also pick on me when you miss Junior. I've noticed that when you come out of his room you ask me why I'm not doing my homework or cleaning up my room." Mr. Sullivan was surprised by Ellen's observations and indicated he would try to be aware of this dynamic in the future.

Mother failed to create any art; instead, she printed out the word, SALE. She confessed "shopping for bargains" was her way of not paying attention to her feelings of loss. Judy interrupted to tell her Mom she was getting out of school earlier the coming fall. The clinician noted Judy's comments as a way of diverting dealing with Mother's feelings of loneliness. She was reminded that her mother would have to deal with her emotions and learn to cope with them as best as she could. This statement was meant to relieve Judy of the belief that she was responsible for filling up Mother's time.

Ellen, too, professed her need to escape from her feelings, only her means differed from her mother's. She chose to run out of the house, getting a date, driving fast, or occasionally drinking; she realized she had formerly thought about it more in terms of "boredom" or sometimes "anxiety." Never before had she fathomed the underlying or true reason for her actions as a way of ignoring the loneliness she experienced. Ellen declared that her family's willingness to confront and share the source of their emotions was helpful to her self-awareness.

Judy drew a *cassette* to demonstrate her use of music to fend off discomfort. The family continued to speak about the way they each resorted to their own defenses or coping mechanisms. The participants were astounded by their "heavy sharing experience" and appeared to be particularly kind and supportive of each other.

They left the session filled with thoughts about their self-examination and new understanding.

SESSION THIRTEEN/*Family Meeting: Father, Mother, Ellen, and Judy*

The family said they had talked about the last session a number of times during the week. To continue the exploration of the feelings around separation, abandonment, and loss, the Sullivans were told to *create an object that exhibits the part of the last meeting that is most memorable for you.*

An *open book* was drawn by *Mother* as a metaphor for Ellen's "opening up." Although in the past she suspected this daughter of acting-out behavior, she was never sure and often felt guilty about these thoughts. "But now," she claimed, "I'm somehow relieved. Now we can at least face the situation because Ellen has admitted it."

A *pair of glasses* was *Judy's* picture. She was impressed by Ellen's insight to her Father's distortion and displacement of his angry feelings onto others. Her Dad's actions were something that she was used to, yet had never understood. In the past Judy had always excused her father by believing his behavior was a part of an aging process.

The drawing of a *lightbulb* was *Ellen's* representation of the insight into her own behavior. She was especially pleased with herself for this newfound consciousness.

The cutout of a *lightning bolt* symbolized *Father's* surprise at discovering how he "got on everyone's back." He admitted that he had not faced his feelings so directly in the past. Mr. Sullivan reported that when the family had talked at home about the session, his wife and daughters remembered additional times when he picked on them without reason.

For instance, Mrs. Sullivan admitted she knew her husband would taunt her for "bargain hunting," even though she understood that was not what was bothering him. At times she thought it was her husband's only way of making contact with her, that is, through complaints of minor things. Judy also confided that Father would "bug" her without reason for being locked up in her room and listening to records of tragic songs.

The author used these examples to tell the family everyone used their own type of defenses to ward off the feelings of loss. Although these actions were attempts to fend off their uncomfortable emotions, they resulted in misunderstandings and anger among themselves. The therapist wondered aloud if the family members ever experienced any direct anger towards Junior for leaving.

Initially, the question appeared too overloading for the Sullivans to handle. Everyone said, "No, of course not." Each person made excuses about Junior's opportunity to go to a fine school, which offered him a scholarship. They certainly did not blame him for getting on with his life. Even though the clinician declared, "Feelings of anger are frequently accompanied with loss," excuses were still made. The therapist continued to be puzzled about the family's emotional restraint: "Is it bad to be angry with someone without any direct provocation on their part?" This question gave the family food for thought and permission to explore their underlying emotions.

Ellen had been doodling throughout the entire conversation. When the clinician asked her about the symbols on her paper, she said they held no significance since it was just a typical type of doodle. As the author pressed Ellen, she placed a big "X" over her scribble and said, "I suppose you think the 'X' means I don't want to examine my feelings?" After a brief pause Ellen stated, "I suppose you think I blame Junior for making our whole family change? Just because we got along together in the past and we're always bickering now doesn't mean it's Junior's fault! Besides, why should I be mad at him? He's a great brother."

Mother, concerned that Ellen's hostility was hurtful to the therapist, interrupted to explain that Junior and Ellen were always close to each other.

Mrs. Sullivan was questioned if she generally tended to pad confrontations. She was quick to confess that arguments made her uncomfortable and believed it was her "job" not to let anyone feel upset.

As the art psychotherapy session was coming to an end, the author suggested that all the family members might consider keeping an art therapy journal for themselves. They could graphically record feelings around daily events or interactions. They might also write down the meanings, in a manner similar to their family sessions.

The art therapy journal was mentioned with, Ellen in particular, in the therapist's mind, since it could serve as a transitional object and a sublimatory vehicle.

SESSION FOURTEEN/*Family Meeting: Mother, Father, Ellen, and Judy*

When the session began the family was extremely resistant to the art tasks. In one way or another Ellen and Judy made it clear they *only wanted to talk*. Rather than engage in a power struggle the therapist went along with the resistance.

The Sullivans spent most of the session "reporting." The meaning behind the conversation was unclear to the author. It seemed possible that the family taking control of the meeting was a way of accepting greater responsibility for their therapy. Or perhaps they were moving towards termination and beginning to be more autonomous, or maybe disengagement was taking place because they resented their dependency upon the clinician.

Just as the family was leaving the office, Mr. Sullivan and his daughters mentioned they had all begun their art therapy journals. They wanted to know if they should be brought into the family meetings or what was the next procedure? Instead of offering instructions, the clinician told the Sullivans that decision would be up to them. Finding the reply unsatisfactory, the family acted disgruntled as they left the art therapy office.

SESSIONS FIFTEEN AND SIXTEEN/*Family Meetings: Father, Mother, Ellen, and Judy*

In the next two sessions the family continued to resist the art tasks; instead, they utilized the mechanism of "reporting" as a defense. They talked about relationship improvements and a positive change in Ellen's attitude. However, what they avoided was dealing with any covert issues. The clinician wondered if she had explored the issue of separation too soon. Perhaps the family was experiencing the mourning process together and blocked the therapist from dealing with their emotions because of overload. Or, it was possible the family had reached a plateau. The previous family dynamics while creating the art products showed Father to be considerate of others. He had loosened his authority position because he was less threatened by the thought of his leadership being usurped. Although the participants caught on to the way they could cooperate during the art task process, integrating this type of interaction into their daily lives required continued awareness and practice.

Rather than allowing the Sullivans to report their arguments, the therapist instructed the family to *portray dissatisfied home scenes through the art during* their treatment hour. The tasks at this time were *limited to the ways in which the family entangled themselves negatively*.

These uneventful sessions are purposely being mentioned since eliminating these facts would give the reader a distorted view of the treatment process. The author did wonder about those meetings and sought to examine past actions. After careful thought, it became apparent that there are times when it is productive for new material *not to arise.* During such periods the participants use the time to examine the processes that have been experienced thus far. This factor is essential in family work, when roles are in a state of transition.

In reviewing the Sullivan case, the therapist realized this family had accomplished a good deal in a relatively short time: the designated patient's behavior had improved; Father was committing himself to change; and the family system was in a restructuring process. The author's own desire to press forward was self-serving and unrealistic. It was therefore necessary to let the family work at a pace that was appropriate for them.

SESSION SEVENTEEN/*Family Meeting:*
Father, Mother, Ellen, and Judy

The two girls notified the therapist they would not attend the next session since they were going to visit Junior. Ellen was also planning to look over the campuses of several eastern universities. Due to these circumstances, Mr. and Mrs. Sullivan asked if they could have a conjoint meeting for themselves. When their daughters were asked what they thought about this request, they encouraged their parents to take advantage of "having Mrs. Landgarten to yourselves."

In order to reestablish their current reasons for being in treatment, the Sullivans were directed to *portray your goals for therapy.*

Father was meticulous in his performance, and one could see his pleasure when he viewed the results. He made a *construction paper building.* Mr. Sullivan explained his art as being representative of himself. He wished to continue his work on self-containment and wanted to be like his structure: *standing alone without leaning on anyone.* He explained he was trying to take responsibility for his own feelings and actions. Mr. Sullivan believed his goals already had a pay-off, since he was working on not blaming others when he himself was frustrated or angry. He was adamant that his goals did not include giving up his perfectionism, despite his family's complaints about this facet of his personality. Mr. Sullivan said he liked doing things neatly and well because it gave him satisfaction.

The therapist recalled Mr. Sullivan's collage of the past when he held a protective line over his family and his former present collage, which depicted his desire to work on his relationship with Ellen. Now, the clinician pointed out, he had moved on to a focus of self-change. This time it was not in relationship to his family, or to Ellen in particular, but to a current commitment to himself.

Mother's therapy goal concerned new involvements. Mrs. Sullivan realized her life had always revolved around her family. She drew *herself working, taking extension courses,* and *learning to play golf.* The last activity was something she could share with her husband. She realized it would not be long before her "nest would be emptied."

Everyone was surprised by *Judy's* "goal" sculpture. She had modeled a *hammer*, which stood for her *wish to stand up for herself.* The family, in amazement, sought to question Judy about her motivation. All agreed she was the easygoing member of the family. They divulged their astonishment at her feeling submerged in the family system. The author thought the hammer symbol contained elements of aggression and rage. Judy was asked if it made her angry to live in a household where she withheld her thoughts and feelings. Instead of responding to the question, Judy reiterated her desire to be more assertive. The therapist brought out Judy's *present collages* and asked her if the photo of a person "calling for help" on the telephone had actually been out of her own personal need. Denying the thought, Judy claimed the "help" picture was directed towards her father and her sister. Nevertheless, with the family treatment she came to realize her role of the *peacemaker* was not to her liking!

For the treatment goal, *Ellen* had drawn an *arrow* which was positioned upwards. The graphic was in concert with her *present collage* of the feet moving forward. Ellen was consistent in her wish to get on with a new life.

For the next directive, the participants were told to *create an object that portrays how you will be affected if the other members reach their treatment goals.*

A *glad face* was drawn by *Mother*, who claimed nothing would make her happier than having her family reach the goals they desired.

A *link chain* molded from plasticene was made by *Father*. He believed that if Ellen "went forward," he would be better able to focus on himself without the usual diversions. In relation to Judy's self-assertion, he formed a *question mark*. Mr. Sullivan admitted he was not sure how he would feel if Judy became a demanding, self-involved person. He created a *zero* for his wife since he believed her changes would not affect him in any way.

A *heart* cut out by *Judy* was an expression of her pleasure should the family make the changes, while the plasticene *smiling face* was *Ellen's* way of proclaiming her delight if everyone chose to improve themselves.

The family became engaged in a lively discussion about it being easier to talk about "change" than to actually make it. However, the tenor of the session was positive. Somehow, the idea of making alterations gave the family a hopeful outlook.

The closure directive requested the participants to *create a construction paper sculpture together*. Father wondered if it would be best if each person would make their own object; then, in the end, they could put all the artwork together to formulate a single product. When Mrs. Sullivan challenged the idea of individual artwork, her husband defended it by explaining that if everyone functioned autonomously he could take his time and not annoy anyone else. He was convinced it would be advantageous to all concerned. The women could see Mr. Sullivan's point and agreed to follow his suggestions.

Ellen was the first person to share her *abstract* cutout, placing it right in the middle of the table.

Judy followed by putting her construction paper *box* next to her sister's.

When it was Father's turn, he waved *Mother* on, making it clear he was determined not to be overbearing. Mrs. Sullivan set her paper *tree* next to Judy's box.

Making sure he had the last turn, *Father* set his *robot* piece on the edge of the table, declaring he had purposely given his women "free rein" of the available space.

The therapist told the family *you may move your art if you wish. If you do decide to change your placement, state your reason.*

In short order, Judy ventured forth to declare her desire to share the central place with Ellen. However, she could not do this unless her sister moved her abstract cutout. Ellen smiled as she willingly made room for her sister. From Judy's expression it was difficult to understand what she was feeling.

Mother claimed she was satisfied with her tree's position, while Father good-naturedly declared he did not wish to move because he had purposely stayed to the side to symbolize his new style of functioning (Figure 107).

The family discussed the project until the meeting came to an end.

SESSION EIGHTEEN/*Conjoint Meeting: Mr. and Mrs. Sullivan*

When Mr. and Mrs. Sullivan came into the office for their conjoint meeting, they announced their intent to dispense with the art tasks during the session. The author agreed and asked the couple what they had on their minds. Basically, they wished to talk about future financial difficulties when they would be supporting two children in college. Al-

Figure 107. Family project

though the Sullivans wanted to have definitive answers about the way to handle Ellen's money matters, the therapist interpreted their questions as a way of presenting their insecure feelings around Ellen's departure.

The author had regrets about her agreement to dispense with the art therapy modality, since it would have cut through the couple's rationalizing defenses. Their conversation served to layer over their separation anxiety and left no space for it to be worked upon.

Nevertheless, when Mr. and Mrs. Sullivan left the office, they appeared satisfied with the opportunity to have the clinician's undivided attention. The therapist suspected they wished to have her support in case they might need her for themselves when Ellen left home.

SESSION NINETEEN/*Family Meeting: Father, Mother, Ellen, and Judy*

When the girls were asked about their trip, they gave glowing reports of Junior and the exciting college atmosphere. Ellen was exhilarated and enthusiastic about her forthcoming school adventure. Regardless, the parents' ambivalence was evident to the therapist. To help them explore their conflicting emotions, everyone was told to *draw the good and bad parts about Ellen going away to school.*

Judy was the first person to display the "good part" of Ellen's departure through the drawing of *herself taking over the larger bedroom,* which currently belonged to her sister. For the "bad" part she created a picture of *herself feeling sad and lonely.*

On the other hand, *Ellen* showed *herself happy at school*, while the "negative side" revealed fear and guilt feelings about leaving home. These feelings were exhibited through an *empty closet* as she stated, "It is frightening to remove my belongings. In a way I feel like I'm deserting my family."

Mother drew *Ellen with a smiling face*, claiming she was certain her daughter would do well in college, while a *sad face with tears* depicted her lonesome feelings.

A single picture was created by *Father*. He portrayed Ellen and himself arguing with each other. The "good" aspect of Ellen's leaving was that she would not be around to argue with him. Yet the "negative part" was the other side of the coin, since she would not be around for "a good disagreement." Mr. Sullivan added that their recent discussions had been "normal," without a vengeful flavor.

The content of the artwork served as a catalyst for further scrutiny. It became clear that everyone had mixed emotions. The Sullivans realized that it was safe to talk about what was underneath their surface and that they could accept these covert feelings more easily.

It was Ellen who declared, "At least we can talk about my leaving. We couldn't or didn't know how when Junior left for college." That remark gave Judy an opening to say it was going to be hard on her when Ellen left. She really hated being left behind by her sister and her brother, speculating about the difficulty of being the only child left at home.

Mr. and Mrs. Sullivan had no idea their youngest daughter had been feeling upset. They claimed she had not given them any such hints. Although concerned, the parents' statements only served to show their lack of sensitivity towards Judy when they failed to follow up with any encouragement to express herself further. For this reason, the next art task required *each person to create a symbol of what you would like from your family right now.*

Judy used the plasticene to make a *form with a moveable little door.* She said she would like the family not to worry or to be embarrassed if she opened up. She hoped to be able to share *what went on inside* of herself more often (Figure 108).

Ellen, who appreciated the session, created a *mouth,* this time claiming she liked everyone's input and wanted them to "keep talking" (Figure 109).

A *liberty bell* was drawn by *Father,* who depicted his desire for everyone to be "free to speak their mind" (Figure 110).

However, *Mother,* unlike the others, referred to emotional desires. She

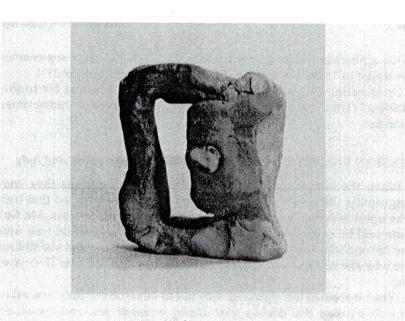

Figure 108. Wishes to open up

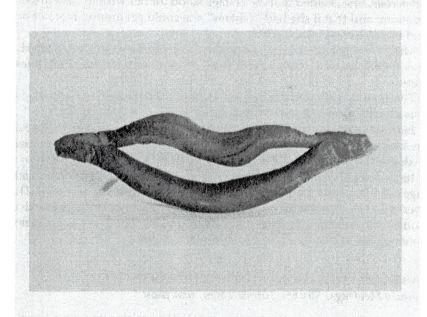

Figure 109. Keep talking

made a plasticene *blanket*, which she placed on a *toy bed*; it represented her desire to "receive warm feelings" from her family (Figure 111).

Once again, the participants' art became the touchstone for further dialogue. Their meaningful conversation encouraged a caring interchange.

SESSION TWENTY/*Family Meeting: Father, Mother, Ellen, and Judy*

When the family walked into the office, it was obvious they were disgruntled. Before they seated themselves, Father explained that Judy was upset because she wanted to take private driving lessons. Mr. Sullivan said he could save several hundred dollars if she would wait until the fall and take the course in school. But Judy insisted that she did not see why she had to wait since her sister drove when she was 15½ years old.

When it seemed the argument was not to be resolved, Judy was asked to *make a collage that exhibits what driving means to you*, and the others could *select images that portrayed alternatives to the driving situation*.

Judy decided to use the photo of a *bird* and *superimposed* it *onto an automobile*. She claimed that the collage stood for her wish to have greater freedom, and that if she had "wheels" she could get around more easily and widen her social activities.

Mother, who had cut out magazine advertisements of *food*, said she was willing to save money from her household budget for Judy's lessons.

The family was disappointed by *Father's blank* page. He declared he was unable to see any alternatives.

Ellen was the last person to share her collage. It contained a picture of an *adolescent next to a car*. Underneath she wrote, "I will teach Judy how to drive."

Judy was pleased with her sister's offer. After talking over the advantages of Ellen teaching Judy, the family agreed to the arrangement. The therapist wondered why this simple solution had not been resolved at home. Nevertheless, families often lean on the therapist for problem-solving, just as they begin to deal with termination.

SESSIONS TWENTY-ONE THROUGH TWENTY-FIVE/
Family Meetings: Mother, Father, Ellen, and Judy

For several sessions the family cooperated in creating various art tasks. For the most part their topics were self-selected. In general, they tended to be testimonials of satisfaction.

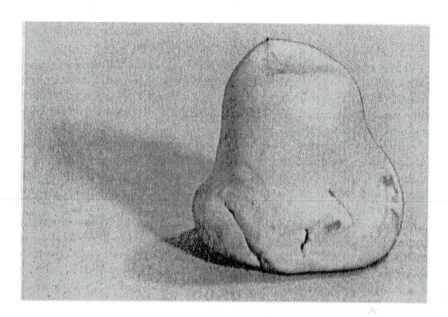

Figure 110. Free to speak

Figure 111. Receive warmth

Ellen's grades had improved and she was motivated to get into the college of her choice. Her psychosomatic complaints had decreased and were limited to premenstrual times. Mr. Sullivan also reported less tension pains in his head and chest and seemed determined to get more pleasure out of his life.

Although still reticent, Judy did assert herself more than in the past, while Mother remained essentially the same.

The interaction among the family members had improved a great deal. Even though Mr. Sullivan and Ellen continued to quibble, neither one used their arguments as a punitive function.

It was during this final phase of treatment that the family started coming late to their appointments. Their excuses were honest on a conscious level, yet the author believed they were unconsciously preparing themselves to end treatment. Since all the short-term goals had been reached, stopping family treatment was appropriate. In the future, if Judy or the parents desired treatment, the author planned to offer the "open door policy."

During one of the sessions, which is reported herein, Judy entered the office in a particularly positive mood. She was quick to report her delight in the driving lessons. Mother was pleased, mentioning her own benefits since Judy was happy to drive to the market, the cleaners, and so forth. She admitted that Judy's willingness to take over some of these chores made her life easier.

After these remarks the family became engaged in a lengthy conversation about Judy's driving. The author wondered what was going on. In order to understand what was behind their discussion, the clinician asked the participants what they wanted to work on. The family could not think of any special issues. They insisted they had "no complaints." Instead, they spoke about their mutual satisfactions.

To get the Sullivans involved in the session, the therapist decided to try a new approach, by telling the family an *experiment* would take place. A volunteer was requested to *act as the art psychotherapist*. Sensing a challenge, the family became excited about the unusual opportunity. They engaged themselves in a decision-making process of examining the pros and cons of each member taking over the clinician's position.

Father wanted to eliminate himself; he reasoned the role was too close to his established authority position. When the girls asked Mother to take over, she flatly refused. With the possibility dwindling down to Ellen and Judy, the two girls conferred with each other. Ellen, wishing to encourage her sister to stand up for herself, withdrew thus leaving Judy to play the part of the therapist.

The venture was taken very seriously by Judy as she asked the therapist to trade seats with her. In actuality the author had *not considered a complete role reversal*; the intent was to be an *observer*. Nevertheless, the author thought Judy's idea might prove to be profitable and obeyed the request to switch places. Judy's instructions stated, *the family is to make a collage together. Each person selects one picture. Then everyone will line up your choices and a storyline will be added.* The plan appealed to the group, and the task of searching for photographs began.

With enthusiasm, *Ellen* picked out a picture that contained a number of automobile *license plates* from various states. Whereas the image of a *young couple with their three children* (a boy and two girls) was chosen by *Mother*, *Father* selected a *hand holding up a dollar sign*. The therapist, as Judy, cut out the ad of a *cyclist riding away*. The storyline was made up by each person in the following order. It read as follows:

> The *license plates* (Ellen's) means "it's good for people to get out and see the world." The *young family* picture (Mother's) relates, "When the family is young, they do everything together. However, when they grow up, the children should go out and enjoy themselves with their own friends." The *hand holding the dollar sign* (Father's) is a reminder that "all of these enjoyments cost money, but the father tries his best to provide for his family." The picture of the *cyclist* (Landgarten's) tells us, "In the long run everyone is on his own. As one situation terminates, another begins" (Figure 112).

Judy, as therapist, responded by saying, "That was very good. You all cooperated very nicely and the picture tells me that you, Ellen, are looking forward to leaving home. You, Mrs. Sullivan, help your girls to grow up. You, Mr. Sullivan, are worried about not making enough money to make your children happy. And, you, Judy (played by Landgarten), want to get away and grow up."

Judy, as Mrs. Landgarten, continued on to say, "Well, tell me what *you* think about your collages." Rather than respond to the collages, Mr. and Mrs. Sullivan and Ellen told Judy how impressed they were with the way she handled being the therapist.

For Judy the experience was very positive; she had a chance to take over, exhibit her skills, be the focus of attention and gain positive reinforcement for a job well done. With Judy's turn completed, the author wished to bring up the issue of *termination*. Fingering the photo of the cyclist, the therapist noted that the rider had the word "challenge" printed on his back, and she connected it to the way the Sullivan family had met their own challenge of treatment. Since the statement did not act as a catalyst for the family to deal with termination, the author pursued the

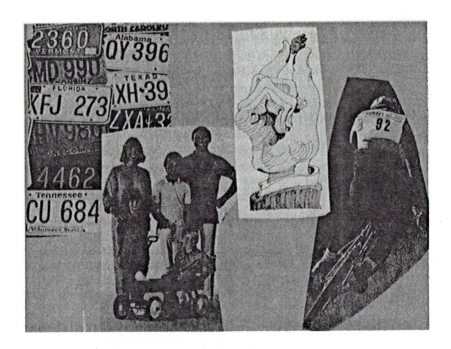

Figure 112. Family storyline

subject by asking the Sullivans, "Does anyone else wish to play the therapist, while dealing with the subject of termination?" Immediately, Ellen volunteered. She took over the session, telling the group *to show how you feel about the idea of not coming here anymore.*

A *moon* and a *sun*, which were sculptured by *Father*, stood for his mixed feelings. The "moon," he said jokingly, meant he would "moon for Mrs. Landgarten's role as the family negotiator." The "sun" stood for his happiness that the family would be "getting on" with their lives (Figure 113). As therapist, Ellen replied, "I can understand your feelings, Mr. Sullivan."

Pipecleaners were used by *Mrs. Sullivan* to form a *sad face*. She voiced her allegiance to the therapist, stating she would miss the office visits (Figure 114). Ellen, playing the clinician, replied, "Yes, I know you found some comfort in coming here but I know your family will be just fine even when you don't come here anymore."

A painting of *eyes* was created by *Judy*. It represented her appreciation to the therapist for providing her with a place to express herself. She emphasized the insight that the art had provided, as well as an outlet for

Figure 113. Ambivalence

Figure 114. A loss

her feelings (Figure 115). Judy professed feeling badly about the thought of termination. As though by chance, she turned to the author to inform her she had kept on with the art psychotherapy journal ever since the suggestion had been made.

Again, Ellen, in the Landgarten role, responded to Judy by stating, "Well, let's see, maybe you could continue to come here. It would be a good idea for a teenager to have a place to express herself."

The exchange between Judy and the surrogate therapist had an impact on Mr. and Mrs. Sullivan and their younger daughter. It was obvious this suggestion was being considered.

Landgarten, acting as Ellen, molded a *large car with a tear superimposed upon it.* The tear represented sadness and regret over discontinuing her meetings with the therapist. However, since the termination was due to going away to college, she also felt happy.

Ellen, as therapist, remarked "Well, Ellen, I'm going to miss you too!" Evidently, Ellen, herself, wished to receive such assurance when termination came about.

Before the family left the office, they asked if Mr. and Mrs. Sullivan could have a turn to be the therapist the following week. The author assured them each parent would have the opportunity to run the therapy session if they so wished.

Figure 115. Gained insight

The clinician decided the role reversal had been a good technique for this particular family during their last phase of treatment. While Judy and Ellen were pleased with the chance to act as the authority, they were also able to disclose what they wanted from the therapist during termination. The author knew Judy's *art therapy journal* was an important event, as it served a therapeutic purpose. In the next session, the author planned to arrange an individual meeting to review its contents.

SESSION TWENTY-SIX/*Family Meeting: Mother, Father, Ellen, and Judy*

Mr. Sullivan was holding a manilla envelope under his arm as he entered the office. As soon as everyone was seated, he expressed his wish to *play the part of the therapist*. Granted full rein, he switched seats with the clinician.

When Mr. Sullivan began acting as the therapist, he asked the family how they were. After a brief conversation, he opened up his manilla envelope and set out magazine photos which he had brought from home and had cut out most carefully! Without hesitation he informed the group to *pick out pictures that show what you believe you or your family got out of coming here to therapy*. (The author was impressed with the directive and the way Mr. Sullivan decided to deal with the issue of termination.)

Mother used several pictures to enumerate a number of gains. One exhibited *a man behind a desk nervously biting on his paper work*. Mrs. Sullivan said her husband used to be like the person in the photo but had become less aggravated and frustrated in the last few months. The other picture of a *happy older woman* portrayed her own good feelings about the improved relationship between her husband and Ellen.

As therapist, Father told Mrs. Sullivan that it was nice that she had received "this bonus from the family therapy."

An unusual photo of a *man's hands popping out of a computer* was selected by *Judy*. Each hand held a number of objects. She believed this picture symbolized her father's former self, whereas, in contrast, a second picture contained only a *single hand with a statement on it*, "One thing at a time." Judy claimed this picture depicted her father's "efforts to stop overloading himself," adding, "and the rest of us too!"

Judy had yet another image of an *adolescent girl next to a man talking on the phone*. It stood for Father communicating more grown-up messages to her. She said, "Dad seems to be paying more attention to the fact that I'm not such a little girl anymore."

Acting as the clinician, father responded, "So it seems your father is changing, not only for himself but he is coming to grips with your growing up." It was obvious Mr. Sullivan felt very good to receive validation from his daughter about his gains.

A poignant picture of a *small child* giving up *her crutches* was used by *Ellen*. She claimed it meant she had wasn't going to cripple herself and was getting down to the business of going to college. Another picture of *a belligerent kid* depicted how she used to feel much of the time. Ellen confessed she really wanted the picture that Judy used—the one of an adolescent and a man holding a phone. She believed it could have expressed the improved communication between Father and herself. Ellen's last picture of a *happy person* displayed her more positive attitude.

Mr. Sullivan, as Mrs. Landgarten, told Ellen it was gratifying to see so many benefits from therapy. He reminded the family that Ellen had been the designated patient, yet it was the entire family who had benefited from treatment. He then picked up Landgarten's (as Father) collage, which contained several magazine photos. The first was a *man's face behind a broken window*. Mr. Sullivan, when he was home, had originally cut out this picture from a magazine, leaving in the words "shattering old ideas about safety." *As Mr. Sullivan*, the author stressed the meaning behind those words, stating, "I try to let go of old ideas and actions." The second image of a *pleasant-looking man* stood for "feeling better in general and very good about the way I'm trying to change." The third picture, "*happy people*," symbolized the girls' general attitudes. In addition, the author could not resist the urge to pick out a picture from Mr. Sullivan's collage box of *dollar bills with Donald Duck's portrait* on them. The clinician, as Mr. Sullivan, stated the meaning, "I've gotten my money's worth out of this art therapy treatment, because I didn't *duck* working on myself" (Figure 116).

Everyone laughed at the comic truth. But Mr. Sullivan was serious when he brought the attention back to the artwork. He seemed overcome by the picture of the man behind the pane of shattered glass. The powerful image was threatening (Figure 117). Perhaps he related it to his unexpressed rage. It seemed he had forgotten that *it was he who had selected and cut out all of the images* that were used in this session. Therefore, it was necessary for the author to reassure Mr. Sullivan the picture was used as a symbol of his *positive change*.

Since there was not sufficient time for Mother to play the therapist role, she was notified that next week would be her turn.

Before the Sullivan family left the art therapy office, the clinician interpreted the act of Mr. Sullivan bringing in his own collage material as a possible indication that he was getting ready to take *complete control*, especially in light of termination. Although Father had not given this idea any conscious thought, he admitted it was probably true.

Figure 116. Did not duck therapy

Figure 117. Threatening image

SESSION TWENTY-SEVEN/*Family Meeting:*
Mother, Father, Ellen, and Judy

Before the Sullivan family had a chance to seat themselves, Ellen excit-edly reported that her parents had agreed to let her go on a student tour to England. Since there was only one date available, she had to leave in only two weeks, which would shorten the family's treatment. In addi-tion, Ellen mentioned graduation was also at that time and she had a "great date" for the prom. She admitted her life was very "full" and gave the therapist credit for "letting good things happen." When the clinician reflected upon the client's self-help, Ellen still clung to the importance of the therapist's role. As the parents watched this interchange, their pride was evident because of the warmth and gratitude Ellen was extending.

Mrs. Sullivan was asked if she was ready to take her turn to be the clinician. "I'm as ready as I'll ever be," she replied. When the session was turned over to her, it was apparent Mrs. Sullivan had prepared her directive in advance. She took the liberty of removing a carton from the supply shelf, placed it on the table, and instructed the family to *make something out of the carton and explain the meaning of your art as you go along.*

Ellen suggested covering the box with construction paper because it would give the project a sense of unity. Judy thought an abstract design that went all around the carton would be interesting. Although Father was doubtful, he went along with this idea. However, he believed it would simplify matters if each person drew on their own piece of con-struction paper first, then pasted it onto the carton. Mother, as Mrs. Landgarten, reminded the group, they must *put some meaning into the design.*

The first person to finish the art was *Judy.* She glued her part onto the box, explaining that the *multicolored lines* meant things were more peace-ful at home.

Ellen was the next person to paste down her graphics of a *sun* in the corner, with its extending rays. She declared it represented her being happy about graduation, the trip, and school.

A bouquet of flowers was made by *Mrs. Landgarten, acting as Mother.* She stated it symbolized the girls and how proud she was of them.

The last person to finish was *Father.* He explained his artwork did not hold any special meaning. He just made an *abstract design* to fulfill his part of the group project (Figure 118). The therapist, played by Mother, assured him it was not always necessary to produce something that contained a "message."

The family, as well as Mrs. Landgarten shared their enjoyment about the manner in which Mrs. Sullivan had functioned as the therapist.

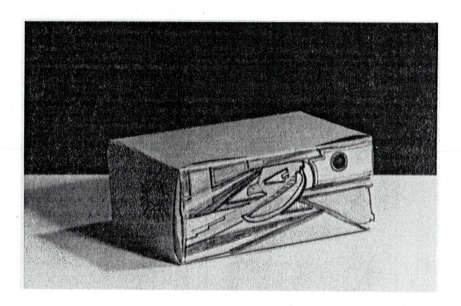

Figure 118. Father's group art

Feeling encouraged, she decided to continue on with the role as she offered a second directive. However, this time Mrs. Sullivan asked if she could give the instructions, then immediately afterwards she wanted to get out of the role-playing situation. In other words, she would state the art task, then return to being herself in time to *follow her own directive.*

When the clinician agreed to this arrangement, Mrs. Sullivan gave the following instructions: "*I want all of you to make something for Mrs. Landgarten* since we're going to stop coming here next week."

The clinician smiled to herself as she realized Mother did a fine job as therapist when she led the family into dealing with the termination.

Flowers made out of construction paper were shown first by *Mother.* Their message was "a wish for Helen to have a good life" (Figure 119).

A *box of candy* was *Judy's* good-bye present.

Ellen's sculpture was difficult to understand without an explanation. She had formed *four blue plasticene squares. In the center of each was a small red circle.* When Ellen was asked its meaning, she related that the squares represented her family and the circles the therapist, symbolizing the parts of the therapy they would retain (Figure 120).

The last gift was a *box of jewelry.* It was created by Mr. Sullivan who

Figure 119. Mother's farewell gift

acknowledged his "gems of appreciation to a gem of a person." The women were delighted with Mr. Sullivan's open compliment to the clinician. Although in the past he had shown his respect for her in many ways, this forthright approach was both amazing and pleasing to his wife and daughters.

The author accepted the Sullivan family's gifts, thanking them with sincerity. Everyone present experienced both warmth and sadness; growth was gratifying, yet separation was still painful.

The family was told that next week, during their termination session, they would have a chance to look over all of the artwork. It would be a way of reviewing their treatment and their gains.

Figure 120. Ellen's farewell gift

SESSION TWENTY-EIGHT/
Final Family Meeting: Mother, Father, Ellen, and Judy

The family came into the office for this double session, looking forward to seeing their portfolio. The therapist had prepared a table easel to prop up the flat artwork. The three-dimensional objects were arranged on shelves. The objects were reviewed according to the dates of their creation.

The meaning behind certain pieces of art still held poignant messages to the Sullivans. Some products brought out chuckles, or smiles or glances of affection, while others still elicited feelings of sadness.

Although the family realized that not all of their goals had been met, they agreed their accomplishments gave them pleasure and a sense of pride.

SUMMARY

Ellen, the 17-year-old adolescent of an intact family, suddenly began to exhibit acting-out behavior. This was manifested in her negative attitude at home, a drop in academic grades, and breaking traffic laws.

Therapy was obtained due to a court order. During the evaluation and treatment phase, family art psychotherapy proved to be effective for the designated patient as well as the other family members.

The art tasks provided evidence of a faulty family system. The father was confronted with his overly controlling behavior. Both he and his older daughter, Ellen, engaged one another with animosity. Their conflict was related to the adolescent's struggle for individuation and Father's fear of loosening the enmeshed relationship.

An insight orientation educated the family to their overt and covert messages and actions. As Mr. Sullivan began to change, he allowed his daughter to function with greater autonomy, causing a shift in the family's roles and system.

Judy, the younger adolescent, realizing her unsatisfactory passivity, began to assert herself and focus upon greater independence.

Although Mother's role remained static, she was aware of this fact, yet resisted deviating from this pattern.

Separation and the emotions it evoked were a major part of the family treatment.

REFERENCE

Haley, J. *Uncommon Therapy*. New York: Norton, 1973.

RECOMMENDED READING

Bandura, A., & Walter, R. H. *Adolescent Aggression: A Study of the Influence of Child Training Practices and Family Interrelationships*. New York: Ronald, 1959.

Blood, R. O., & Wolfe, D. M. *Husbands and Wives: The Dynamics of Married Living*. New York: Free Press of Glencoe, 1960.

Bloom, M. V. *Adolescent Parental Separation*. New York: Gardener Press, 1980.

Blos, P. *On Adolescence*. New York: The Free Press, 1962.

Blos, P. *The Young Adolescent*. New York: The Free Press, 1970.

Brown, S. L. Family therapy for adolescents. *Psychiatric Opinion*, 7(1), 8–15, 1970.

Dragastin, S., & Elder, G. H. *Adolescence in the Life Cycle*. New York: Halstead Press,

Esman, A. H. (Ed.). *The Psychiatric Treatment of Adolescents*. New York: International Universities Press, 1983.

Ginott, H. G. *Between Parent and Teenager*. New York: Macmillan, 1969.

Glaser, K. Masked depression in children and adolescents. *American Journal of Psychotherapy*, 21, 563–74, 1976.

Glasser, P. N., & Glasser, L. Role reversal and conflict between aged parents and their children. *Marriage and Family Living*, 24, 46–51, 1962.

Hadley, T. R., Jacob, T., Milliones, J., Caplan, J., & Spitz, D. The relationship between family development crisis and the appearance of symptoms in a family member. *Family Process, 13*(2), 207–214, 1974.

Harkins, E. G. Effects of empty nest transition on self—Report of psychological and physical well-being. *Journal of Marriage and the Family, 40,* 549–556, 1978.

Hess, B. B., & Waring, J. M. Changing patterns of aging and family bonds in later life. *Family Coordinator, 27,* 303–314, 1978.

Howells, J. G. (Ed.). *Modern Perspectives in Adolescent Psychiatry.* New York: Brunner/Mazel, 1971.

Impey, L. Art media: A means to therapeutic communication with families. *Perspectives in Psychiatric Care, XIX*(2), 70–77, 1981.

Ishikawa, G. Some therapeutic effects of family drawings: With special reference to the adolescent patients. *Psychiatria et Neurologia Japonica, 84*(9), 681–705, 1982.

Kaplan, L. J. *Adolescence: The Farewell to Childhood.* New York: Simon & Schuster, 1984.

Kidwell, J., Fischer, J. L., Dunham, R. M., & Baranowski, M. Parents and adolescents: Push and pull of change. In H. I. McCubbin & C. R. Figley (Eds.), *Stress and the Family: Coping with Normative Transitions.* New York: Brunner/Mazel, 1983, pp. 74–90.

Leader, A. L. Intergenerational separation anxiety in family therapy. In J. G. Howells (Ed.), *Advances in Family Psychiatry, II.* New York: International Universities Press, 2, 1980.

Lowenthal, M. F., & Chiribuga, D. Transition to empty nest: Crisis, challenge, or relief? *Archives of General Psychiatry, 26,* 8–14, 1972.

McArthur, A. Developmental tasks and parent-adolescent conflict. *Marriage and Family Living, 24*(May), 189–191, 1962.

McPherson, S. R., Brackelmanns, W. E., & Newman, L. E. Stages in family therapy of adolescents. *Family Process, 13*(1), 77–95, March 1974.

Malmquist, C. P. *Handbook of Adolescence.* New York: Jason Aronson, 1985.

Marmor, J. *The Crisis of Middle Age.* Annual Meeting of the American Orthopsychiatric, Washington, D.C., March 1967.

Meeks, J. *The Fragile Alliance.* Baltimore: Williams & Wilkins, 1971.

Meissner, W. W. Family process and psychosomatic disease. In J. G. Howells (Ed.), *Advances in Family Psychiatry, I.* New York: International Universities Press, 1979.

Miller, D. *The Age Between: Adolescence and Therapy.* New York: Jason Aronson, 1983.

Ravenscroft, K. Normal family regression at adolescence. *American Journal of Psychiatry, 131*(3), 31–35, 1974.

Schildkrout, M. S., Shenker, I. R., & Sonnenblick, M. *Human Figure Drawings in Adolescence.* New York: Brunner Mazel, 1972.

Stierlin, H. *Separating Parents and Adolescents.* New York: Quadrangle, 1974.

Stierlin, H. Countertransference in family therapy with adolescents. In M. Sugar (Ed.), *The Adolescent in Group and Family Therapy.* New York: Brunner/Mazel, 1975, pp. 161–178.

Stierlin, H. Family therapy with adolescents and the process of intergenerational reconciliation. In M. Sugar (Ed.), *The Adolescent in Group and Family Therapy.* New York: Brunner/Mazel, 1975, pp. 194–205.

Stierlin, H., & Ravenscroft, K. J. Varieties of adolescent separation conflicts. *British Journal of Medical Psychology, 45,* 299–313, 1972.

Wadeson, H. S. Art techniques used in conjoint marital therapy. *American Journal of Art Therapy, 12,* 147–164, 1973.

Williams, F. S. Family therapy: Its role in adolescent psychiatry. In S. C. Feinstein & P. G. Giovacchini (Eds.), *Adolescent Psychiatry, Development and Clinical Studies, 2.* New York: Basic Books, 1973.

Winnicott, D. W. Transitional objects and transitional phenomena. *Collected Papers.* New York: Basic Books, 1961.

Wood, B., & Talmon, M. Family boundaries in transition: A search for alternatives. *Family Process, 22,* 347–357, 1983.

CHAPTER 8

Three-Generation Treatment for a Terminally Ill Grandparent

INTRODUCTION

In recent years professionals in the mental health, medical, and religious fields have been treating the dying patient with greater sensitivity and frankness than in the past.

Therapists who work with the terminally ill have the responsibility of assisting these clients to express their feelings and to make their thoughts known. It is important for them to talk about the impending death, to bid farewells, and to discuss the disposition of their possessions if they so desire. At the same time the rest of the family is helped to listen to the expiring relative with openness and support. The family unit that establishes a collaborative communication system works towards easing the psychological pain in the dying person and the rest of the members during the process of separation, premourning, and grieving.

Psychotherapy with families during this crisis time is complicated due to the different ways in which the individuals handle the situation. While some relatives choose to deal with reality, others prefer to utilize their defense of denial as a coping mechanism and function under the illusion of false hope. These two polarized stances often set up a conflict and put additional stress on all concerned. Therefore, it is essential for the family to accept and deal with the fact that the life of the terminally ill individual is soon coming to an end.

The therapist facilitates the dying patient in setting the tempo for communication where final statements are made and responses encouraged. Far too often, caring family members collude to prevent the patient from reaching out to deliver his or her good-byes. These well-meaning people believe they are being protective by offering the patient a façade of pretense. One of the fantasies, is the fear of prematurely destroying the life of the terminally ill person, by dealing directly with his or her inevitable demise. Unfortunately, this screened approach only serves to strip away the dignity that rightfully belongs to every human being before death occurs.

A multigenerational treatment approach includes all the family members. Even though the experience is a shared one, each generation is dealing with material indigenous to its own stage of development. For the spouse, the thought of losing a husband or wife is not only painful but also threatening. For the "sandwiched generation," the comfort of being a child as well as a parent must soon be abandoned. It also means this middle generation steps up in line towards its own end. At the same time, the third generation is faced with the starkness of death, which brings into focus the issue of mortality. For these reasons, it is a therapeutic advantage for the entire family to be seen together. It affords them the opportunity to face the loss and gives them the chance to know each other on an intimate level.

Support between the dying and the bereaved can be a most gratifying life experience, for a heightened family closeness brings long-remembered solace to those who are left behind.

CASE ILLUSTRATION

The case history presented herein concerns multigenerational family treatment. The focus is on dealing with the grandmother's terminal illness. The entire family attended the seven, intermittent sessions, which were held over a period of four months.

PRECIPITATING EVENT

Originally Mrs. Hinde Belmont sought crisis treatment for herself. She focused on her mother's terminal cancer and imminent demise. After a few sessions, she frantically notified the therapist that her entire family seemed "to be falling apart." Mrs. Belmont described her father as running away from his wife on any pretense he could find. Her husband was also annoying, as he insisted upon repeating "the doctors don't know everything," and her daughters appeared to be irritated most of the time. Nevertheless, it was her mother's recent withdrawal that was the paramount concern. Mrs. Belmont believed it was up to her "to keep matters on an even keel."

When the author asked if seeing the entire family would be helpful, Mrs. Belmont seized upon the suggestion. She was certain her husband, parents, and children would agree since they still mentioned their past art psychotherapy experiences during the girls' adolescent years.

SESSION ONE/*Family Meeting: All Members Present*

Hinde Belmont was obviously anxious about the first family meeting. She led her parents the Rosens, her husband Andy, and their two young adult daughters Leda and Diane, into the office. Mr. Rosen appeared agitated and disgruntled as he complained about the parking difficulties. In contrast, Mr. Belmont and the girls gave the author a friendly greeting. Leda and Diane took a few minutes to fondly reminisce about their past family art therapy meetings. Although Mrs. Rosen said it was nice to see the therapist again, her affect was depleted and depressed.

When the family was encouraged to talk about the "reason" for the session, everyone had a great deal of difficulty coming to grips with the problem of Mrs. Rosen's incurable illness. Anytime someone hinted at the painful subject, the conversation was sabotaged.

To aid the family in clarifying the purpose of treatment, they were directed to *do a collage which shows what you would like to achieve through the art therapy meeting*. The family, relieved to be diverted from conversation, busied themselves by looking through the selection of magazine pictures.

When the group finished their task, the grandchildren encouraged Mrs. Rosen to begin sharing the artwork. She held up her collage which was composed of two photos: one was *a group of people exchanging presents, the other portrayed a family hugging and kissing one another*. Mrs. Rosen haltingly explained her symbolism. It indicated a desire for her loved ones to be "caring and loving with each other." In actuality her words, which came across as a plea, brought tears to her family. They were touched by this poignant request. Feeling finished, Mrs. Rosen turned to her husband indicating him to go next.

Mr. Rosen displayed his collage, which filled the entire page. It contained *a plane in flight, an older couple walking hand in hand, the theater marquee, and a foursome playing bridge*. He said the photos signified all the activities in which he and his wife participated. With determination he added, "And we're going right on doing all of these things!"

Because Mr. Rosen expected his wife to be pleased with his statements, he was disappointed by her lack of response. Mrs. Rosen, extremely vulnerable, wanted support from her family, not denial. Looking very sad, she purposely avoided eye contact with her husband. The family, observing the interchange between the couple, fell silent.

Hinde, bothered by the lack of interaction between her parents, believed she had to impress her father with the reality of the situation. She told him Mother would have to discontinue their social life very soon. Andy interrupted his wife to bring attention to his own art: the drawing of *iced-tea and a photo of a baby taking its first steps*. He said he had hoped the art therapy would "help the family keep their cool and enable them to take one step at a time" (Figure 121). Turning to Hinde, he proclaimed, "Maybe some of the things Pa wants to do *are* possible right now. If Ma becomes weaker, then naturally some changes in plans will be made at that time." Andy's statement made sense, since the idea alluded to parameters designed for each stage of the illness.

Leda (the older grandaughter) offered to show her collage next. It exhibited a photo of *Israel*. She believed the art therapy would offer a

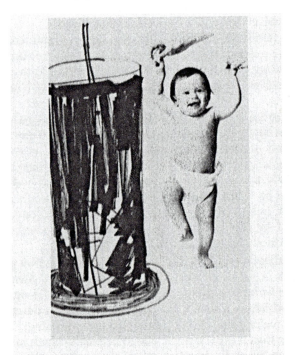

Figure 121. Keep cool and take one step at a time

means for supporting her grandparents to enjoy life as long as they could. Similarly, Diane's collage included visuals of activities for her grandmother and grandfather.

Mrs. Rosen, who knew she could not physically handle the suggestions being made, sat mutely depressed. Her husband, noting his wife's withdrawal, began to cough and excused himself from the room for "a drink of water." When he returned, the therapist interpreted his actions as an indication of his pain and the resistance to deal with the subject of his wife's future death, adding that most of the family seemed to have a problem with discussing the longer ranged plans. Leda, unwilling to accept this thought, intervened by siding with her father, "It's like Daddy said, when grandma isn't feeling very well we'll decide at that time what to do." In spite of this statement, Hinde attempted to manipulate the family into talking about her mother's last days. To circumvent this premature discussion, the therapist told Mrs. Belmont to *create something that would express your need to talk about the final stage of your mother's illness at this particular time.* The rest of the family were told to *make any object of your own choice."*

Andy decided to be the first person to display his mixed media artwork. It portrayed *a woman with eyeglasses.* He voiced his desire to have his wife pay more attention to him. Andy related his recent feelings of neglect (Figure 122). Although these thoughts had not been expressed before, Hinde was not surprised, in spite of her husband's support and extreme understanding. She sat looking at Andy with a great deal of love and understanding. No one spoke, as it would have been an intrusion upon the personal glances that were being exchanged between husband and wife. After a few moments Mrs. Belmont decided to go on with her task. She held up a plasticene *playing card* and a *gold star.* She told the group the art represented her need to discuss her mother's rapidly declining health. Hinde claimed it was essential to "lay the cards on the table," knowing she "would feel better if plans were set." In a quivering voice she told her family, "I'm a doer; I hate standing aside and just watching. I want to be constructive." She continued on to talk about the *gold star,* which was reminiscent of her childhood, explaining how her mother would paste gold stars on a chart for her being a "good girl" when she "performed well." Hinde believed that if the family decided on the way the future should be handled she would carry out the plans "like a good girl should."

Leda was surprised by what her mother had shared. Seeing her parent's self-involvement as inappropriate she retorted, "Mom, maybe right now the stars need to go to grandma, not to you!" However, Mrs. Rosen, upset with the remark, defended her daughter as she stated, "No, she is

Figure 122. Wants more attention

a doer. She wants the best for me. I know that." Then turning to Hinde she said, "When I'm ready, we'll talk dear. Don't worry." The family, impressed with Mrs. Rosen's understanding and the protectiveness that she exerted on behalf of her grown child, backed off from any further confrontation.

At the end of the session, the participants were asked if they wished to return. After a brief conversation they admitted it was helpful to have a therapist who knew them and understood their circumstances. They decided to continue with the art psychotherapy.

SESSION TWO/*Family Meeting: All Members Present*

On the way into the office several family members mentioned that the last art therapy session had served as a catalyst for communication. After being seated, Andy reported that his wife was ruminating less and paying more attention to him. Mr. Rosen volunteered, "Me and Lena went to the show last night." The younger granddaughter reported that she had given her grandmother a box of watercolors, encouraging her to do some painting since she had been an artist at one time.

The therapist asked the family if there was anything special they wished to talk about. The members said they liked the experience of being all together where communication was encouraged. However, they could not think of anything they wanted to discuss. Since none of the participants would take the lead, the therapist divided them into three-generational teams. Each pair was given a cardboard box and was instructed to *create something that is indicative of your own generation's problems.*

Mr. and Mrs. Rosen did not speak while they worked together. Mr. Rosen selected a box to create a *two-story house*. His wife used contruction paper to add *curtains*, a *tree*, and *flowers* (which were unconsciously presented in a leaning position, indicating her tenuous hold on life). Amazingly, when they talked about the project Mrs. Rosen noticed the way in which she had eschewed her structures. She understood its meaning as an expression of her illness. As Mr. and Mrs. Rosen talked about the artwork, they decided the house represented the energy which they put into keeping their child and grandchildren close to them, admitting that a "tight-knit group" had always been a very important part of their value system.

By coincidence Mr. and Mrs. Belmont also created *a house*. Their structure contained one story with four doors, one on each side of the house. Andy said his generation was "into doing our own thing; that's why there are four doors and each person can go in and out as they please. You see a door for each person means that everyone is an individual."

Leda and Diane had also conversed as they made their sculpture. They complained about sharing a single box and settled the matter by cutting it into two parts.

Diane used her half to depict a symbolic message about *feminism*. She described the box as a place where women in her generation had three walls, which kept them "partly boxed in"; nevertheless, the fourth side, which was left open, represented "new frontiers for women" (she was attending law school). Her sister Leda used her half of the box to *avoid* the issue of a generational problem when she made a *gym*. She stated a healthy body was important and working out was essential. Leda expressed a holistic approach to one's physical and psychological well-being.

The constructions were then utilized for family observations and interaction. Mrs. Belmont noticed the way in which the artwork was lined up: first, the house that was made by her parents; in the middle, the construction created by her husband and herself; and last, the girls' artwork. Mrs. Belmont noted the products, which were lined up generationally, had obvious structural differences.

Hinde pointed out the way in which her house was *sandwiched* in between two generations. She laid claim to a symbolic meaning, stating "it represents my responsibility to parents and children." She added that the side doors on her own construction portrayed her "access to both generations." Somehow, Leda heard her mother's comment as a complaint and interjected, "But you want it that way." The remark, apparently true, went undisputed. Feeling uneasy, the family shifted to admire the house that the Rosens had created. Leda looked at grandmother as she told her their *tight-knit* family had helped everyone to share their joys and sorrows more intensely. Embarrassed by the sentiment, Andy diverted the subject by saying, "Hinde, it's interesting how you came up with a different meaning to the four doors in our house sculpture. Originally you and I decided they symbolized our family's individuality. Then you free associated and came up with your sense of responsibility."

Hinde, perceiving her husband as being judgmental, retorted that she was a combination of her family's tight-knit group, yet also believed herself to be autonomous. Thinking out loud she wondered if she had tried to break away from parental influences in her youth to establish her own identity.

The girls who understood that struggle looked at their mother lovingly. There seemed to be a special understanding among the women, whereas the men acted as observers or perhaps they didn't wish to invade the generational feminine rapport.

As the session was coming to an end, Mrs. Belmont voiced her opinion that the two art therapy sessions had been meaningful. Nevertheless, speaking for herself she did not feel the need to come back the following week, but hoped the entire family would return when her "mother's health was failing." The therapist, who was open to this suggestion, asked the rest of the family for their opinions. After some discussion the family consensus was to come back for treatment when they deemed it more urgent.

SESSION THREE/*Family Meeting: All Members Present*

After several months, Mrs. Belmont contacted the author once again. She reported her mother's increasingly weakened condition. Mrs. Rosen was spending a great deal of time in bed; her energy level varied on different days. The doctor claimed she would live for approximately three months. The family, realizing they must deal with Mrs. Rosen's approaching death, requested additional art therapy treatment.

During the return session the following directive was given as a warm-up: *Make individual plasticene sculptures that reveal some aspect of yourselves.*

As in the past, the family was relieved to be involved with the artwork instead of conversation. However, when the tasks were completed, Mr. Rosen volunteered to begin the sharing with his sculpture of *two solid feet*. He described it as symbolic of his recent actions of "staying close to my wife" (unlike his former defense of removing himself) (Figure 123). Touched by his statement, his wife decided to go next. She had created a *pomegranate cut in half and filled with seeds*. Mrs. Rosen said it represented the many seeds that she had planted, such as her daughter and son-in-law, granddaughters, community contributions, good friendships, the school children she had taught, and so forth. She was sad when she related there were still many seeds left in her with no time to plant them, adding that this realization "was hard to take" (Figure 124).

After a long pause Mrs. Belmont pushed her *octopus* sculpture to the center of the table, proclaiming it stood for several things: attempts to care for her mother, doing what must be done at home, and working at her part-time job. She added, "It also represents what I take in from my family and friends. Since we last came to you (the therapist), all of us have been sensitive to each other although I think we pussy foot around Mama's condition. I'm afraid we don't let Mama speak about what's on her mind. Whenever she hints at the subject of dying or her will, we're afraid to face it and tend to change the subject" (Figure 125).

Andy, in agreement, took the opportunity to show his *self-portrait with only one ear and one eye*, stating, "It is too hard to accept seeing Mama quiet and accepting, not complaining. I know she is feeling awful" (Figure 126). The family, obviously going through their premourning experience, was drawn to Leda's *braid*, which she claimed stood for her grandma, mother, and herself who were interwoven, for she had recently realized the many similar characteristics that they shared. Leda gave examples: "The way all of us like to sing in the car and our efficient ways of cooking and cleaning up as we go along and the fact that we all appreciate art. More and more, I keep finding out how much I have in common with Mom and Grandma."

Diane appeared to feel left out. Coincidently, her *book* sculpture explained the reason: "I see that I have thrown myself completely into school. In part it was to escape thinking about Grandma's suffering; in part it was to perform well to make my grandparents and Mom and Dad proud of me."

The family was encouraged to continue talking about the feelings that the artwork evoked. Afterwards the therapist placed a very large piece of paper on the table, telling the participants *to place your individual sculptures wherever you please on the page.*

Initially, everyone hesitated to move as they waited for Grandmother

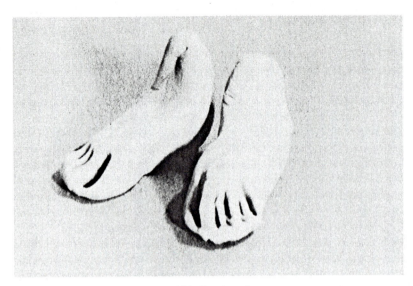

Figure 123. Staying close

Figure 124. Remaining seeds

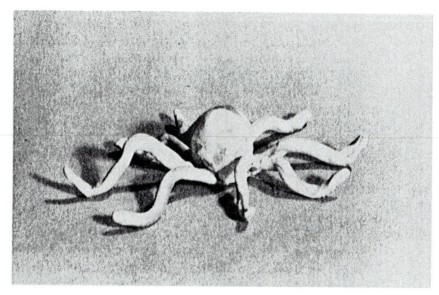

Figure 125. Give and take

Figure 126. Hard to observe

to go first. Seeing what was expected of her, Mrs. Rosen placed her *pomegranate* in the center. Her daughter placed her *octopus* next to her mother's plasticene piece, while Andy also set his *self-sculpture* near his mother-in-law's artwork. Mr. Rosen followed, placing his plasticene *feet* next to his wife's pomegranate. By that time everyone could see Mrs. Rosen's piece was being surrounded, and the girls followed to complete the pattern.

The family was told to *make whatever changes you wish*. Quietly, Mrs. Rosen plucked off enough pomegranate seeds to plant one on each of her family's figures. Mr. Rosen shifted his plasticene feet even closer to his wife's sculpture, until the two pieces touched. However, without any conscious intent, one foot was in the center touching his wife, while the other was on the outside (perhaps as an affirmation of his closeness to his wife and as a symbol of his own on-going life). Hinde's, Andy's and Leda's positions remained basically the same, although they all moved their pieces closer to Mrs. Rosen's. Again it was Diane who held herself back for last. When she took her turn, she moved the book sculpture until one side leaned on Grandmother's, while the other touched her parents'.

Everyone examined the group sculpture without talking. Diane was the first to speak up, saying she wanted to be close to Grandma, but lately she realized mortality could touch her parents also. She reported that the thought about her parents dying had not occurred since she was a little child. A hush came across the family as they each free associated to Diane's threatening statement. The silence was broken by Leda who said she knew what Diane meant. Then she added a fourth *strand* to her *plasticene braid*, reweaving it to represent the closeness and affection she felt towards her sister Diane.

After Leda's gesture, Hinde decided to redo her octopus's tentacles by making them long enough to touch everyone.

The family, finding the experience both touching and meaningful, gazed at the group sculpture, each thinking their own thoughts. The therapist respected the privacy of the introspection and thus ended the session.

SESSION FOUR/*Family Meeting: All Members Present*

When the family returned the following week, they commented on how "heavy" and worthwhile the last art psychotherapy session had been. They agreed it left them thoughtful. Diane claimed she "felt good" about being able to show emotions, which usually went unexpressed, and about her family who allowed the feelings to be expressed "without making nice." As a rule, both parents and grandparents were overly protective. Diane admitted, "Their actions seemed to carry the message that I couldn't handle things; that maybe I was too fragile or somehow incompetent." Both parents and grandparents protested, insisting Diane's interpretation was wrong. However, Leda who acted as an objective observer, said she believed her sister to be right. Excuses to explain away anything negative did include a message that such feelings were "secretly bad." Diane glanced appreciatively at Leda for the validation of her perception.

After the interchange, as a lead back into the session, the family was instructed to *create artwork with a theme of your own choice.*

Mr. Rosen used construction paper to create a *television set.* He said he planned to buy a new colored set which would be placed in his wife's bedroom.

As Hinde listened to her Dad, she rummaged through the collage box and picked out the photograph of a *woman with a nurse at her bedside,* and stated that she had "received material on home hospital care" (Figure 127). Mrs. Rosen, who was startled by this news, voiced resentment towards her daughter for using the art therapy session to "sneak in" the home hospice information. She questioned Hinde, "Why didn't you show it to me at home?" Mrs. Belmont apologized to her mother, admitting she "was too chicken to bring up the subject before." The author

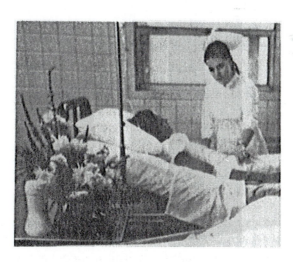

Figure 127. Home hospice

suggested that Mr. and Mrs. Rosen, the physician, and Hinde go through the use of the hospice plan together. Everyone thought it was the appropriate way to proceed.

It was Leda who spoke up to state, "After talking about the hospice setup, my artwork seems ridiculous." She demeaned her drawing, which contained a *group of women voting for a better pay scale.* The therapist believed her picture was one of denial. It exhibited Leda's resistance to dealing with her grandmother's fatal illness. However, this interpretation was not stated aloud. Refusing to allow her granddaughter to feel guilty, Mrs. Rosen claimed, "It isn't ridiculous at all. I'm pleased with your involvement for women's rights. I wish I had done more for the improvement of the feminine position." When Mrs. Belmont became upset to hear her mother voice "regrets," the girls were quick to point out, "Grandma has a right to feel unfinished and regretful."

The family talked to each other about the need to tolerate other people's thoughts and feelings. Afterwards, Diane showed her watercolor painting of a *setting sun.* Although she did not have anything in mind when the picture was created, it now reminded her of the time when the entire family went on a boat cruise together. Several members reminisced about that particular vacation with wonderful memories. The author commented that the "setting sun" could also have another meaning: Grandmother's "sunset of life." Diane looked sad as she acknowledged the interpretation (Figure 128).

Andy had drawn his *mother-in-law sitting up in bed,* as an acceptance of her illness. Shifting back to Diane's watercolor painting, he remembered Mrs. Rosen's talent as an artist. Facing his mother-in-law he said, "Next time you feel well enough, I would love to have you paint a watercolor picture for my office. That would really please me." Mrs. Rosen smiled at Andy's request, obviously flattered by his affection and respect for her art.

The last person to share the artwork was Mrs. Rosen. Her painting had a *moon* in the center of the page with several *rings around it.* The first ring contained five large stars; a second ring, placed farther out, had five smaller stars in it. In the rest of the space there were tiny stars scattered throughout. Mrs. Rosen, explaining her picture, said, "I stand for the moon. The first ring of *five stars* stands for *all of you.* The second ring of *smaller stars* represents all of *you moving farther away.* This is as it should be. *Close is good. Too close is not so good.* You see the tiny scattered stars is the way it should be when I die. *Everyone must go on living, doing what each of you must do*" (Figure 129).

Several members began to doodle as a way of dealing with their feelings. Mr. Rosen began to sob, then reached over to his wife and lifted her hand to kiss and pat it so very tenderly.

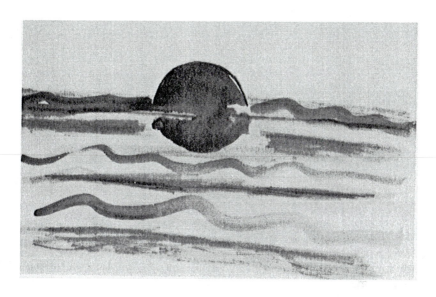

Figure 128. Setting sun

Figure 129. Letting go

The impact of Mrs. Rosen's message was not to be diluted. It seemed clinically important *not* to lead the family into a discussion but, rather to allow everyone to *contemplate their own philosophy of life and death*.

Comments

Although the family dynamics were continually revealing themselves, for the purpose of this family's treatment goals, they were neither interpreted nor dealt with. The clinician proceeded with the plan of helping the family deal with the thoughts and feelings that needed to be expressed before Mrs. Rosen died.

SESSION FIVE/*Family Meeting: All Members Present*

Mrs. Rosen's health began to sink very rapidly. She was no longer able to leave her home and spent most of her time in bed. Arrangements were made for the therapist to continue treatment on a home-site visit basis. This session took place two weeks after the fourth meeting.

The author believed a "positive life review" via a photograph album would comfort the family and help them to face the future. During a telephone conversation the clinician told Mrs. Rosen of her plans and asked her to look over the pictures in advance. If the photos were loose she was to put them in chronological order.

Although Mrs. Rosen sounded weak and depressed when answering the phone, she was delighted with the idea and seemed to get a lift at the thought of looking over the family snapshots.

When the family art therapy session took place, everyone gathered close to Mrs. Rosen who sat at the head of the dining room table with the albums spread in front of her. She claimed that putting the albums *in order* had been a wonderful task for herself and her husband. She seemed to be aware of the therapist's intent to symbolically put an *orderly end to her life*, mentioning that many photos of people who were unknown to her descendents were now labeled, and a large number of snapshots had been thrown away.

With the therapist in mind, Mrs. Rosen had gone to the trouble of marking specific album pages that held pictures of particular significance.

The album, in a life-cycle order, began with Mrs. Rosen's childhood, including pictures of her own parents, herself, and her siblings. A late adolescence photograph of Mr. and Mrs. Rosen as high school students was viewed. It followed with courtship time and marriage, and pictures of Hinde as a baby, growing up, and getting married. The last part of the album included her granddaughters. Everyone present was on a sentimental journey. Andy said he would like to rent a video camera to tape Mama talking about her family background. Complimenting him on the "great idea," the girls voiced their wish to be a part of the video recording.

When the photograph album review was completed, to sustain the emotions that had been generated the participants were given the directive to *create a mural based on positive memories of the past.*

The family urged Mrs. Rosen to lead them with the mural. Before the drawing actually began, she asked for suggestions, then combined all of the ideas. The title was "Memories of Celebrations." It started with a drawing of *Mr. and Mrs. Rosen during their wedding ceremony standing under a white and blue cloth canopy.* Another scene represented *Hinde and Andy's wedding ceremony.* This was followed by the drawing of *two cribs belonging to Leda and Diane.* For the next part, magazine photo collages were used showing a *family at a dinner table depicting the annual Passover Seder* (a traditional Jewish holiday which includes the dinner meal). Everyone helped to draw a *wedding cake with the number 45 on it* to signify the Rosens' recent wedding anniversary celebration (Figure 130).

The mural produced a bittersweet effect on the family members. As the session came to an end, Mr. and Mrs. Rosen declared they had had a "good life together" in spite of some difficult times.

Figure 130. Celebrations

SESSION SIX/*Family Meeting: All Members Present*

The therapist was struck by Mrs. Rosen's physical degeneration since the preceding week. Concerned that the end was near, the therapist believed the time for good-byes was at hand. For this reason the session began with the directive to *create art which portrays something you wish to express to your wife/mother/grandmother.* Mrs. Rosen, the exception, was to *convey any messages that are still unfinished or that you want to tell your family.*

Mr. Rosen volunteered to start the discussion by holding up a construction paper *heart.* He pronounced it stood for the love he had for his spouse (Figure 131). Hinde, who drew a *bowl of matzoball chicken soup* told her mother, "You have always given me what I need—you've been a nourishing and wonderful mother" (Figure 132). After explaining her picture, she went over to her parents to give them hugs and kisses. Andy looked teary as he showed his *picture of a family at the dinner table.* He had cut out and pasted on the words *one family.* Looking at Mrs. Rosen he said, "Mama, you've always felt like my very own mother" (Figure 133). Leda hesitated before showing her sculpture of a *person with open arms.* Focusing on Grandmother, she proclaimed, "You were always there for me. I always knew I could run away to you when I got mad at Mom or Dad. You would listen to me, give me cookies, wash my face, give hugs, and phone my parents to tell them they were lucky to have such a child" (Figure 134).

Diane, who had painted a *sign with 100%* on it, showed her work last. She explained, "Grandma, you could always be counted on. You never

Figure 131. Love

Figure 132. Nourishing

Figure 133. Integrated into family

Figure 134. Always there

broke a promise. I always felt like there was nothing that I could do wrong in your eyes!" After a few moments she added, "Grandma, I can't imagine our lives without you!!" Unable to continue, she broke out in sobs. Her father reached out to hug his daughter and let her cry on his shoulder.

Mrs. Rosen was stoic as she listened to each person's testimony. With an equally brave front she presented her own artwork. It was a watercolor painting of a *rainbow with a heart in the center*. Mrs. Rosen explained, "Each rainbow band of color represents a family member. When they are all put together, they form something extra beautiful, but, by themselves, they are still lovely." She pointed out the way in which the colors were inexactly placed, stating, "I don't have long to live. There have been times when I was angry or hurt. Everything is not always perfect, but as a whole I've been very fortunate. Yes, very fortunate. I want you all to know that" (Figure 135).

The good-byes had been an exhausting experience. As the major goal of treatment had been met, any future art therapy sessions would be focused on closure.

SESSION SEVEN/*Family Meeting: All Members Present*

At the beginning of the session Mrs. Rosen reported the home hospice setup had already been put into action. She declared, "I feel myself slipping away."

The family members were instructed to *make something that you would*

Figure 135. Family metaphor

like to give to Mrs. Rosen, and Mrs. Rosen, you can do the same for your family.

The mourning process had already begun and sadness bore down heavily on the family members. The act of creating art gave the family an opportunity to release their bottled-up thoughts. Mr. Rosen looked around the room to select a paper tray upon which he drew some *pills*. He told his wife he would like to give her a gift of "freedom from pain," adding "If only I could pull the pain away from you, I would gladly put it *onto* myself." Mrs. Rosen smiled faintly as she told her husband she was well aware of this fact.

Hinde handed her mother the painting of a *mandala* to represent "peace of mind." She assured her mother that any requests she might make would be carried out. Andy cut out a *pillow*, which stood for his desire to make his mother-in-law "more comfortable." Diane offered a construction paper *ear* to represent her wish "to hear out whatever grandma wanted to say" and Leda gave her the drawing of a *colored design* as the metaphor "for trying to bring some beauty in Grandma's life."

Mrs. Rosen said she derived a great deal of pleasure from her family, adding their gifts were thoughtful and most sensitive to her needs. Feeling physically and emotionally exhausted, she apologized for not doing any artwork. It appeared that Mrs. Rosen had already given her family as much as she could.

The faces in the room portrayed affection and grief. The author did not see a need for any closing remarks since the family had already done their own work.

THE FOLLOWING WEEK

Mrs. Belmont phoned to say her mother was close to the end and was heavily medicated. The next week Mrs. Rosen died.

SEVERAL MONTHS LATER

The author received a call from Hinde Belmont asking if she could have the art therapy portfolio, explaining that her family wanted to review it. The therapist readily agreed with the request, hoping it could be a comforting factor during their mourning process.

A FEW WEEKS LATER

Mrs. Belmont telephoned the author once again to report the event was painful yet very satisfying. She said the family felt very good about the roles they had played in helping Mama and themselves get through her dying days. Hinde's last statement to the author was, "We felt so close to Mother when we saw our inheritence," referring to the visual messages that Mrs. Rosen had left behind.

Mrs. Rosen had also left the author a legacy of a privileged and memorable experience of an exceptional client and her family.

SUMMARY

Multigenerational family art psychotherapy sessions were held. The treatment revolved around the grandmother's impending death. The goals of therapy were as follows: 1) help the terminally ill patient and her family face the forthcoming death; 2) facilitate dealing with their emotions; 3) establish an open support system; and 4) provide a time to say good-bye.

Sessions included home-site visits and a positive family life review.

The portfolio proved to have post-treatment value for the remaining members, serving as affirmation of their experience, which they handled with truth, dignity, and love.

RECOMMENDED READING

Aldrich, G. K. The dying patient's Grief. *Journal of American Medical Association, 184,* 109–111, 1963.

Beatman, F. L. Intergenerational aspects of family therapy. In N. W. Ackerman (Ed.), *Expanding Theory and Practice in Family Therapy.* New York: Family Service Association of America, 1967, pp. 29–38.

Blazer, D. G. Working with the elderly patient's family. *Geriatrics, 33,* 117–123, 1978.

Boszormenyi-Nagy, I., & Spark, G. M. *Invisible Loyalties: Reciprocity in Intergenerational Family Therapy.* New York: Harper & Row, 1973. (Reprinted by Brunner/Mazel, New York, 1984.)

Brink, T. L. Family counseling with the aged. *Family Therapy, 3,* 163–169, 1976.

Cameron, P. The generation gap: Time orientation. *The Gerontologist, 12*(2), 117–119, 1972.

Carp, F. Some components of disengagement. *Journal of Gerontology, 23,* 382–386, 1968.

Feifel, H. Death. In N. L. Farberow (Ed.), *Taboo Topics,* New York: Atherton Press, 1963.

Hammer, E. F. *The Clinical Application of Projective Drawings.* Springfield, IL: Charles C Thomas, 1971.

Headly, L. *Adults and Their Parents in Family Therapy.* New York: Plenum Press, 1977.

Herr, J. J., & Weakland, J. H. *Counseling Elders and Their Families: Practical Techniques for Applied Gerontology.* New York: Springer Publishing, 1979.

Hinton, J. *Dying*. Baltimore: Pelican Books, 1972.

Horowitz, L. Treatment of the family with a dying member. *Family Process, 14*(1), 95–107, March 1975.

Junge, M. The book about Daddy Dying: A Preventative art therapy technique to help families deal with the death of a family member. *Art Therapy, 2*(1), 4–10, March, 1985.

Killer, M. R. *Families: A Multigenerational Approach*. New York: McGraw-Hill, 1974.

Kimmel, D. C. *Adulthood and Aging*. New York: John Wiley & Sons, 1974.

Kubler-Ross, E. *Living with Death and Dying*. New York: Macmillan, 1980.

Landgarten, H. B. Art psychotherapy for depressed elders. *Clinical Gerontologist: The Journal of Aging and Mental Health, 2*(1), 45–55, Fall 1983.

Neugarten, B. L. *Middle Age and Aging*. Chicago: University of Chicago Press, 1967.

Peterson, J. A. Marital and family therapy involving the aged. *Gerontologist, 13*, 27–31, 1973.

Pincus, R. *Death and the Family*. New York: Random House, 1974.

Reilly, D. M. Death propensity, dying and bereavement: A family systems perspective. *Family Therapy, 5*, 35–55, 1978.

Schulz, R. *The Psychology of Death, Dying and Bereavement*. Reading: Addison-Wesley, 1978.

Seelbach, W. C. Correlates of aged parents' filial responsibility expectations and realizations. *Family Coordinator, 27*, 341–350, 1978.

Schneidman, E. S. *Death*. Palo Alto: Mayfield, 1984.

Siegler, I. C., & Blazer, D. G. (Eds.) *Working with the Family of Older Adults*. Reading: Addison-Wesley, 1981.

Soulen, R. *Care for the Dying*. Atlanta: Knox, 1975.

Spark, G. M., & Brody, E. M. The aged are family members. *Family Process, 9*, 195–210, 1970.

Spark, G. M. Grandparents and intergenerational family therapy. *Family Process, 12*(2), 225–239, 1974.

Stoddard, S. *The Hospice Movement*. New York: Vintage, 1978.

Weisman, A. *On Dying and Denying*. New York: Behavioral Publications, 1972.

Worden, J. W. *Personal Death Awareness*. Englewood Cliffs, NJ: Prentice-Hall, 1976.

Zuk, G. H. *Family Therapy: A Triadic Based Approach*. New York: Behavioral Publications, 1971.

Epilogue

As I wrote up the case histories in this book I was struck by the fact that family therapy always included some issue of *separation and loss*. Since I realize more now than ever before that such painful experiences slow down or divert areas of growth, I am grateful for the art therapy approach, where these issues can be worked upon through metaphor when direct efforts are premature or blocked.

Being a family art psychotherapist has been a source of gratification. Families have proven their willingness and capacity to change their attitude, their system, and the way they perceive one another. I have been able to obtain follow-up information from former patients who have called for brief crisis intervention a number of years after therapy. Art therapy the second time around generally proves that their changes have been maintained. Those patients who have since married and had children, report that they draw upon the insight gained during their family-of-origin art therapy treatment.

It is important for the reader to realize, the family art therapist must *be creative in two areas simultaneously;* while being psychologically attuned to the participants, he or she must make an immediate decision about the appropriate art task which shall serve a therapeutic purpose. This dual challenge is one that lowers the "burnout" factor and makes my career as family art psychotherapist one which is still exciting and satisfying.

Among the additional advantages of art psychotherapy, which are sometimes overlooked, is the fact that this modality *works* for the poor and the rich, the psychologically unsophisticated, as well as those who know the psychology books by heart.

Also, as is evident in this volume, this modality allows the family art psychotherapist to employ numerous treatment approaches, whether they be oriented towards: insight, communication, interaction, symptom reduction, and so forth.

The proliferation of family therapy books indicates the increase in family work. Many institutions have family art psychotherapists on their staffs. I predict a greater influx of this profession in every mental health sector that provides treatment for families.

Family art psychotherapy is most certainly not a panacea, but it is a psychotherapeutic technique which is healing, if applied with thought, knowledge, and skill.

Additional Bibliography

Abel, T. M. Figure drawing and facial disfigurement. *American Journal of Orthopsychiatry, 23,* 253–264, 1953.

Ackerman, N. W. Family psychotherapy and psychoanalysis: The implications of difference. In N. W. Ackerman (Ed.), *Family Process.* New York: Basic Books, 1970 (a).

Ackerman, N. W. (Ed.). *Family Therapy in Transition.* New York: Little, Brown, 1970 (b).

Albee, G. W., & Hamlin, R. M. An investigation of the reliability and validity of judgments of adjustment inferred from drawings. *Journal of Clinical Psychology, 5,* 389–392, 1949.

Alexander, F. The psychoanalyst looks at contemporary art. In R. Lindner (Ed.), *Explorations in Psychoanalysis.* New York: Julian Press, 1955.

Alschuler, R., & Hattwick, L. W. *Painting and Personality.* Chicago: University of Chicago Press, 1 & 2, 1947 (rev. ed. 1969).

Ames, L. B., Metraux, R. W., Rodell, J. L., & Walker, R. N. *Child Rorschach Responses.* New York: Brunner/Mazel, 1974.

Ames, L. B., Metraux, R. W., & Walker, R. N. *Adolescent Rorschach Responses.* New York: Brunner/Mazel, 1971.

Anastasi, A., & Foley, J. P. An analysis of spontaneous drawings by children in different cultures. *Journal of Applied Psychology, 20,* 689–726, 1936.

Anderson, C. M., & Stewart, S. *Mastering Resistance: A Practical Guide to Family Therapy.* New York: Guilford Press, 1983.

Anderson, F., & Landgarten, H. B. Art therapy program in the mental health field. *Studies in Art Education, 15*(5), 1973–74.

Andolfi, M. *Family Therapy: An Interactional Approach.* New York: Plenum Press, 1979.

Aponte, H. J. Psychotherapy for the poor: An eco-structural approach to treatment. *Delaware Medical Journal,* March 1974.

Ard, B., & Ard, C. (Eds.). *Handbook of Marriage Counseling.* Palo Alto, CA: Science & Behavior Books, 1969.

Arieti, S. *The Intrapsychic Self.* New York: Basic Books, 1967.

Arieti, S. *Creativity: The Magic Synthesis*. New York: Basic Books, 1976.

Arnheim, R. *Visual Thinking*. Berkeley: University of California Press, 1969.

Auerbach, J. G. Psychological observations on "doodling" in neurotics. *Journal of Nervous and Mental Disorders, III*, 304–332, 1950.

Bandler, R., Grinder, J., & Satir, V. *Changing with Families*. Palo Alto, CA: Science & Behavior Books, 1976.

Bandura, A. Psychotherapy based upon modeling principles. In A. E. Bergin & S. L. Garfield (Eds.), *Handbook of Psychotherapy and Behavior Change*. New York: John Wiley & Sons, 1971.

Bandura, A., & Walter, R. H. *Adolescent Aggression: A Study of the Influence of Child-Training Practices and Family Interrelationships*. New York: Ronald, 1959.

Bank, S. P., & Kahn, M. D. *The Sibling Bond*. NY: Basic Books, 1982.

Barker, P. *Basic Family Therapy*. Baltimore: University Park Press, 1981.

Barnes, M., & Berke, J. *Mary Barnes*. New York: Ballantine Books, 1971.

Barten, H., & Barten, S. *Children and Their Parents in Brief Therapy*. New York: Behavioral Publication, 1973.

Beck, H. S. A study of the applicability of the H-T-P to children with respect to the drawn house. *Journal of Clinical Psychology, II*, 60–63, 1955.

Beels, C., & Ferber, A. Family therapy: A view. *Family Process, 8*, 280–332, 1969.

Bell, N., & Vogel, E. *A Modern Introduction to the Family*. Glencoe, IL: Free Press, 1960.

Bell, N. W., & Vogel, E. F. *The Family*. Glencoe: Free Press, 1960.

Bender, L. (Ed.). *Child Psychiatric Techniques*. Springfield, IL: Charles C Thomas, 1952.

Benedek, T. The emotional structure of the family. In R. N. Anshen (Ed.), *The Family: Its Functions and Destiny*. New York: Harper, 1949, pp. 202–225.

Bertalanffy, L. von. *General Systems Theory: Foundation, Development, Applications*. New York: Brazillier, 1968.

Betensky, M. *Self-discovery Through Self-expression*. Springfield, IL: Charles C Thomas, 1973.

Betensky, M. Patterns of visual expression in art psychotherapy. *Art Psychotherapy, 1*(2), Fall, 1973.

Bing, E. The conjoint family drawing. *Family Process, 9*(2), June 1970.

Bloch, D. *Techniques of Family Psychotherapy, A Primer*. New York: Grune & Stratton, 1973.

Blos, P. *The Adolescent Personality*. New York: Appleton-Century-Crofts, 1941.

Boszormenyi-Nagy, I., & Ulrich, D. N. Contextual family therapy. In A. S. Gurman & D. P. Kniskern (Eds.), *Handbook of Family Therapy*. New York: Brunner/Mazel, 1981, pp. 159–186.

Boszormenyi-Nagy, I., & Framo, J. L. *Intensive Family Therapy: Theoretical and Practical Aspects*. New York: Harper & Row, 1965.

Bowen, M. The use of family theory in clinical practice. *Comprehensive Psychiatry, 9*, 1966.

Bradley, S., & Sloman, L. Elective mutism in immigrant families. *Journal of the American Academy of Child Psychiatry, 14*, 510–14, 1975.

Brant, R. S. T., & Tisza, V. B. The sexually misused child. *American Journal of Orthopsychiatry, 47*(1), 80–90, 1977.

Broderick, C. B. Beyond the five conceptual frameworks: A decade of development in family theory. In C. B. Broderick (Ed.), *A Decade of Family Research and Action*. Minneapolis: National Council on Family Relations, 1971.

Bross, A. *Family Therapy*. New York: Guilford Press, 1982.

Brown, S. L. Dynamic family therapy. In H. Davanloo (Ed.), *Short-term Dynamic Psychotherapy*. New York: Jason Aronson, 1980.

Burns, R. C. *Self-growth in Families. Kinetic Family Drawings (KFD): Research and Application*. New York: Brunner/Mazel, 1982.

Burns, R. C., & Kaufman, S. H. *Kinetic Family Drawings*. New York: Brunner/Mazel, 1970.

Cane, F. *The Artist in Each of Us*. New York: Pantheon, 1951.

Cath, S. H., Gurwitt, A. R., & Ross, J. M. (Eds.). *Father and Child: Developmental Perspectives*. Boston: Little Brown, 1982.

Cohn, F. W. Art Therapy: Psychotic Expression and Symbolism. *The Arts in Psychotherapy, 8*(1), 1981.

Corfman, E. et al. *Families Today*. Rockville, MD: U.S. Department of Health, Education and Welfare, Vol. I, 1979.

Coser, R. *The Family, Its Structure and Functions*. New York: St. Martin's Press, 1964.

Cutter, F. *Art and the Wish to Die*. Chicago: Nelson Hall, 1982.

Davanloo, H. (Ed.). *Short-term Dynamic Psychotherapy*. New York: Jason Aronson, 1980.

Dax, E. C. *Experimental Studies in Psychiatric Art*. London: Faber & Faber, Ltd. 1953.

DeFrancis, V. Protecting the child victims of sex crimes committed by adults. *Fed. Prob., 35*, 15–20, 1971.

Dell, P. J. Beyond homeostasis: Toward a concept of coherence. *Family Process, 21*(1), 21–41, 1982.

Dicks, H. V. *Marital Tensions: Clinical Studies Towards a Psychological Theory of Interaction*. London: Routledge & Kegan Paul, 1967.

Di Leo, J. H. *Young Children and Their Drawings*. New York: Brunner/Mazel, 1970.

Di Leo, J. *Child Development: Analysis and Synthesis*. NY: Brunner/Mazel, 1977.

Duhl, B. S. *From the Inside Out and Other Metaphors*. New York: Brunner/Mazel, 1983.

Duvall, E. M. *Marriage and Family Development* (5th ed.). New York: Lippincott, 1977.

Ehrenzweig, A. *The Psycho-Analysis of Artistic Vision and Hearing*. New York: George Braziller, 1967.

Eisler, R. M., & Hersen, M. Behavioral techniques in family-oriented crisis intervention. *Archives of General Psychiatry, 28*, 111–16, 1973.

Engel, G. A life setting conducive to illness—the giving up/given up complex. *Annals of Internal Medicine, 69*, 293–300, 1968.

Epstein, N. B., & Bishop, D. S. Problem-centered systems family therapy. *Journal of Marital Therapy, 7*(1), 23–32, 1981.

Erickson, G. D., & Hogan, T. P. (Eds.). *Family Therapy: An Introduction to Theory and Technique (2nd ed.)*. Monterey, CA: Brooks/Cole, 1981.

Feather, B. W., & Rhoads, J. M. Psychodynamic behavior therapy: II. Clinical aspects. *Archives of General Psychiatry, 26*, 503–511, 1972.

Feder, E., & Feder, B. *The Expressive Arts Therapies*. Englewood Cliffs, NJ: Prentice-Hall, 1981.

Ferrira, A. J. Family myths and homeostasis. *Archives of General Psychiatry, 9*, 457–463, 1963.

Fischer, R. Art interpretation and art therapy. In I. Jakab (Ed.), *Psychiatry and Art*.

Basel: Karger, 1969, p. 33.

Ford, F. R., & Herrick, J. Family rules: Family lifestyles. *American Journal of Ortho-psychiatry, 44,* 61–69, 1974.

Framo, J. L. (Ed.). *Family Interaction: A Dialogue Between Family Researchers and Family Therapists.* New York: Springer, 1972.

Framo, J. Family origin as a therapeutic resource for adults in marital and family therapy: You can and should go home again. *Family Process, 15,* 193, 210, 1976.

Frazier, E. F. The Negro family. In R. N. Anshen (Ed.), *The Family: Its Function and Destiny.* New York: Harper, 1949, pp. 142–158.

Frazier, E. F. Problems and needs of Negro children and youth resulting from family disorganization. *J. Negro Educ., 19,* 269–277, 1950.

Freud, A. *The Psychoanalytical Treatment of Children.* New York: Schocken, 1964.

Freud, S. *On Creativity and the Unconscious: Papers on the Psychology of Art, Litera-ture, Love, Religion.* New York: Harper & Row, 1958.

Fried, E. *Artistic Productivity and Mental Health.* Springfield, IL: Charles C Tho-mas, 1964.

Fromm, E. *The Forgotten Language.* New York: Grove Press, 1951.

Furman, E. *A Child's Parent Dies: Studies in Childhood Bereavement.* New Haven: Yale University Press, 1974.

Gardner, H. *Art, Mind and Brain: A Cognitive Approach to Creativity.* New York: Basic Books, 1982.

Gardner, H. *The Arts and Human Development.* New York: Wiley, 1973.

Ghiselin, B. (Ed.). *The Creative Process.* Berkeley: University of California Press, 1952.

Glaser, K. Masked depression in children and adolescents. *American Journal of Psychotherapy, 21,* 563–74, 1976.

Glasser, P. H., & Glasser, L. N. (Eds.). *Families in Crisis.* New York: Harper & Row, 1970.

Glick, I. D., & Kessler, D. R. *Marital and Family Therapy.* New York: Grune & Stratton, 1974.

Goldenberg, I., & Goldenberg, H. *Family Therapy: An Overview.* Monterey, CA: Brooks/Cole, 1980.

Goldstein, J., Freud, A., & Solnit, A. *Beyond the Best Interests of the Child.* New York: The Free Press, 1973.

Golombek, H. The therapeutic contract with adolescents. *Canadian Psychiatric Association Journal, 14,* 497–502, 1969.

Goode, W. *The Family.* Englewood Cliffs, NJ: Prentice-Hall, 1964.

Goodman, N. *Languages of Art* (2nd ed.). Indianapolis: Hackett, 1976.

Greenburg, L. Therapeutic grief work with children. *Social Casework, 56,* 396–403, 1975.

Greenspoon, D. Case study: The development of self-expression in a severely disturbed adolescent. *American Journal of Art Therapy, 22*(1), October 1982.

Gurman, A. S., & Kniskern, D. P. (Eds.). *Handbook of Family Therapy.* New York: Brunner/Mazel, 1981.

Guerin, J. P. (Ed.). *Family Therapy: Theory and Practice.* New York: Gardner Press, 1963.

Haley, J. *Strategies of Psychotherapy.* New York: Grune & Stratton, 1963.

Haley, J. Family therapy. In C. Sager & H. Kaplan (Eds.), *Progress in Group and Family Therapy.* New York: Brunner/Mazel, 1972.

Haley, J. *Uncommon Therapy.* New York: Norton, 1973.

Haley, J., & Hoffman, L. *Techniques of Family Therapy*. New York: Basic Books, 1967.

Hanes, K. M. *Art Therapy and Group Work: An Annotated Bibliography*. Westport: Greenwood Press, 1982.

Harris, J., & Joseph, C. *Murals of the Mind*. New York: International Universities Press, 1973.

Hatterer, L. J. *The Artist in Society: Problems and Treatment of the Creative Personality*. New York: Grove Press, 1965.

Havelka, J. *The Nature of the Creative Process in Art*. The Hague: Martinus Nijhoff, 1968.

Heinicke, C. M., & Westheimer, I. J. *Brief Separations*. New York: International Universities Press, 1965.

Herjanic, B., & Wilbois, R. P. Sexual abuse of children: Detection and management. *Journal of the American Medical Association, 239*, 331–33, 1978.

Herr, J., & Weakland, J. H. *Counseling Elders and Their Families: Practical Techniques for Applied Gerontology*. New York: Springer, 1979.

Hill, A. *Art Versus Illness*. London: George Allen and Unwin, 1945.

Horowitz, M. J. *Image Formation and Cognition*. New York: Appleton-Century Crofts, 1970.

Howells, J. G. (Ed.). *Theory and Practice of Family Psychiatry*. London: Oliver & Boyd, 1968.

Howells, J. G. (Ed.). *Modern Perspectives in International Child Psychiatry*. New York: Brunner/Mazel, 1971.

Howells, J. G. (Ed.). *Advances in Family Psychiatry*. New York: International Universities Press, Vol. 1, 1979.

Howells, J. G. (Ed.). *Advances in Family Psychiatry*. New York: International Universities Press Inc., Vol. 2, 1980.

Jackson, D. D. Family interaction, family homeostasis, and some implications for conjoint family psychotherapy. In J. Masserman (Ed.), *Individual and Family Dynamics*. New York: Grune & Stratton, 1959.

Jackson, D. The marital quid pro quo. In G. Zuk & I. Boszormenyi-Nagy (Eds.), *Family Therapy for Disturbed Families*. Palo Alto: Science and Behavior Books, 1966.

Jackson, D. *Human Communication*. Vols. I & II. Palo Alto, CA: Science & Behavior Books, 1967.

Jackson, D. D. (Ed.). *Communication, Family and Marriage*. Palo Alto: Science and Behavior Books, 1968.

Jackson, D. D. (Ed.). *Therapy, Communication and Change*. Palo Alto: Science and Behavior Books, 1968.

Jacobi, J. Pictures from the unconscious. *Journal of Projective Techniques, 19*, 264–270, 1955.

Jakab, I. (Ed.). *Psychiatry and Art*. New York: S. Karger, I(1968), II & III(1971), IV(1975).

Jolles, I. A study of the validity of some hypotheses for the qualitative interpretation of H-T-P for children of elementary school age. Sexual identification, *Journal of Clinical Psychology, 8*, 113–119, 1952.

Jung, C. G. *Man and His Symbols*. New York: Doubleday, 1964.

Junge, M. The book about Daddy dying: A preventative art therapy technique to help families deal with the death of a family member. *Art Therapy, 2*(1), 4–9, March, 1984.

Junge, M., & Maya, V. Women in their forties: A group portrait and implications for psychotherapy. *Women and Therapy,* 4(3), Fall, 1985.

Kaffman, M. Short-term therapy. *Family Process,* 2, 216–234, 1963.

Kahana, R. J., & Levin, S. Aging and the conflict of generations. *Journal of Geriatric Psychiatry,* 1971, 4, 115–135.

Kellog, R. *The Psychology of Children's Art.* New York: Random House, 1967.

Kestenberg, J. S. *Children and Parents.* New York: Jason Aronson, 1975.

Kiell, N. *Psychiatry and Psychology in the Visual Arts and Aesthetic: A Bibliography.* Madison: University of Wisconsin Press, 1965.

Koestler, A. *The Art of Creation.* New York: Macmillan, 1964.

Kramer, E. *Art Therapy in a Children's Community.* Springfield, IL: Charles C Thomas, 1958.

Kramer, E. *Art as Therapy with Children.* New York: Schocken Press, 1971.

Kreitler, H., & Kreitler, S. *Psychology of the Arts.* Durham, NC: Duke University Press, 1972.

Kris, E. *Psychoanalytic Explorations in Art.* New York: International Universities Press, 1952.

Kubie, L. *Neurotic Distortion of the Creative Process.* Lawrence, KN: Universities of Kansas Press, 1959.

Kubie, L. Psychoanalysis and marriage: Practical and theoretical issues. In V. Eisenstein (Ed.), *Neurotic Interaction in Marriage.* New York: Basic Books, 1956.

Kubler-Ross, E. *Death: The Final Stage of Growth.* Englewood Cliffs, NJ: Prentice-Hall, 1975.

Kubler-Ross, E. *On Death and Dying.* New York: Macmillan, 1969.

Kurelek, W. *Someone with Me.* Toronto: McClelland and Stewart Limited, 1980.

Lamb, D. *Psychotherapy with Adolescent Girls.* San Francisco: Jossey-Bass, 1978.

Landgarten, H. Lori: Art therapy and self-discovery. 16 mm. sound film in color. Los Angeles: Art Therapy Film Distributors.

Landgarten, H. Mutual task-oriented family art therapy. *Proceedings of the American Art Therapy Association,* 24, 1974.

Landgarten, H. B. Adult art psychotherapy. *International Journal of Art Psychotherapy,* 2(1), 1975.

Landgarten, H. B. Art therapy as a primary mode of treatment for an elective mute. *American Journal of Art Therapy,* 14(4), July 1975.

Landgarten, H. Group art therapy for mothers and their daughters. *American Journal of Art Therapy,* 14(2), 1975.

Landgarten, H. Changing status of art therapy in Los Angeles. *American Journal of Art Therapy,* 15(4), 1976.

Landgarten, H. B. *Mutual Task-Oriented Family Art Therapy: Creativity and the Art Therapist's Identity.* American Art Therapy Association, 1977.

Landgarten, H. My struggle with maintaining a dual professional identity: Artist and art psychotherapist. *Proceedings of the American Art Therapy Association,* 38–39, 1977.

Landgarten, H. B. Competency based education. *Art Therapy Education,* Series I, March 1978.

Landgarten, H. B. Status of art therapy in Greater Los Angeles, 1974: Two-year follow-up study. *International Journal of Art Psychotherapy,* 5(4), 1978.

Landgarten, H. B. *Clinical Art Therapy: A Comprehensive Guide.* New York: Brunner/Mazel, 1981.

Landgarten, H. B. Hanna Kwiatkowska's legacy. *Personality of the Therapist.* American Society Psychopathology of Expression, Pittsburgh, PA, 1981.

Landgarten, H. B. Lori finds herself. In E. Feder & B. Feder (Eds.), *Expressive Arts Therapy*. Englewood Cliffs, NJ: Prentice-Hall, 1981, pp. 104–112.

Landgarten, H. B. Art psychotherapy for depressed elders. *Clinical Gerontologist, 2*(1/2). Haworth Press, New York, 1983.

Landgarten, H. B. Burnout and the role of art psychotherapist. *Clinical Gerontologies, 2*(2). Haworth Press, New York, Winter 1983.

Landgarten, H. B. Visual dialogues: The artist as art therapist, the art therapist as artist. *Art Therapy Still Growing*. American Art Therapy Association, Alexandria, VA, 1983.

Landgarten, H. B. Ten year follow-up survey on art therapy in Los Angeles. *Art Therapy, 1*(2). Alexandria, VA, 1984.

Landgarten, H. B., & Anderson, F. Survey on the status of art therapy in the midwest and southern California. *American Journal of Art Therapy, 13*(2), January 1974.

Landgarten, H. B., & Harriss, M. Art therapy as an innovative approach to conjoint treatment: A case study. *International Journal of Art Therapy, 13*(2), January 1974.

Landgarten, H. B., Junge, M., Tasem, M., & Watson, M. Art therapy as a modality for crisis intervention. *Clinical Social Workers Journal, 6*(3), Fall 1978.

Lange, A., & van der Hart, Anna. *Directive Family Therapy*. New York: Brunner/ Mazel, 1983.

Langsley, D. G., & Kaplan, D. M. *The Treatment of Families in Crisis*. New York: Grune & Stratton, 1968.

Lantz, J. E. *Family and Marital Therapy: A Transactional Approach*. New York: Appleton-Century Crofts, 1978.

Laquer, H. P., LaBurt, H. A., & Morong, E. Multiple family therapy. In J. Masserman (Ed.), *Current Psychiatric Therapies, 4*, 150–154, New York: Grune & Stratton.

Lewis, H. P. (Ed.). *Child Art: The Beginnings of Self-Affirmation*. Berkeley: Diablo Press, 1973.

Lewis, J. M., et al. *No Single Thread*. New York: Brunner/Mazel, 1976.

Lidz, T., Fleck, S., & Cornelison, A. *Schizophrenia and the Family*. New York: International Universities Press, 1965.

Linderman, E. W. *Invitation to Vision: Ideas and Imaginations for Art*. Dubuque, IA: William C. Brown, 1967.

Lowenfeld, V. *The Nature of Creative Activity* (2nd ed). London: Routledge and Kegan Paul, 1952.

Lowenfeld, V., & Brittain, W. L. *Creative and Mental Growth* (6th ed). New York: Macmillan, 1975.

Luthe, W. *Creativity Mobilization Technique*. New York: Grune & Stratton, 1976.

Luthman, S. *The Dynamic Family*. Palo Alto, CA: Science & Behavior Books, 1974.

Macgregor, R., Richie, A., Serrano, A., & Schuster, F. *Multiple Impact Therapy with Families*. New York: McGraw-Hill, 1964.

Malone, A. J., & Massler, M. Index of nailbiting in children. *Journal of Abnormal Psychology, 47*, 193, 1952.

Marshall, S., Marshall, H. H., & Lyon, R. P. Enuresis: An analysis of various therapeutic approaches. *Pediatrics, 51*, 813–17, 1973.

Martin, P. *A Marital Therapy Manual*. New York: Brunner/Mazel, 1976.

McHugh, A. F. Children's figure drawings in neurotic and conduct disturbances. *Journal of Clinical Psychology, 22*, 219–221, 1966.

McNiff, S. *The Arts and Psychotherapy*. Springfield, IL: Charles C Thomas, 1981.

McNiff, S. The effects of artistic development on personality. *Art Psychotherapy,* 3(2), 1976.

McNiff, S. Cross-cultural psychotherapy and art. *Art Therapy,* 1(3), October 1984.

Meares, A. *Hypnography.* Springfield, IL: Charles C Thomas, 1957.

Meares, A. *The Door of Serenity.* London: Faber and Faber, 1958.

Meares, A. *Shapes of Sanity.* Springfield, IL: Charles C Thomas, 1960.

Miller, D. *The Age Between.* New York: Jason Aronson, 1983.

Milner, M. *On Not Being Able to Paint.* New York: International Universities Press, 1967.

Milner, M. *The Hands of the Living God.* New York: International Universities Press, 1969.

Minuchin, S., Montalvo, B., Guerney, B., Rosman, B., & Shumer, F. *Families of the Slums: An Exploration of their Structure and Treatment.* New York: Basic Books, 1967.

Mizushima, K. Art therapies in Japan. *Interpersonal Development.* 2(4), 213–222, 1971/72.

Moore, R. W. *Art Therapy in Mental Health.* Washington, D.C.: National Institute of Mental Health, 1981.

Moustakas, C. E. *Creativity and Conformity.* New York: Van Nostrand Reinhold, 1967.

Naevestad, M. *The Colors of Rage and Love: A Picture Book of Internal Events.* London: White Friars Press, 1979.

Napier, A. Y., & Whitaker, C. A. *The Family Crucible.* New York: Harper & Row, 1978.

Napier, A. Y. The marriage of families: Cross-generational complementarity. *Family Process, 10,* 373–395, 1971.

Naumburg, M. *Psychoneurotic Art: Its Function in Psychotherapy.* New York: Grune & Stratton, 1953.

Naumburg, M. *Schizophrenic Art: Its Meaning in Psychotherapy.* New York: Grune & Stratton, 1953.

Neumann, E. *Art and the Creative Unconscious: Four Essays.* New York: Princeton University Press, 1969.

O'Hare, D. (Ed.). *Psychology and the Arts.* New Jersey: Humanities Press, 1981.

Papp, P. (Ed.). *Family Therapy: Full-Length Case Studies.* New York: Gardner Press, 1977.

Paul, N. L., & Grosser, G. Operational mourning and its role in conjoint family therapy. *Community Mental Health Journal, 1*(4), 339–345, 1965.

Paul, W. The use of empathy in the resolution of grief. *Perspect. Biol. Med., II,* 143–155, 1967.

Peckman, M. *Man's Rage for Chaos: Biology, Behavior, and the Arts.* New York: Schocken Press, 1965.

Perkins, D., & Leondor, B. (Eds.). *The Arts and Cognition.* Baltimore: Johns Hopkins University Press, 1977.

Pfister, O. R. *Expressionism in Art, Its Psychological and Biological Basis.* London: Kegan Paul, Trench, Trubner and Co., 1922.

Phillips, W. (Ed.). *Art and Psychoanalysis.* Cleveland: World Publishing Co., 1963.

Pickford, R. W. *Psychology and Visual Aesthetics.* London: Hutchinson, 1972.

Pickford, R. W. *Studies in Psychiatric Art: Its Psychodynamics, Therapeutic Value and Relationship to Modern Art.* Springfield, IL: Charles C Thomas, 1967.

Pinney, E. L., & Slipp, S. *Glossary of Group and Family Therapy.* New York: Brunner/Mazel, 1982.

Plank, E. N., & Plank, R. Children and death: As seen through art and autobiographies. In R. S. Eissler, et al. (Eds.), *Psychoanalytic Study of the Child*, Vol. 33. New Haven: Yale University Press, 1978.

Plokker, J. H. *Art from the Mentally Disturbed*. Boston: Little Brown, 1965.

Prinzhorn, H. *Artistry of the Mentally Ill: A Contribution to the Psychology and Psychopathology of Configuration*. New York: Springer-Verlag, 1972.

Progoff, I. *The Symbolic and the Real*. New York: Julian Press, 1963.

Rabin, A. I., & Haworth, M. R. (Eds.). *Projective Techniques with Children*. New York: Grune & Stratton, 1960.

Rank, O. *Art and the Artist*. New York: Knopf, 1932.

Rees, H. E. *A Psychology of Artistic Creation*. New York: Bureau of Publications, Teachers College, Columbia University, 1942.

Reitman, F. *Psychotic Art*. London: Routledge and Kegan Paul, 1950.

Reusch, J. *Therapeutic Communication*. New York: W. W. Norton, 1961.

Rhodes, S., & Wilson, J. *Surviving Family Life*. New York: G. P. Putnam's Sons, 1981.

Rhyne, J. *The Gestalt Art Experience*. Palo Alto, CA: Science and Behavior Books, 1962.

Robson, B. *My Parents are Divorced Too. What Teenagers Experience and How They Cope*. Toronto: Dorset, 1979.

Roman, M., & Blackburn, S. *Family Secrets*. New York: Times Books, 1979.

Roman, M., & Haddad, W. *The Disposable Parent*. New York: Holt, Rinehart and Winston, 1978.

Rubin, J. A. *Child Art Therapy: Understanding and Helping Children Grow Through Art*. (2nd ed.). New York: Van Nostrand Reinhold, 1984.

Sachs, H. *The Creative Unconscious: Studies in the Psychoanalysis of Art*. (2nd ed.). Cambridge, MA: Sci-Art Publishers, 1951.

Sager, C. J. *Marriage Contracts and Couple Therapy*. New York: Brunner/Mazel, 1976.

Sager, C. J., et al. *Treating the Remarried Family*. New York: Brunner/Mazel Inc., 1983.

Satir, V. *Peoplemaking*. Palo Alto, CA: Science & Behavior Books, 1972.

Schachtel, E. G. On color and affect. *Psychiatry*, 6, 393–409, 1943.

Schachtel, E. G. Projection and its relation to character attitudes and creativity in the kinesthetic response. *Psychiatry*, 13, 69–100, 1950.

Schaefer-Simmern, H. *The Unfolding of Artistic Activity*. Berkeley: University of California Press, 1948.

Schmidl-Washner, T. Formal criteria for the analysis of children's drawings. *American Journal of Orthopsychiatry*, 2, 95–103, 1942.

Schneider, D. E. *The Psychoanalyst and the Artist*. New York: Farrar, Straus & Co., 1950.

Sechehaye, M. A. *Symbolic Realization*. New York: International Universities Press, 1960.

Shore, M. F. (Ed.). *Red is the Color of Hurting*. Bethesda, MD: National Institute of Mental Health. 1967.

Silver, R. A. *Developing Cognitive and Creative Skills in Art*. Baltimore: University Park Press, 1948.

Simos, B. G. *A Time to Grieve*. New York: Family Service Association, 1979.

Skynner, A. *Systems of Family and Marital Psychotherapy*. New York: Brunner/Mazel, 1976.

Smith, N. R., & Franklin, M. P. (Eds.). *Symbolic Functioning in Childhood*. Hillsdale, N.J.: Lawrence Erlbaum Associates, 1979.

Speck, R., & Attneave, C. *Family Networks*. New York: Phantom Books, 1973.

Spiegel, J. P. *Transactions: The Interplay Between Individual, Family and Society.* New York: Science House, 1971.

Steinhauer, P. D., & Rae-Grant, Q. (Eds.). *Psychological Problems of the Child in the Family.* New York: Basic Books, 1983.

Stewart, R. H., Peters, T. C., March, S., & Peters, M. J. An object-relations approach to psychotherapy with marital couples, families and children. *Family Process, 14,* 161–178, 1975.

Stierlin, H. *Psychoanalysis and Family Therapy.* New York: Jason Aronson, 1977.

Stierlin, H., & Ravenscraft, K. J. Varieties of adolescent separation conflicts. *British Journal of Medical Psychology, 45,* 299–313, 1972.

Sugar, M. *The Adolescent in Group and Family Therapy.* New York: Brunner/Mazel, 1975.

Textor, M. *Helping Families with Special Problems.* New York: Jason Aronson, 1983.

Tymchuk, A. *Parent and Family Therapy.* New York: Spectrum, 1979.

Ulman, E., & Dachinger, P. (Eds.). *Art Therapy in Theory and Practice.* New York: Science Books, 1975.

Ulman, E., & Levy, B. L. Judging psychopathology from paintings. *Journal of Abnormal Psychology, 72,* 1967.

Van Krevelen, D. On the use of the family drawing test. In J. G. Howells (Ed.), *Advances in Family Psychiatry, Vol. I.* New York: International Universities Press, 1979.

Wadeson, H. *Art Psychotherapy.* New York: Wiley, 1980.

Washner, T. S. Interpretations of spontaneous drawings and paintings. *Genetic Psychology Monographs, 33,* 70, 1946.

Waelder, R. *Psychoanalytic Avenues to Art.* New York: International Universities Press, 1965.

Walsh, F. (Ed.). *Normal Family Processes.* New York: Guilford Press, 1982.

Watzlawick, P., Weakland, J. H., & Fisch, R. *Change.* New York: Norton, 1974.

Weakland, J. The double bind hypothesis of schizophrenia and three-party interaction. In D. D. Jackson (Ed.), *Studies in Schizophrenia.* New York: Basic Books, 1960.

Williams, F. S. Family therapy: A critical assessment. *American Journal of Orthopsychiatry, 37*(5), 912–919, 1967.

Williams, F. ïamily therapy: Its role in adolescent psychiatry. In S. C. Feinstein & P. G. Giovacchini (Eds.), *Adolescent Psychiatry, Development and Clinical Studies.* New York: Basic Books, 2, 1973.

Williams, G. H., & Wood, M. M. *Developmental Art Therapy.* Baltimore: University Park Press, 1977.

Willmuth, M., & Boedy, D. The verbal diagnostic and art therapy combined: An extended evaluation procedure with family groups. *Art Psychotherapy, 6*(1), 1979.

Winner, E. *Invented Worlds: The Psychology of the Arts.* Cambridge: Harvard University Press, 1982.

Winnicott, D. W. Why children play. In *The Child, the Family and the Outside World.* Middlesex, England: Penguin Books, 1964, pp. 143–146.

Winnicott, D. W. *Therapeutic Consultations in Child Psychiatry.* New York: Basic Books, 1971.

Worden, W. J. *Grief Counseling and Grief Therapy.* New York: Springer, 1982.

Zeligs, R. *Children's Experience with Death.* Springfield, IL: Charles C Thomas, 1974.

Zuk, G. H. Family therapy. In J. Haley (Ed.), *Changing Families: A Family Therapy Reader.* New York: Grune & Stratton, 1971.

Zuk, G., & Boszormenyi-Nagy, I. *Family Therapy and Disturbed Families.* Palo Alto, CA: Science & Behavior Books, 1969.

Index